The Desert World

Sand dunes in Death Valley, California.

DAVID F. COSTELLO

The Desert World

ILLUSTRATED BY THE AUTHOR

Thomas Y. Crowell Company, New York

ESTABLISHED 1834

Designed by Marshall Henrichs

Manufactured in the United States of America

L.C. Card 77-184973

ISBN 0-690-23513-5

1 2 3 4 5 6 7 8 9 10

To Cecilia

Contents

Ripple marks on the sand dunes in Death Valley make new patterns almost daily under the shifting winds.

CHAPTER 1

The Desert Realm

In this rapidly changing America, the desert is among the least disturbed of our great natural heritages. The prairie, where the earth once trembled beneath the feet of countless bison, now is largely plowed, crisscrossed with highways, and dotted with towns and cities. The primeval forests that clothed our eastern and western lands now are fallen before the loggers' axes. Streams that once flowed pure and sparkling now are dead waters stored behind hydro-political dams. Our greatest lakes are polluted and their fish are loaded with poisonous chemicals. But the desert, even though man has conquered portions of it, still retains much of its physical character and the plant and animal life that make it distinctive among all landscapes and biological environments on earth.

The desert is the land of sun and little water. It is the land where you see in stark detail the work of the elemental forces of earth and time. It is the land where only properly adjusted living things can long endure. It is a harsh land only to those who will not accede to its demands, or to those who live elsewhere and believe that only their own surroundings are normal. It is a land where you must cultivate an acquaintance with its principles, processes, and creatures in order to understand it; otherwise, if you pass through the desert, it is something you have merely seen.

Understanding does not come at first sight. Many years ago I learned one of the first principles of life in arid lands—acceptance of the desert's moods: its harshness, and its tranquility. I boarded a bus at Yuma, Arizona, and started a long journey into Mexico across the limitless landscape that burned beneath

1

the copper sun. The distant dun-colored mountains shimmered in the noontime heat, and the road ahead dissolved endlessly in a silver mirage that never became a lake.

Wiser than I, a little native girl of ten or eleven years, without asking, placed her head on my lap and slept for more than a hundred miles. Thus she avoided the discomfort of the desert heat and the monotony of the repetitious expanse of sand and parched earth. Finally, she awakened to a panorama of exotic scenery in which giant cacti and paloverde trees made the desert strangely beautiful. I still remember her charming smile and her eager interest in the world that was surely home to her. Now I realize that she accepted the necessities of the desert as do the plants and animals that exist so successfully in this dramatic land.

In the years since the little girl placed her head on my lap I have learned other secrets of the desert. Also, I found through many years that the desert has some mysteries which even the scientists have not solved. The desert is so large and varied that a lifetime is too short to learn all of its history, its ecological processes, its landscapes, climate, changing moods, and the plants and animals that constitute its wildlife. But especially I have learned that one of its greatest gifts is solitude.

I treasure the memory of a sage-grouse hunt in the Wyoming desert north of Point of Rocks with my two sons when they were young. Now they are caught up in the whirl and noise and tension of the business world. But that night, when we camped in the sagebrush-covered hills, the stars were fiery diamonds and the Milky Way was a powdery path across the black ceiling of the world. In our sleeping bags we listened to the coyote chorus as it began in the dry swale near our camp and was answered from the hills and the bluffs beyond the hills. There seemed to be many coyote voices, but I knew that some were only echoes. Then came the silence.

In the absence of external sound our heartbeats became audible and even our thoughts seemed vocal. The stillness of the desert was awesome. Then we heard muffled beats like the sound of frogs padded with cotton jumping on the ground. The miniature thuds were caused by kangaroo rats making their nightly rounds—collecting seeds and sparring with intruders, coming and going between their burrows. Next we heard mouse teeth rasping on sagebrush bark; the sound of their gnawing seemed to be magnified out of all proportion to the size of the tiny animals. Thus we heard the creatures of the night as they undoubtedly hear one another in the aloneness of the desert. Finally, the melancholy hooting of a great horned owl ended. Then our timeless world returned to silence, and we were content to sleep.

Beyond the gift of silence and solitude, the desert has many other attractions. It is a paradox of nature that the more arid and bizarre the desert terrain, the more numerous and varied its wildlife seems to be. In the solitude of the desert, if you are lucky, you encounter a Gila monster ambling over the flinty pavement of the cholla flats. In the shimmering heat of noon, while sitting in the shade of a giant saguaro, as the jackrabbits do, you see the vultures wheeling in the sky, riding the updrafts from the heated earth. You hear the rasping cadence of desert locusts flitting away from the grasp of a marauding lizard. At sundown you see the vista of desert monuments, left standing after eons of erosion have removed the intervening sediments, and beyond them the majestic mountain ranges growing purple with the advance of night. And in early morning you see the beauty of the desert in the profile of the Joshua tree against the crimson dawn.

Desert ponds provide food, shelter, and water for an immense variety of birds, reptiles, amphibians, and mammals. Migrating waterfowl frequent the permanent ponds in spring and autumn. A pair of coots are swimming near the rushes.

The desert offers brilliant beauty in its contrasting colors in rocks, sands, and gravels. It offers fresh greenery after the spring rains. Sometimes it blooms with whole valleys of flowers. It offers the fury of floods, winds, and heat, and then ameliorates into an invigorating land where the gray and crimson pyrrhuloxia, like the cardinal of the eastern forests, whistles his wondrously clear *cheereat*, or the vermilion flycatcher, brilliant as a jungle butterfly, makes forays for flying insects from his cottonwood tree beside a desert stream.

The desert offers uniqueness in its waters: ponds, pools hidden in caves, rivers that sink into the sands, and lakes that are remnants of inland seas. Fish found in no other place in the world live in these waters. Even where no lakes or rivers exist the action of water, past and present, is universally evident. Natural bridges, former waterfalls, and potholes in dry riverbeds attest to the elemental force of water shaping the land. But the desert is more than a physical wonderland or a place to study habitat relationships of plants and animals.

One of the great heritages of the desert is the story of human occupation that began centuries before the coming of white men. The Indians of prehistoric times knew the problems of the desert and solved them. In the desert they found all the materials for food, clothing, and shelter. They made use of the desert waters and practiced irrigation and agriculture. They developed elaborate rituals, spiritual traits, crafts, and political concepts that still have an impact on modern culture, architecture, and industry.

The culture of the people who once spoke the Aztec language existed long before the time of Christ. Indians living in southern New Mexico were raising maize some 6,000 years ago. When the Hohokam people moved from northern Mexico into southern Arizona in about A.D. 1000, they brought with them stone-etching techniques, pottery construction methods, and the practice of trading with other tribes as far west as California.

At the time of the Spanish invasion in the 1520's there were, perhaps, 20 million people in central Mexico alone. Tenochtitlán (Mexico City) then was one of the most modern cities in the world, where people excelled as artisans, engineers, astronomers, statesmen, and warriors. The conquering Spaniards intermarried with the Indians, and the later Spanish-Mexican northward movement contributed to the heritage that developed in the desert—a heritage which now influences not only the Southwest, but much of the culture of the entire United States.

The Indian tribes of the cold northern deserts of Wyoming, Oregon, Utah, and Nevada gave us legends about the origins of men. Many of these myths concern humans who acquired the characteristics of animals, including the coyotes, the lizards, and the birds of the desert. Other legends came from patriarchs of the Paiutes, who told how magic mountains of fire poured molten rock over the valleys and burned the skins of their ancestors to a dark brown. The survivors who walked on the cooling lava became the first people of their race. Who is to say that the Great Spirit was not present in the flames and pumice clouds that blasted out of Mount Shasta, Mount Mazama, and the other great volcanoes on the western edge of the desert within the last 10,000 years?

The Indians were still there when the white explorers challenged the northern deserts, not in search of beauty and understanding of its processes, but in quest of animal hides, gold, and religious freedom. After Lewis and Clark made their intrepid march to the mouth of the Columbia, the trails of the explorers spread widely over the land. Peter Skene Ogden of the Hudson's Bay Company in 1828 led his trappers down the Owyhee to the headwaters of the Humboldt River, which flows from the mountains and sinks in the desert. In 1844 Captain John C. Frémont discovered the most beautiful of all the desert waters and named it Pyramid Lake after the rock of that shape near the eastern shore. Later the Mormons came to Utah to farm the desert. Next came the mining strikes and booms, followed by huge cattle and sheep spreads which resulted in water wars. Then came railroads, towns, and cities, and the legends of a different race of men began to take form.

Now modern-day explorers from the great cities search for history where sagebrush grows on the sites of ghost towns. Some look for new Klondikes with rare minerals for an atomic age. But the wisest of these explorers come to the desert because it is a wilderness of mystery, the domain of unusual plants and animals, and an environment where peace and quiet and good health can be enjoyed in a fantastic setting.

What is a desert? My earliest impressions were formed years ago when I played "hearts and flowers" music on the violin for the silent movies. The cue for an increase in musical tempo came when the Sheik rescued the beautiful American girl and galloped ahead of the pursuing Bedouins. Fortissimo was demanded when the white-capped heads of the Foreign Legion topped the crest of a mighty sand dune and then engaged in clanging sword fights with camel-mounted raiders who had captured the oasis. In those days I believed that the Sahara was the world's only desert.

Later, at the University of Chicago, Professor Henry C. Cowles used to tell us students that some of the most tremendous deserts of all time existed aeons ago. From him we learned how deserts were shaped by geological and climatic forces, and how the physiognomy, or appearance, of the landscape was altered by the vegetation developed under the prevailing soil and weather conditions. The definition we learned was: A desert is an area in which bare earth is the most conspicuous feature of the landscape.

This definition still provides a rule of thumb for the layman, if he looks down at the earth instead of straight ahead. In the desert the sand or the rocks at one's feet nearly always occupy more total area than the cactus, sagebrush, or any vegetation. In grassland, not overgrazed by livestock, the ground frequently is entirely obscured by herbaceous vegetation. In forests the ground usually is covered by herbs, or fallen leaves, and is shaded by the overstory of shrubs and trees. Of course, if one looks straight ahead, even in a cactus desert, the perspective and the numbers of plants may give the appearance of a densely vegetated world.

The wide spacing of plants, or their virtual absence from deserts, results from scarcity of water. Deserts are dry or arid lands. That is why the climatologists define deserts as areas of limited or poorly distributed rainfall. But deserts are not necessarily hot or sandy places. The one common characteristic of all deserts, cold or hot, is their aridity; even a warm house in winter with a low humidity becomes an "indoor desert."

Most of us have never thought of the arctic or antarctic regions as being deserts. But precipitation at these ends of the earth is relatively low, the air contains a minimum of moisture, and vegetation is low in stature or is absent. Even more startling to the layman is the idea that desert conditions extend westward over the oceans from portions of North and South America, Africa, and Australia. The arid climatic conditions of the Sahara, for example, exist across the North Atlantic Ocean almost to the

West Indies. If land instead of water were there, the area would be an enormous desert.

The deserts we know on our own continent contain few endless stretches of burning sands, although Death Valley, California, becomes as hot and has areas as barren as the Sahara or the deserts in Arabia, or Australia. Our deserts are both hot and cold. And in general they are populated by a fantastic variety of herbs, shrubs, and trees, which in turn provide food and shelter for a multitude of animals, both large and small.

In our hot southern deserts summer daytime temperatures are high and nighttime temperatures are relatively low. Soil temperatures at or near the surface also fluctuate widely and affect germination of seeds, growth of roots, geographic distribution of plants, and rates of absorption of water and solutes. The saltiness of the soil in poorly drained areas excludes all but the most salt-tolerant of species such as shadscale, greasewood, saltsage, winterfat, and halogeton.

But the desert is not a pitiless environment where only a few living things engage in an incessant struggle for survival. It has so many physical forms that flora and fauna are more numerous and varied than in many of our luxuriant forests. Each land form provides habitats for plants and animals with special adaptations for life in arid surroundings. These plants and animals characterize the desert just as the desert itself is characterized by dryness and irregular extremes of weather. When one begins to understand plant and animal adaptations to varied habitats, such as succulence among the cacti, evasion of drought through ephemeral growth of annual plants, or conservation of water by rodents (some of which never drink), then the desert becomes a land for adventure, study, and unending discovery.

The geologic features that were to contribute to the formation of the modern American desert began during the Cenozoic era, which is known as the age of mammals. In the Miocene and Pliocene epochs of this era mountains rose in western North America and created the topographic conditions conducive to desert environments under favorable climatic conditions. Beginning in the Pleistocene, about one million years ago, the continental glaciers advanced and retreated four times during the Ice Age. The Southwest was not glaciated, but local glaciation in the mountains, greater rainfall, and stream erosion filled the valleys with sediments and led to maximum water levels in prehistoric lakes.

Worldwide climatic changes then contributed to the development of our present deserts. A drought that lasted for more than 3,000 years, beginning about 7,500 years ago, reduced ancient Lake Lahontan to mere remnants such as Pyramid Lake near Reno, Nevada. Widespread wind erosion, dune building, and cutting of stream channels by water from melting glaciers contributed to the relief features we see in the desert today. The shallow desert soils never accumulated humus, such as we find

Weird geological formations in the desert attest to the forces of wind, water, gravity, and temperature over aeons of time. This rock window is in the Arches National Monument, Utah.

in the midcontinental prairies, since abundant rain and deep penetrating moisture were absent.

Climate and weather, of course, are the major factors which cause aridity, the principal feature of deserts whether they are hot or cold. The mountains and the sea, in turn, influence the climates that result in the development of deserts. Most of our western deserts are rain-shadow deserts. The air currents that come from the Pacific Ocean rise on the windward side of the Cascade and Sierra Nevada ranges and become cool with increase in altitude. Condensation of their moisture occurs, clouds form, and the western slopes on the ocean side receive precipitation. As the winds descend on the leeward side of the mountain ranges, the air compresses and becomes warmer. This results in decreased precipitation and in drying of the land over which the wind travels. Thus the Great Basin, for example, is arid, since it lies in the rain shadow of the Oregon and California mountains to the west. The Rocky Mountains to the east also reduce the amount of precipitation that might otherwise be carried northward and westward with winds from the Gulf of Mexico.

Clarity of the air over deserts also contributes to their aridity. The rays of the sun are not obstructed by clouds, and much solar energy reaches the ground, which becomes heated and in turn radiates heat to the lower atmosphere. But since the humidity is so low, this rarely causes fog or dew, except in short periods after rainfall. When summer precipitation occurs it usually is in the form of violent thunderstorms, caused by convection in which air heated at the earth's surface rises to great heights. Tropical moist air going westward from the Gulf of Mexico over the Sonoran and Chihuahuan deserts also results in violent summer thunderstorms.

The coastal desert of Baja California is cool because it receives ocean air chilled by currents coming from polar regions southward along the western American coast. The air that moves over the shore is a shallow layer that holds only enough moisture to condense to fog. No rain is produced because the air above is dry, and there are no thunderstorms because the fog prevents heating of the ground and the formation of convectional currents in the atmosphere.

Mountains within deserts, as well as those around deserts, also affect the climate. The fault-block mountains of Utah and Nevada, for example, are long parallel ridges running north and south for dozens or even hundreds of miles. These mountains affect wind movement and cause lesser rain shadows on their leeward sides. You can see this local climatic variation reflected in the vegetation and associated animals which differ on eastward and westward facing slopes. Also, the flat dry lake beds, or playas, between slopes support forms of life different from those at higher elevations. In the playas there is greater aridity and alkalinity—the alkali having been leached from the mountains and deposited in the soils at the lowest elevations in the desert.

The mountains around the desert's rim and those that rise from its floor provide many opportunities for study of the perspective of geological time. The prehistory of the desert is revealed in wonderlands of fossil beds where the remains of extinct animals occur. Embedded in rock formations are bones of three-toed horses, camels, giant pigs, sabertooth tigers, elephants, and oreodons, the latter being large plant-eating animals. Sediments in some localities in New Mexico yield fossils of deer, camels, and bears that lived during the late Miocene and early Pliocene epochs some 15 million years ago.

Even as a casual wanderer in the desert you can find evidence that ancient seas once existed there. As a start, look at the anthills. In far-western Colorado, for example, the harvester ants thatch their foot-high mounds with fossil teeth of sharks that lived in the Cretaceous period. These teeth, with their serrated or file-like edges, are mostly less than one-eighth of an inch long. The rains now bring them down from the shale beds and streaks of conglomerate and deposit them on the desert floor.

The story of the past is written there in the bold upthrust of mountains, in rock platforms or pediments, in long slopes formed by erosion of the materials of mountains, and in alluvial plains which once were bottoms of ancient lakes. Their shorelines and terraces, carved and silted by Pleistocene waves, still are visible. Craters formed by meteor impact are best preserved in deserts. Volcanic cones and lava streams remind us of ceaseless changes that developed these land forms in the past.

When one looks at the desert as a whole it presents a landscape of mountains, basins, troughs, and plains. Some of the plains lie at high elevations; others are striking because they bottom below sea level, as does Death Valley in California and the Dead Sea between Israel and Jordan. Superimposed on these

Mountains are visible from almost any place in the desert. Here, in the Sonoran Desert in Arizona, Montezuma Head at the far right on the horizon is a landmark in the Aho Mountains.

various land forms, for all the millennia since they came into existence, have been the effects of winds, water, temperature changes, and the down-pull of gravity. Together, these forces have dissected the mountain slopes, filled the valleys with soil and encrusted salts, produced mud flows, piled up wind-rippled sands, and produced marshes where mountain streams now sink into oblivion in the desert.

The North American desert extends from southwestern Wyoming and western Colorado to the Cascades in Oregon and southward from the sagebrush-covered areas in eastern Washington and Idaho to eastern Durango in Mexico. The desert covers much of Utah and Nevada and reaches the base of the Sierra Nevada and the San Bernardino mountains in California. From southern New Mexico and Arizona it extends to the coast of Baja California and through the Mexican states of Chihuahua and Coahuila.

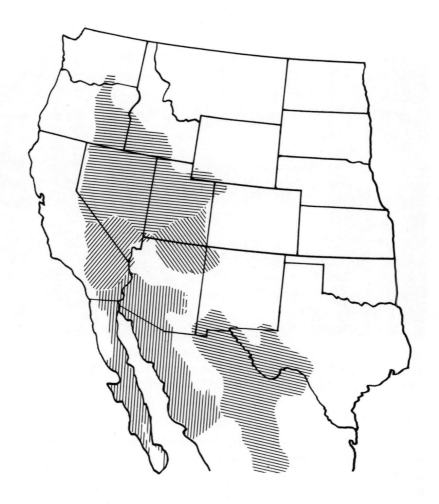

Major North American Deserts

	Great Basin Desert
	Painted Desert
	Mohave Desert
	Sonoran Desert
	Chihuahuan Desert

Desert also occurs in the valley of the Rio Grande and Pecos rivers in Texas.

Within this vast territory are four major deserts: the Great Basin Desert, characterized by big sagebrush and saltbush; the Mohave Desert, dominated in part by the picturesque Joshua tree; the Sonoran Desert, typified by the saguaro cactus; and the Chihuahuan Desert, characterized by a variety of cacti, shrubs, and small trees. Many writers recognize various subdivisions of these major deserts, and some of the lesser deserts have been named with respect to their geographic location or soil condition.

The Red Desert in southwestern Wyoming, so named because of its red soil, and the Painted Desert of northern Arizona and southeast Utah, with its many-hued rocks, are sometimes considered to be distinct areas rather than integral parts of the Great Basin Desert. The Colorado Desert of California (named after the great river, not the state of Colorado) may also be considered as separate from the Sonoran. The arid playground east of Los Angeles, where people spend some 5 million visitor-days each year, is widely known as the California Desert. It overlaps much of the area often designated as the Colorado Desert.

The great deserts of North America are distinctive in topography, climate, plant and animal life, and natural resources. The largest is the Great Basin Desert. If you go west through central Wyoming you first encounter big sagebrush (*Artemisia tridentata*), the characteristic shrub that grows over an area of some 90 million acres in the West. The pigmy forests of this and other species of sagebrush are found in all of the eleven western states, but they grow in greatest profusion in southern Idaho, southeastern Oregon, Utah, and Nevada. Present on the lower flats, where moisture is more abundant than on the slopes, are hardy drought-resistant shrubs such as shadscale (*Atriplex confertifolia*), hop sage (*Grayia spinosa*), winterfat (*Eurotia lanata*), and the yellow-flowered rabbitbrushes (*Chrysothamnus*) that bloom in late summer and early autumn.

Many years ago, Homer L. Shantz aptly called this plant formation the Northern Desert Shrub. He gave the name Salt Desert Shrub, or greasewood formation, to those alkaline areas within the sagebrush desert where the percentages of salt are so high that only halophytes (salt-tolerant plants) such as greasewood (*Sarcobatus vermiculatus*), pickleweed (*Allenrolfea occidentalis*), and glasswort (*Salicornia rubra*) can exist. If you go south around Great Salt Lake and west across the great salt flats near Wendover, Utah, you can see the transition from sagebrush desert to flat and barren surface so alkali-encrusted that no vegetation can grow.

The Great Basin is rimmed east and west by high mountain ranges, but it is not a single basin. Within this vast province are nearly one hundred desert valleys that lie between parallel fault-block mountains traversing the basin from north to south. Between these mountain ranges are long slopes (either barren or covered only with pinyon pines and juniper) extending down to the valley floors, many of which are alkali-encrusted flats or dry lakes. Floods from the uplands occasionally cover these flats, or playas, with water that evaporates and adds to the salt encrustations. There is no drainage to the sea.

The Great Basin Desert is less spectacular than some of the other deserts, but it is not a monotonous land. Its very vastness can be attractive to the urbanite seeking escape from the confines of large cities and the tension of modern living. Its mountains offer panoramic views of forested areas that merge at their lower edges into juniper zones that in turn bound the upper reaches of the shrub-covered basins broken here and there by the ghostly

The Bonneville Salt Flats in western Utah are part of the most extreme desert in America. Few plants are able to survive in the alkali-encrusted soil.

white of alkali flats or the green belts of vegetation growing beside meandering desert streams.

There are few rivers in the Great Basin. The Humboldt, famous in the history of exploration of Nevada, flows from the mountains in the north and sinks into the desert. The Truckee, which flows eastward from the Sierra, through Reno, empties into Pyramid Lake, where the prehistoric cui-ui fish still live along with a multitude of white pelicans, California gulls, many kinds of ducks and geese, and a host of shore birds. Other rivers that end in the Great Basin Desert contribute to green marshes and shallow ponds where birds come to nest and mammals come from the desert to seek food and drink.

The variety of the Great Basin is enhanced by lakes, both large and small, which are the remnants of ancient Lake Bonneville in the north and Lake Lahontan in the south. These modern lakes include Great Salt Lake, the largest of them all; Pyramid Lake; Honey Lake in California, around which one must drive on the way south from Oregon to Reno; and Walker and other lakes which formerly were connected with Honey Lake, as is shown by the remains of ancient shorelines and the presence of fish species that once swam in the prehistoric waters.

Sand dunes are found in the Great Basin. The most spectacular of these lie north of Winnemucca, Nevada, and south of the Carson Sink where the Carson River disappears in a broad area of marshlands. Caves are present in the desert, and the Indian artifacts found in their debris tell us much about ancient men who reaped a living by eating succulent herbs, harvesting seeds and nuts, and hunting animals and birds.

The varied terrain of the Great Basin Desert supports abundant plant and animal life. Pronghorn antelope race across the level areas. Mule deer frequent the bushlands beside the streams in spring and fall; in winter they graze the desert shrubs, and in summer they live in the adjoining mountains while their fawns grow toward maturity. Jackrabbits, ground squirrels, badgers, skunks, and innumerable mice and other rodents share the desert with migratory birds and the resident sage grouse that boom during the mating season on dancing grounds that have persisted for centuries.

In the sagebrush zone the desert becomes a flower garden that covers the sandy soils of the valleys and softens the harshness of the stony outcrops on the lower slopes of the foothills. Conspicuous flowering plants of spring and early summer are the lupines, scarlet gilia, sand verbena, and various penstemons. Phloxes with pink flowers grow in cushions where their roots find footing in the crevices of lava rims. On dry slopes the discovery of the beautiful sego lily (*Calochortus nuttallii*), with its white petals streaked with green down the middle, and dark purple at the base, is as rewarding as would be the finding of a precious stone.

The Mohave Desert, smallest of the American deserts, is located in southeastern California, southern Nevada, and western Arizona. With its varied topography, plant life, and animal life, it marks a transition between the Great Basin Desert and the Sonoran Desert. Some authors treat this area as the California Desert and divide it into two parts, the larger Mohave Desert and the smaller Colorado Desert. The smaller desert includes the

Yuccas and various shrubs grow up through the shifting sands of the dunes north of Winnemucca, Nevada.

low-altitude area bordering the lower Colorado River and the drainage area surrounding the Salton Sea, with an extension into Baja California. The larger Mohave Desert lies eastward and northward of the San Gabriel and San Bernardino mountains and includes the Death Valley area and a small portion of southeastern Nevada.

Big sagebrush, so characteristic of the Great Basin, mingles on the north and west of the Mohave Desert with the creosote bush (*Larrea tridentata*), which dominates the plains of the Mohave. This shrub, with its dark green leaves and resinous scent, grows in nearly pure stands and is practically the only shrub on some of the extremely arid slopes of Death Valley. The Joshua tree (*Yucca brevifolia*), one of the most distinctive plants of the desert, with its forked branches and fantastic asymmetry, is erratically distributed. Characteristically the Joshua tree grows in a zone below that of the pinyon pines and juniper trees of the foothills and above the endless stands of creosote bush on the plains. The Joshua tree is the center of life for much of the desert fauna in its locality, including screech owls, wrens, flycatchers, wood rats, snakes, and the desert night lizard (*Xantusia vigilis*).

Although Death Valley lies below sea level, much of the Mohave Desert is high country. The landscape is spectacular where the Sierras dominate the western skyline and is varied in the eastern sections by parallel mountain ranges with gently sloping bahadas and dry, alkaline lake beds. The land is varied by monumental sand dunes near Kelso, California, and by the Colorado River in the southern part of the Mohave. As you travel southward and eastward you enter the Sonoran Desert and a world of tall cacti, desert trees, beautiful birds, and strangely adapted reptiles and mammals.

The Sonoran or Arizona Desert extends over the lower elevations of southern Arizona, northwestern Mexico, and much of Baja California. A small area of this desert also extends into southern California. In Mexico the Sonoran Desert extends across the Gulf of California to the peninsula of Baja California. The shores of the Gulf of California and the Pacific Ocean shore of the peninsula thus become the desert border. There are two subdivisions of this coastal desert, the Vizcaíno-Magdalena Desert and the Gulf Coast Desert. The former occupies much of the peninsula of Baja California from Rosario on the Pacific coast south to the latitude of La Paz. The latter consists of two narrow strips, one on either side of the Gulf of California. The western strip extends approximately from the Bay of San Rafael to San José del Cabo near the southern tip of the peninsula. The eastern strip borders the eastern coast of the Gulf of California from a point about fifty miles north of Puerto Libertad to the bay south of Guaymas.

When most of us think of American deserts, the Sonoran is

the first one we picture in our minds, because we associate giant cacti and drought-resistant plants with high temperatures, low rainfall, and barren soil.

The Sonoran Desert is distinctive because of its variety of cacti and the numerous trees and other plants with small leaves or no leaves at all. More than sixty species of cactus have been listed for Arizona, and many of these are found in the Sonoran Desert. Some have cylindrical stems, such as teddy-bear cholla (*Opuntia bigelovii*) and the barrel cactus (*Echinocactus acanthodes*). Others are flat-stemmed with pancake-like joints, such as the beavertail cactus (*Opuntia basilaris*).

The trees of the Sonoran Desert are not tall—the largest seldom exceed thirty feet in height—but they possess many mechanisms for dealing with the desert environment. The palo-verdes are large shrubs or small trees—the greenest of green things in the desert. Other common woody plants are mesquite (*Prosopis juliflora*), ironwood (*Olneya tesota*), coffeeberry or jo-joba (*Simmondsia chinensis*), and cat's-claw (*Acacia greggii*).

The display of winter and summer annual plants is spectacular when the rainfall is right. On the western side of the desert rainfall occurs mostly during the winter months; on the eastern side most rain occurs in summer, and less than 30 percent of the yearly supply comes in winter. The ephemeral plants, which include grasses and broad-leaved herbs or forbs, many with showy flowers, make their best growth and display of colors after the winter or summer rains have fallen.

Different land forms, rainfall amounts, and elevations produce a variety of vegetational subregions in the Sonoran Desert. The Lower Colorado Valley Desert, bordering the northern end of the Gulf of California, is low-level, nearly barren, sandy land that supports little vegetation except for creosote bush (*Larrea divaricata*) and burroweed (*Franseria dumosa*). The Arizona Upland Desert, typified by the area between Phoenix and Tucson, features mountains and slopes with an amazing display of large shrubs, trees, and cacti.

In the Gulf Coast Desert the largest of all desert cacti, the cardón (*Pachycereus pringlei*), reaches a height of sixty feet or more. In central Sonora a desert area known as the Plains of Sonora is a region of plains and low mountains. Trees are widely spaced, and tall columnar cacti, especially the organ-pipe (*Lemaireocereus thurberi*) and the senita, or old man cactus (*Lopho-*

cereus shottii), are common. The latter, with its long bristles, or "whiskers," on the upper ends of the stems, is found in the United States only along the Puerto Blanco Drive in the Organ-Pipe Cactus National Monument.

The area known as the Foothills of Sonora, east and north of Guaymas and south of Arizpe, Mexico, presents the richest and most continuous plant cover of the Sonoran Desert. Organ-pipe cactus, the tall ocotillo (*Fouquieria macdougallii*), and even desert palms occur here. Vegetation in the southern end of the Foothills region gradually changes to Thorn Forest north of the Culiacán River.

The strangest of all desert plants are found along the central third of the Pacific coast of Baja California. This is the Vizcaíno Region of the Sonoran Desert, extending southward from the vicinity of Rosario to Punta Pequeña and inland to the drainage divide of the peninsula. Many of the plants are unique. The cirio, or boogum tree (*Idria columnaris*), has no rival as the most bizarre plant of the Sonoran Desert. In general appearance it resembles an elongated upside-down carrot, and it reaches an average height of twenty to twenty-five feet, although some trees grow to a height of sixty feet. The grotesque elephant tree (*Bursera microphylla*), with its exaggerated thickness of trunk and limbs, is one of the most striking and beautiful trees of the desert.

The desert of the southern third of the Pacific coast of Baja California is the Magdalena Region. The cirio is absent, and elephant trees are scarce. Large cacti and numerous species of small trees dominate. In America this is one of the few deserts that reaches to the lagoons and sand dunes bordering the sea.

In order to place our North American deserts in perspective we pause here to consider briefly the deserts of other continents.

The largest desert in the world is the Sahara, with a total area of 3.5 million square miles. Its vast area stretches more than 3,000 miles across northern Africa and exhibits a variety of landscapes, including mountains, stone pavements, gravel surfaces, and enormous areas of windblown sand. Winter precipitation occurs in the northern portion from Morocco and Libya to Egypt. The southern portion, a thousand miles to the south, has warm winters, hot summers, and only a minimum of summer rainfall. Herbs and shrubs grow in favorable localities, but much of the Sahara is practically barren of plant life. Wind is almost a constant feature, and dust storms sometimes reduce the day to almost complete darkness, as did the "black blizzards" of the Dust Bowl days in the Great Plains of the United States in the 1930's. In spite of the harshness of the Sahara, however, terrestrial birds and uniquely adapted reptiles, insects, and mammals abound in favorable habitats.

In southwest Africa the Kalahari and Namib deserts embrace a variety of landscapes, including sand dunes, rock surfaces, and reddish-brown soils. The Namib receives less than two inches of annual rainfall and exhibits extreme desert conditions along the west coast of the continent. The Kalahari lies inland, but its climate is not extremely arid; trees, bushes, grass, and herbs grow there, and in the Karroo district summer and winter rains support a variety of succulent shrubs.

An arid land along the coast of the Red Sea and extending southward into Kenya is named the Somali-Chalbi by some scientists. The land forms exhibit much diversity, varying from a coastal zone to windblown soil deposits and volcanic formations inland from the Indian Ocean. Vegetation is scanty where annual rainfall is less than four inches. Trees, shrubs, and grasses grow in parklike savannas where rainfall exceeds eight inches annually.

Of all the arid lands of Asia the Arabian Desert exhibits the most extreme conditions of climate and paucity of plant growth. The largest area of sand dunes in the world occurs here on the Arabian Peninsula, where no perennial rivers are known. Land forms include barren coastal plains with excessive heat and humidity, mountains that reach altitudes of 12,000 feet, rocky plateaus watered by runoff from the mountains, fertile plains, and the Rub al-Khali, a vast ocean of sand. In early Biblical times the gum resins, frankincense, and myrrh produced by trees found only in southern Arabia and in Somalia across the Gulf of Aden became sources of profitable trade as ancient transportation by cargo-carrying camels was developed.

East of Arabia the Iranian Desert, with an area of 150,000 square miles, covers parts of Iran, Afghanistan, and Pakistan. This desert has hot summers and cool winters. Little is known about its vegetation, but at higher elevations sagebrush (*Artemisia herba-alba*) grows in communities similar to the sagebrush stands in the Great Basin. East of the Iranian Desert lies the Thar or Indian Desert. In this arid portion of western India and eastern West Pakistan dunes and gravelly soils support diverse communities of vegetation including small trees, salt desert plants, and scattered grasses.

The Turkestan Desert lies north of the Iranian Desert. Its western boundary is the Caspian Sea and its southern boundary is the mountains on the borders of Afghanistan and Iran. Many salt deserts occur in this region, which includes land areas with dry lake beds below sea level. Farther east in central Asia is the Takla-Makan Desert extending from western China to Mongolia. Included in this region is the Gobi Desert. In this enormous area, far from the oceans and protected from moist winds by the Tibetan plateau, vegetation is sparse and the winters are cold.

In South America the Atacama Desert lies along the coastline of Peru and Chile. Although it borders the Pacific Ocean, it is one of the driest deserts on earth. Annual rainfall at Arica is less than 0.04 inches but exceeds 2.5 inches along the Peruvian coast. Vegetation is extremely sparse and animal life also is scarce.

Inland, on the eastern side of the Andes Mountains, the Patagonian Desert covers 260,000 square miles in Argentina. The Monte, or northern region, lies directly in the shadow of the mountains and receives about eight inches of annual rainfall. It is a cool desert dominated by bushes, many of which are without leaves. In Patagonia proper the desert stretches for a thousand miles to the south and borders the mountains on the west and the Atlantic Ocean on the east. The climate is cold, dry, and windy. Grasses and low shrubs predominate.

The Australian Desert, second in size to the Sahara, covers an area of 1.3 million square miles. This arid land occupies nearly half of the entire continent. It is a stony, sandy land of low precipitation and few human inhabitants. Low mountains and tablelands occur in the Australian Desert, much of which is a vast plain with numerous saline flats and occasional intermittent streams. The rain shadow of the mountains on the Queensland coast causes low precipitation in the northeastern portion of the desert. Small trees and spineless shrubs and tussock grasses are characteristic. Because of the relative abundance of grasses, particularly spinifex (*Triodia basedowii*), the Australian deserts are sometimes called grass deserts. There are no native succulent plants such as are found in our deserts in North America. And in general the North American deserts are the most densely vegetated of the earth's arid regions.

The desert grassland, interspersed with mesquite trees, forms the eastern border of the cactus desert in New Mexico and Arizona.

CHAPTER 2

The Rim of the Desert

One pleasant summer, I lived on the mountain rim of the desert in southern Utah making records of weather and plant development. My research required that I drive up and down the mountainside to study experimental plots in the different vegetation zones: alpine meadows at 10,000 feet; spruce-fir forest intermingled with aspen groves down to 7,000 feet; then ponderosa pine, juniper, and oak; and finally sagebrush where the desert began. Occasionally I crossed the threshold of the desert to see the contrasts between its plants and animals and those of the less demanding mountain environment.

From the top of the Wasatch Plateau, which I visited at least once each week, I could see a portion of that great arid land that physiographers call the Basin and Range Province. Extending from southeastern Idaho to Oregon, from central Utah to eastern California, and from southern Arizona and New Mexico into the Sonoran Desert of Mexico, the province covers about 300,000 square miles. Here lies much of the desert of the West and Southwest. In this land of varied topography more than two hundred mountain ranges form essentially parallel ridges running north to south with wide valleys or basins between the ranges.

Life zones on the mountains that rim the desert increase in altitude from north to south. Tundra in the Arctic occurs at sea level. In the southern Rocky Mountains it exists at altitudes of 12,000 feet or more. Upper timberline on Mt. McKinley, Alaska, is found at 2,500 feet but reaches 12,000 feet on San Francisco Mountain in Arizona. This high timber zone is characterized by

Engelmann spruce and alpine fir. Below this zone in much of the mountainous West a tree zone of blue spruce and white fir meets tree stands of Douglas fir and ponderosa pine. Below this, forests of ponderosa pine on dry hillsides frequently grow as an overstory to shrubs such as mountain mahogany, antelope bitterbrush (*Purshia tridentata*), and various species of sagebrush.

The sagebrush zone, one of the largest plant communities in the North American deserts, occurs in general between altitudes of 8,000 feet in its most southerly extent and 4,000 feet in its northern localities. This is the cold northern desert, where temperatures and evaporation rates are much lower than those in warm southern deserts. South of the sagebrush zone is the warm southern desert, where annual rainfall is less than ten inches, yearly temperatures and evaporation rates are high, and the growing season is usually frost-free. This is the land of mesquite, cat's-claw, yuccas, paloverde, and cacti. It is also the land of drought-adopted rodents, peccaries, desert snakes, lizards, roadrunners, vultures, and many resident birds.

If you contemplate this whole panorama of desert life zones, you become aware that the desert is where it is because of broad continental climatic influences. Northward the sagebrush rim lies below woodlands and forests, which are better adapted to higher precipitation and lower evaporation rates. Eastward and westward the northern desert shrublands likewise give way to forest trees on the mountainsides of the Rockies, the Cascade Mountains, and the Sierras. Southward, in Mexico, the warm dry desert yields to semitropical rainfall in the lowlands and to forest growth on the high mountains. Only in Baja California and on the shores of the Gulf of California does the desert yield to the sea. It exists at the water's edge because the California Current in the Pacific Ocean is cold, and the air moving landward is unable to hold large amounts of moisture.

The mountain ranges and plateaus bordering the desert basins provide an unending variety of evironments with contrasting aggregations of plants and animals. The boundaries of the upper plant zones on the mountain faces usually are distinctive, and the areas of transition between them usually are abrupt. In the Sierra Nevada, for example, the zones progress downward from alpine tundra through white bark pine, lodgepole pine–mountain hemlock, and red fir to ponderosa pine–white fir. In the Toyabe Mountains the downward sequence is from alpine tundra through limber pine–bristlecone pine, high elevation sagebrush–grass, pinyon-pine and juniper woodland, and lower elevation sagebrush–grass to shadscale desert.

The boundaries between mountain and desert vegetation zones frequently are characterized by gradual transition from one type to another. In some places dense stands of juniper trees gradually thin out on the lower slopes into parklike groves where occasional trees stand alone in the pigmy forest of sagebrush plants. The different faces of canyons also display different kinds of plant life. On north-facing slopes pine forests sometimes grow down to the edge of the desert. On dry south-facing slopes sagebrush, scrub oaks, bitterbrush, and other shrubby plants frequently occupy sites a thousand feet above the trees growing across the canyon. Whenever I cross the boundaries between any of these zones, I find it instructive to note the plants involved in the transitions and the range of animal life.

Each animal has its own environmental requirements for water, food, and shelter. Kangaroo rats require little water beyond that obtainable from the food they eat; they are adapted to life in the desert. The porcupine occasionally wanders down into the desert but spends most of its winter in the pine and spruce-fir zones, since bark is available there as its principal food. The coyote forages most frequently in summer on the upper slopes, where rodents, birds, insects, and fruits furnish a dependable food supply in the forested zones and in mountain meadows. He tends to winter in the oak, sagebrush, and desert border, where wood rats, jackrabbits, cottontails, and mice are abundant.

Birds also are distributed according to features of vegetation, topography, and food supply. The canyon wren is partial to rock gorges; the Arizona woodpecker chooses evergreen oaks; the violet-green swallow seeks dead conifers with woodpecker holes for its nests; the roadrunner inhabits the desert, where snakes and lizards provide an abundant food supply. Thus the boundary between mountain and desert offers us an opportunity to appraise or to speculate about the unique requirements of many species of living things. The mountain borders, however, extend for so many thousands of miles that only a brief summary of their locations and effects on climatic, physical, and biotic factors in the desert can be mentioned here.

The Rocky Mountains constitute a great barrier between the semiarid Great Plains, dominated by grasslands, and the plateaus and deserts that stretch to the Pacific mountain system. The western foot of the Rockies meanders from the Okanogan Range in northeastern Washington to the southern end of the Sangre de Cristo Range near Santa Fe, New Mexico. Along the endless miles of this border the transition from mountains to semiarid and arid lands shows great vistas of spectacular land forms, colorful rocks, and a great wealth of varied vegetation.

The western boundary of the northern province of the Rockies adjoins the Columbia Plateau west of Spokane, Washington, and Lewiston, Idaho. Before it was plowed for wheat production, much of the plateau was covered by the magnificent grasslands of the Palouse Prairie. Thousands of acres of the plateau still are covered by sagebrush and grass, a plant community which marks the northern boundary of the cold desert. South of Boise, Idaho, and extending eastward to the foot of the Teton Range, sagebrush desert dominates the broad Snake River Plains. South of the Tetons the Wasatch Mountains form the eastern rim of the desert in central Utah.

The Colorado Plateau, with its highly varied topography and colorful desert scenery, lies south of Provo, Utah. This is Painted Desert country, full of deep canyons, including the Grand Canyon. The area is characterized by hot summers and cold winters, and by vegetation that ranges from creosote bush and mesquite through pinyon-pine and juniper woodlands; changes to stands of pine, spruce, and fir to about 11,500 feet; and then becomes treeless alpine meadows above upper timberline. The Colorado Plateau has its own high rim, and within the bowl formed by encircling mountains are isolated mountains. These rise above an interior desert of shrubs and drought-enduring grasslands.

From the Colorado Plateau and the central Rocky Mountains the desert lies westward across the Great Basin to the Cascade Mountains in Washington and Oregon and the Sierra Nevada in California. These are the high mountains that deprive the winds of their moisture as they move inland from the Pacific Ocean.

The transition from mountains to desert east of the Pacific mountain system is marked by Tertiary lavas and by volcanic cones of Pleistocene age. The part of this desert border where I have traveled extensively lies south and east of Bend, Oregon. Here the ponderosa pines give way to the sagebrush of the "high desert" of Oregon. It is a country of dramatic geologic variety, fascinating anthropological sites, and spectacularly beautiful desert flowers. Here also deer, antelope, coyotes, and bobcats roam; jackrabbits and desert rodents are abundant; and in early spring the sage-grouse males display to their mates on their ancestral booming grounds.

Among the unique features of this desert is the cave which now is protected as the Fort Rock Cave National Monument. Some early human history starts here. In Cow Cave some seventy-five sagebrush-bark sandals, more than 9,000 years old, have been discovered along with other artifacts and campfire ashes that indicate the presence of Indians in the vicinity more than 13,000 years ago.

An interesting geological feature in this same locality is the Crack-in-the-Ground, caused by the splitting of cooling lava that flowed across the area about 1,000 years ago. This crack varies from a few inches to ten feet or more in width and is twenty to forty feet deep in some places. Ice frozen in winter remains there into summer. Reub Long, coauthor with E. R. Jackman of *The Oregon Desert* and a resident of the high desert for many years, told me that the pioneers around Fort Rock used the ice to make ice cream each Fourth of July. This conservationist rancher and teller of fabulous tales also informed me that the Hole-in-the-Ground near his place was the size of a bathtub when he lived there as a boy. When I saw it recently it was nearly a mile wide from rim to rim and some 300 feet deep. Most geologists disagree with Reub and believe it is a small crater caused by volcanic action.

In the country around Fort Rock and the town of Christmas Valley one can visit and explore other fascinating aspects of the desert. The Devil's Garden, for example, is a jumbled field of lava with a moonlike landscape where doves, quail, magpies, coyotes, deer, bobcats, and rabbits abound. Then there is Fossil Lake, where fossils of prehistoric animals have intrigued paleontologists for years. And beyond are sand dunes, dry lake beds, white lava sands that look and feel like popcorn, and endless miles of sagebrush with phloxes, larkspurs, evening primroses, and other showy forbs that bloom brilliantly when the spring rains come.

From southern Oregon and far south into California pinyon and juniper woodlands are common east of the Cascade–Sierra Nevada axis. These woodlands merge with the upper part of the sagebrush desert edge for hundreds of miles on the west side of the Great Basin. In southern California Joshua trees grow on the upper rim of the Mohave Desert at elevations up to 5,000 feet in the rain shadow of the San Gabriel Mountains. The Colorado Desert to the south lies mostly below 2,000 feet and has higher winter temperatures than those in the Mohave Desert. Its western border is the California chaparral, the brushland which is burned every few years by intense fires.

The Sonoran Desert is rimmed in part by water—by the Pacific Ocean and the Gulf of California. There are many anomalies in Baja California and the coastal deserts. In this romantic and almost unknown part of the world are high mountains, broad plateaus, deep canyons, volcanic formations, sandy plains, and dry riverbeds. Rainfall is meager, and no effective moisture may fall for half a dozen years. Summer rains, if they occur, come as cloudbursts. The resulting floods and torrents sweep the dry washes free of living things. In this land of oppressive heat and little rain we see a bizarre vegetation of dreamlike unreality.

The weird elephant tree (*Bursera microphylla*) and the giant cardóns (*Pachycereus pringlei*), largest of the cacti, grow in the Vizcaíno Desert. Forests of the strange cirio, or boogum tree (*Idria columnaris*), grow on rocky slopes in company with a kaleidoscopic display of thorny shrubs, lesser cacti, white-barked palo blanco trees (*Lysiloma candida*), and tree yuccas (*Yucca valida*). Here, also, the peninsular ocotillo (*Fouquieria peninsularis*) produces its spreading stems on a short sturdy trunk. Near the coast this tree, as well as the paloverde and the large cacti, are festooned with gray lichens of the genus *Ramalina*, which are sustained by moisture from fogs that roll in from the sea. In this land of misty nights, mistletoes and other epiphytes shroud the elephant trees in a manner similar to that of the Spanish moss on the oak trees in Florida or the beard moss in the Montana mountain forests.

Animal life in the deserts bordering the sea includes numerous genera found in the deserts of California and Arizona. But the species and varieties of some mammals, birds, reptiles, and in-

The cirio or boogum tree is one of the strange plants in Baja
California. The tree resembles an inverted carrot and may reach a
height of sixty feet. The twiglike branches produce small leaves
during favorable moisture periods.

sects differ from those farther north. These differences include color adaptations, life habits, and morphological variations distinguishable only by classification experts. Mice are abundant, and other desert animals—including foxes, rabbits, skunks, snakes, and lizards—are present. Antelope, deer, and desert bighorns also live there.

Western gulls and California brown pelicans raise their chicks in the intense heat of the desert in rookeries on Angel de la Guarda, an island located in the Gulf of California. The young down-covered gulls regulate their internal temperatures by panting to achieve evaporative cooling from the moist living membranes of their respiratory tracts. They also obtain some relief from solar radiation by vaporization of moisture from their skins, although they, like other birds, do not have sweat glands. The young naked pelicans depend on shade provided by the adults, which are ever solicitous for their young.

Baja California is a desert wonderland and a wilderness explorable only by the adventurer who goes well prepared. The very roadlessness of this land of strange plants and animals has pre-

Senita cactus is bearded at the ends of the branches, which have fewer ridges than the organ-pipe cactus. It grows sparingly in southwestern Arizona but is common in northern Sonora and western Chihuahua.

served its primitive nature. Beyond the tourist facilities along the
coast, which can be reached by small planes or boats, vast areas
are unknown to most people. There is a road on Baja California
from Tijuana to La Paz. From the end of the limited-access highway it is paved until it approaches Rosario de Arriba. Also, it is
paved for more than 300 kilometers north of La Paz. Between
these paved stretches all the roads are dusty, rocky, sandy, rutted,
steep, and poorly maintained. Jeeps and four-wheel-drive vehicles
with high clearance can negotiate them. But the country that lies
beside these roads and stretches away to the horizon and beyond
is a desert with a wildness and beauty not approached by any
other desert in North America.

One of the striking features of the vegetation on American
deserts, not consciously recognized by many travelers, is the
widespread occurrence of grasses. In Wyoming blue grama and
western wheatgrass, so common in the short-grass prairie of the
plains, gradually decrease in abundance westward as sagebrush
becomes prominent near the Continental Divide. The light annual precipitation in the area between Wamsutter and Green
River is insufficient for good growth of sod grasses, but it is
ample for many grasses that grow singly or in bunches.

Indian ricegrass is widely distributed, and the bunches are conspicuous when their leaves become dry and silvery under the
autumn sun. Wet alkaline flats sometimes support solid mats of
inland saltgrass, and other flats become straw-colored in early
summer as the annual foxtail barley becomes dry and cures on
the stalk. Giant wild-rye grows six feet tall in narrow valleys,
along stream courses, and in moist soils in company with greasewood. On dry slopes above the watercourses other grasses
scattered among the sagebrushes include galleta, Sandberg blue-
grass, and thickspike wheatgrass.

While traveling westward across this part of Wyoming, you
can see how the decreasing abundance of plains grasses and the
increase of arid-land grasses indicate the subtle transition from
prairie to desert over a zone many miles wide. The rim of the
desert where it borders the grassland is indistinct in comparison
with the sharp demarcation between woodlands, chaparral, and
pine forests at the bases of the western mountains.

Similarly, the contact of the original magnificent Palouse

Prairie on the Columbia Plateau of Oregon and Washington with the cold northern desert of the Great Basin never was a striking borderline. Instead, it was a broad transition zone over which pure stands of bunchgrass gradually decreased as sagebrush increased. Only remnants of the Palouse Prairie now remain. But intermingled stands of bunchgrass and sagebrush still grow beside the highways that cross south-central Washington and north-central Oregon. Good examples occur in the vicinity of Moses Lake, Washington, and on the steep slopes bordering the Columbia River south of Wenatchee. The grassland-sagebrush transition also is exemplified on the rugged slopes above the John Day River and the Deschutes River for many miles above their junctures with the Columbia River in Oregon.

The contact of desert grassland and hot desert shrubland in the Southwest is diffuse and highly varied with a correspondingly great diversity of mammals, birds, reptiles, insects, and other animals. Mesquite grasslands extend from Texas through New Mexico and Arizona into Mexico. The margins of grassland and desert are often characterized by dense stands of cactus. The grasses themselves occur in perplexing variety. Gramas are abundant, especially blue grama, which occurs as islands on the

Yuccas grow in profusion in some of the desert grasslands in Arizona and New Mexico. They are also abundant in west Texas.

highlands. Other excellent forage grasses are black grama, slender grama, and hairy grama. Before livestock appeared in abundance, Rothrock grama once grew in pure stands at the upper borders of the cactus and desert-shrub belts.

In Arizona the desert grass belt is best developed between 3,000 and 4,500 feet around the southern mountain ranges. In Cochise County, for example, the high valley floors originally supported unbroken seas of grass. Some of the grasslands on high mesas were characterized by the picturesque palmillo or soaptree (*Yucca elata*) and the cholla cactus (*Opuntia spinosior*).

A conspicuous grass in the foothills is curly mesquite. In southern Arizona another member of the genus *Hilaria*, tobosa grass, forms dense sods and masses of twisted dried stems. It becomes green twice in the year after favorable rainfall in summer and winter. Sacaton, a grass made conspicuous by its tall growth, occurs along the drainage courses in the desert grassland. Accounts by the early explorers that mentioned grass "tall as a horse's back" probably referred to the sacaton.

Originally grasses were dominant over extensive areas of desert grassland, and shrubs were widely scattered. Much of the area today is dominated by shrubs. Mesquite, burroweed, and snakeweeds are abundant and overtop the grasses. In southern New Mexico and southwestern Texas mesquite, creosote bush, tarbush, cacti, and a variety of other thorny plants are the most conspicuous plants in the grassland.

The increase of shrubs in recent decades has been ascribed to overgrazing, transportation of seeds by grazing animals, and decrease in frequency and intensity of fires. Before intensive grazing was practiced, luxuriant stands of grass accumulated over a period of years. Fires set by lightning or by the Indians, burning furiously through the dried and matted grass, destroyed trees and shrubs. When stockmen came, their animals reduced the grass cover, and widespread fires became a thing of the past. Rodents also increased on the overgrazed ranges, and they undoubtedly planted many seeds that contributed to the spread of trees, brush, and cacti in the desert grassland.

Woodland borders have encroached upon, and retreated from, the desert from ancient times until the present. Geologic uplift and subsidence, convulsion by earthquakes, climatic changes, and man's recent influences have produced profound changes in the nature and distribution of vegetation around the desert boundaries. Along with these movements of vegetation zones at the edge of the desert a host of birds, mammals, reptiles, and insects have accompanied the shifting woodlands, which provide a source of water, shade, and food not found in the desert.

Ancient wood rats have given us some of the history of the upward and downward movements of the woodland zone in the Chisos Mountains of the Chihuahuan Desert in Texas. A study by Philip V. Wells of Pleistocene midden deposits accumulated by wood rats in caves and shelters, and dated by radiocarbon measurements, indicates the presence of former xerophytic woodland as much as 800 meters below present woodlands of pinyon pine, juniper, shrubby live oak, and prickly pear. The middens contain fossils of leaves, of twigs, and of seeds of trees, shrubs, grasses, and cacti. These were dated at ages ranging from 11,560 years to more than 40,000 years. The dated macrofossil record suggests that where desert now exists moist climatic conditions persisted from as late as 11,560 to 20,000 years ago and also earlier than 36,600 years ago.

In recent times man and his grazing animals have caused plant successions and other ecological changes along the borders of the desert. Millions of acres of desert grassland in Arizona, New Mexico, and Texas have been and still are being invaded by shrubs and trees. The change from grassland to woodland has been so gradual that few people have been aware of it. The most conspicuous trees invading the grasslands are alligator juniper, oneseed juniper, Utah juniper, and Rocky Mountain juniper.

Before white men began overgrazing the desert, fires very probably killed juniper seedlings when they appeared in the grasslands. Seeds undoubtedly were transported for thousands of years by native mammals and birds, but the grasslands persisted without trees. The introduction of livestock, however, resulted in thinning of the grass cover, loss of litter and grass competition, and trampling of the soil. Soil erosion accompanying severe overgrazing also lowered the water table and favored the encroachment of junipers. Thus conditions favorable for juniper invasion were created, and once the deep-rooted trees were established they remained and produced seeds for further advancement into the grasslands.

However, the junipers and other trees and shrubs (along with a great variety of herbaceous plants) that grow along the fringe of the desert support an unusual abundance and variety of wildlife. Common residents are desert mule deer, coyotes, bobcats, badgers, foxes, jackrabbits, cottontails, wood rats, mice, lizards, and a variety of birds. Trees and shrubs here withstand drought because of their deep root systems. Their shade is beneficial to grasses and forbs, and their fruits and seeds furnish food and shelter for many kinds of animals.

At the edge of the desert grassland in southern Arizona the diversity of habitats provides living conditions for white-tailed deer, ringtails, peccaries, poorwills, scrub jays, canyon wrens, mockingbirds, verdins, brown towhees, roadrunners, Gila monsters, western rattlesnakes, and collared lizards. In holes and crevices in rocky cliffs the resident bats include the California brown bat, the masked brown bat, the western pipistrelle, and, in summer, the Mexican freetail bat.

The birds and mammals of the desert rims around the bases of the mountains in the Southwest are a varied group. In the Santa Catalina, Santa Rita, Chiricahua, and Huachuca ranges you may encounter wild turkeys, Mexican chickadees, red-faced warblers, and Bendire's thrashers. Among the night birds of the canyons are the elf owls, whiskered owls, poorwills, and whippoorwills. A variety of bats wing overhead in the darkness. If you camp there, in the light of your evening fire you may see kangaroo rats and silky pocket mice collecting seeds; you may glimpse the shadowy figure of a coatimundi, or hear the snarl of a bobcat or the mumbling of a wandering porcupine.

Jackrabbits and cottontails in the desert are lighter in color
than their relatives that live in the forests and prairies. Even
this baby rabbit matches the color of the big sagebrush in Wyoming
where the author photographed it.

CHAPTER 3

Life and Specialization
in the Desert

Innumerable adaptations of plants and animals make the desert a place of mystery, charm, and beauty. The diversified habitats in the desert—open grasslands, rocky mesas, shifting sands, alkaline flats, salty lakes, meandering rivers, and intermittent streams—are basic influences on the nature and abundance of local vegetation. Plants, in turn, govern the presence of animals that use them directly or indirectly for food, water, and shelter.

Many plants are so widespread and common that we see them constantly while traveling across the desert. In the cool deserts of the Great Basin sagebrush grows on millions of acres. The more alkaline soils support extensive stands of shadscale, winterfat, or greasewood. In the warm deserts extending southward into Mexico succulent plants, such as the cacti, yuccas, and agaves, dominate the landscape and seem to be the kinds of plants one would expect to see there. But merely recognizing plants and giving them names contributes little to our understanding of how the desert biome, or whole combination of plant and animal life, works as a living, interacting community.

When one considers the great variety of plants in the desert—possibly 6,000 kinds—and the innumerable differences in their sizes, structures, and appearances, it seems paradoxical that all are somehow adapted for existence in similar surroundings. Drought is the universal enemy. Yet a multitude of herbs, grasses, shrubs, and trees typify the landscape and are able to live there because each has its own attributes for survival.

The desert biome becomes more meaningful if we look at each plant or animal in terms of its adaptations and capabilities for survival in the place where it lives. The sagebrush plant, which lives in deep, moderately alkaline soil, has long roots which provide water in times of drought. The saguaro cactus, with its shallow, horizontally radiating root system, collects water for storage in its fluted stem, which is "waterproofed" by cuticle, a waxy outer skin. Its spiny covering also retards evaporation. The brightly colored lichen, living as a quiescent crust on a rock, comes alive during brief wet periods and with the aid of its blue-green algae fixes nitrogen from the air. This nitrogen is later returned to the earth, and eventually incorporated into the bodies of other plants. Ultimately it is cycled into animal herbivores, and from them into carnivores. The showy annual grasses and

Widely scattered creosote bushes grow on millions of acres on the flatlands in the Mohave and Sonoran deserts.

forbs that cover the desert with flowers when the rains are right spontaneously develop from billions of seeds buried in the soil. In all these adaptations we can see how plant structure, periodicity of growth, and conservation of water enable plants to respond to the temperature extremes and aridity of the desert.

The simplest system of classifying desert plants divides them into those that evade or escape drought and those that resist or tolerate drought. The cacti, for example, tolerate or endure drought by storing water during rainy seasons and using it during dry periods. Annual plants evade drought by rushing through their entire life cycle in a brief period following favorable rainfall.

Some drought-tolerating plants, such as the creosote bush (*Larrea divaricata*), are veritable camels in the plant kingdom. When drought comes they do not wilt and die. Instead they dry out gradually, and when favorable conditions return they resume active growth. Many other plants resist water loss or reduce transpiration by protective devices such as hairy coats or waxy coverings, or by closure of stomata (pores) in the leaves.

The plants that take the easy way of life in the desert are the annuals. Their life stages occur in such rapid sequence that new seeds are formed before the soil is too dry to prevent uptake of water by the shallow roots. Some of the annual plants produce flowers and seeds when growth has reached a height of only one inch or even less. One of the most remarkable of these is poison suckleya (*Suckleya suckleyana*), found in moist sinkholes and in the bottoms of ponds that dry up in summer. This plant hurries its growth so rapidly that when it is only half an inch high, flowers and fruit are formed in the axils of tiny leaves, while the two linear cotyledons from the seed still are green and are the most conspicuous parts of the plant. If soil moisture persists, this opportunistic plant then goes on to produce a much-branched prostrate mat of succulent stems, leaves, and many flowers and seeds.

Some desert annuals seem to be extravagant with water. They transpire at a faster rate than plants in the humid areas of the United States. This is no paradox. These annuals need water for rapid growth, and while it is available they use it. Many years ago Dr. Homer L. Shantz, who did much research on the water requirements of plants, showed me how to recognize some of the drought-escaping plants. He simply felt the leaves between his fingers. If the leaves felt cool, they probably had open stomata and were transpiring rapidly. If they did not feel cool, then we examined them for such attributes as waxy coatings, hairy surfaces, leathery texture, small surface area, or other characteristics. Of course, there are many microscopic characteristics and physiological features of leaves relating to drought evasion and drought tolerance which can be tested only by sophisticated laboratory studies. But I still find it amusing and instructive to go about feeling desert plants, especially those without thorns or prickles.

Many of the devices and processes used by plants to resist the desert dryness are not immediately obvious. Much digging, for example, is required to find that roots of many perennial plants are weakly branched but penetrate to considerable depths to find moisture. And, by growing deeply, roots obtain a relatively large volume of soil from which to draw this moisture. Deep-rooted plants sometimes assist youngsters of the same species. For example, small greasewood plants (*Sarcobatus vermiculatus*) are connected by roots or runners with larger and older greasewood plants. Thus the parent plants sustain the younger plants until their roots reach groundwater.

Structural differences between desert plants growing side by side often appear contradictory. Grasses, snakeweeds, and pinyon pines with small leaves grow in company with cacti with wide flat stems. The limited surface exposed by small leaves reduces the absorption of radiation, while transpirational cooling and internal metabolic adjustments keep sunlit leaves almost as cool as the surrounding air; at the same time, surface soil temperature may be more than 28° C. above air temperature. The broad cactus pads, however, transpire little water, and may be 10° C. to 16° C. above air temperature. Recent research indicates that they have evolved a protein structure which is stable at relatively high temperatures. It would be delightfully easy if we could look at each desert plant and relate its appearance to its resistance to the arid climate in which it grows; but then much of the mystery and fascination concerning its existence would disappear. The visible and hidden features of the plant work together to enable its survival.

Among the drought-resisting plants, the cacti are particularly successful. They are true storage tanks for desert rains, which wet the upper soil layers where the cactus roots are concentrated.

Saguaro cacti develop additional branches as they grow to maturity.
A creosote bush grows in the foreground and a paloverde tree in the
middle background.

The fleshy stems of some of the cacti are ribbed and are capable
of an accordion-like expansion to accommodate the water supply.
The covering of spines on these ribs tends to break up air currents and thus reduce evaporation of the stored water.

Succulence also occurs in shrubs and herbs of a number of
other plant families. Greasewood shrubs and some of the herbaceous plants of the goosefoot family have mealy, scurfy, or

fleshy leaves. The Utah glasswort (*Salicornia utahensis*) has succulent stems with opposite leaves reduced to small scales; the herbage often turns red or purplish, imparting a vivid color to the barren alkaline shores of desert lakes. The water supply in these succulent plants enables them to continue growth and to produce a new seed crop even if rain does not fall.

One of the best examples of plant specialization in the desert is the adjustment to different concentrations of salt. The grasses known as blue grama, galleta, Indian ricegrass, and sand dropseed have extensive but shallow root systems. They grow in soils with a salt content of less than 1,000 parts per million. The roots of shadscale, small rabbitbrush, greasewood, saltbush, and winterfat can grow in more salty soil and penetrate deeply into soil layers with a salt content greater than 1,000 parts per million. The roots of big sagebrush can stand less salt than any of the above species, but they penetrate to depths of several feet where soils have only 200 parts per million of salt content.

At the shore of Great Salt Lake the margin presents a dazzling white surface due to the heavy crust of salts that crystallize as the water recedes in summer. On these alkaline flats are communities of pickleweed (*Allenrolfea occidentalis*). Pickleweed is a shrubby plant with numerous cylindrical, jointed, fleshy, practically leafless branches. The long taproot obtains groundwater from considerable depths where the soil is less alkaline than at the surface.

Halogeton, a plant related to Russian thistle and poisonous to sheep, prospers when the salt concentration is 5,800 parts per million or higher. After the plants die, large quantities of their sodium are returned to the soil. Accumulation of this salt prevents germination of other plants that might compete with halogeton.

Salt tolerance does not always prevent grazing of desert plants by animals. Winterfat and gray molly, for example, are nutritious and well liked by domestic and wild animals. Since these plants do not compete strongly with less desirable forage plants, it is easy to understand why they diminish in numbers or even disappear when the desert is overgrazed by livestock.

Overgrazing gives a decided advantage to such spiny plants as shadscale, greasewood, and cactus. Indeed, in general the painfully sharp thorns and prickles of many desert perennials undoubtedly decrease predation by large mammals. A camel, however, is little deterred by some of the most horrible thorns. Rabbits, goats, and javelina also eat cacti and other plants with spines. Insects, of course, are notorious for nibbling leaves and stems regardless of plant armor.

Among the wonders of nature are seeds which sustain the lives of plants through unfavorable periods often lasting for years. Through seeds the embryonic life of plants is almost suspended,

Greasewood and saltbushes persist on extremely dry alkaline soils, since their roots penetrate to permanent moisture at depths of ten to twenty feet.

and is then revived to produce new generations. Under extreme desert conditions the mortality of seeds and seedlings is high. The miracle of their survival rests in the innumerable devices and physiological adaptations by which the parent germ plasm is protected against the harsh environment.

Many desert seeds are able to survive temperatures in surface layers of soil that frequently get as hot as 120° F. to 150° F. High salt or alkali concentration usually has little effect on dry seeds. They do not germinate until heavy rains have washed away or greatly diluted the concentration of salt. Heavy rain also dissolves the built-in inhibitors that prevent germination of some kinds of seeds during periods of light rainfall. Many seeds have a time clock that keeps them dormant until a season favorable for germination comes along. Some seeds are produced in such prodigious numbers that even the depredations of insects, birds, and rodents and the vicissitudes of weather fail to utterly destroy the crop. Even the life expectancy of parent plants relates to the production of seed and the chance that their kind will be propagated.

The giant saguaro cactus, for example, produces an abundance of seeds, but few of its seedlings survive. More than 200 fruits are produced near the apex of the trunk and branches of a large plant. Each fruit contains approximately 1,000 seeds. From these, maybe half a dozen seedlings survive in the following year after seed-eating birds and rodents have taken their toll. Even coyotes eat the sweet juicy pulp of the fruits, and ants remove the seed embryos. Rabbits eat the seedlings, and many are also destroyed by drought and floods. The parent cactus compensates by living for 50 to 200 years, during which time a few favorable periods for reproduction are likely to occur.

Many desert herbs counterbalance the danger of extermination by producing a superabundance of seeds. I once tied a large dry Russian thistle plant in a bag and attached it to the wall of my garage. Buffeting by the wind loosened approximately 85,000 seeds during the winter. Some plant species attain prodigal seed production by growing in such fantastic numbers as to make up for the relatively small seed output of individuals. On one of my experimental plots I once counted more than 11,000 six-weeks fescue plants on a square meter. I have found other annuals, such as certain types of plantains, to be equally numerous.

Most kinds of seeds live longer than from one growing season to the next. Some remain alive for several years. Many weed seeds remain viable for twenty years or more. Evening primrose seeds have been known to germinate after seventy years in soil. This ability to tolerate long periods of drought explains the appearance of millions of showy ephemerals with attractive flowers when wet seasons produce appropriate conditions for seed germination in the desert.

The seeds of many desert plants are adapted to germinate in different seasons. Some of the annuals begin growth when the summer rains occur. Others germinate when the autumn rains come, and their plants produce new seeds in the following spring. Some produce two kinds of seeds on the same plant: one kind germinates after several rains have fallen, and the other kind does not germinate at all in the same season. Seeds of still other annual plants germinate whenever abundant soil moisture is available.

The different ways in which seeds are dispersed can be observed anywhere in the desert. Seeds move with windblown sand. Ants collect seeds from plants or from the ground and accidentally drop some on the way to their nests. Ground squirrels and kangaroo rats bury more seeds in the soil than they use as food. Creosotebush fruits have hairy coverings and are blown about by the wind or washed long distances by floods. Many plants of the sunflower family produce seeds with hairy parachutes which carry them long distances on the wind. Seeds with spines and hooks become attached to animals and thus are carried from place to place. One hardly needs to ask how a given plant arrives at a favorable place for growth in the desert. One only needs to remember that seeds are among the greatest travelers in nature.

If you walk in the midday glare of the summer sun, the desert seems barren of animal life. The shimmering heat waves only accentuate the silence of the endless landscape, and even the cloud shadows over distant mountains are stationary. But the desert is full of cold-blooded and warm-blooded creatures.

Beneath your feet, hidden in their excavations in the earth, are ants, scorpions, wasps, termites, and even toads. In the sand, shaded by shrubs, are snakes that have buried themselves to escape the death-dealing radiant energy from the sky. In the shadows of the saguaros antelope jackrabbits shift eastward with the westward march of the sun. Birds, which are active in the cooler parts of the day, rest in shrubs or trees where there is shade and sufficient height to avoid much of the heat reflected from the ground.

Animals with fossorial, or digging, habits naturally avoid the heat by living in their relatively cool moist burrows. These include the innumerable rodents—kangaroo rats, pack rats, mice, and pocket gophers—and some of their predators such as the kit foxes, coyotes, bobcats, and badgers. Large grazing mammals such as the desert sheep and deer evade the highest temperatures and avoid expenditure of energy by moving slowly or by resting in shade in midday. The stillness or sluggishness of animals when heat and evaporation are highest is one adaptation for their survival.

One reason that most of us are unaware that there is much animal life in the desert is that many animals are active in darkness. We are amused if we find a mouse nest on the carburetor of our automobile after a night in a desert campground. Or we are perturbed if a wood rat exchanges pretty pebbles for the silverware in our cook kit. But mostly we are unaware that a roll call of mammals around our camp might include a menagerie of harvest mice, deer mice, pocket mice, cactus mice, grasshopper mice, hispid cotton rats, black-tailed jackrabbits, desert cottontails, pocket gophers, antelope ground squirrels, kangaroo rats, bobcats, coyotes, a few collared peccaries, and even a mule deer or two. Species, and even varieties of species, are uniquely adapted to their often extremely limited environments.

Almost every animal in the desert has a comparatively narrow range of environmental limits within which it survives. But if you study the adaptations of desert creatures long enough, your biggest surprise may be that life for them is not so precarious as you have imagined it to be. Life for adapted plants and animals in the desert is quite the normal thing, since each creature lives in its own little niche where water and food are adequate for its specific requirements. These specializations promote the lives of individual species, since by living in different niches competition for food is lessened.

Some desert niches provide limited concealment because of sparseness of vegetation. But certain animals take advantage of this. Kangaroo rats are accomplished jumpers in open country and thus can escape nocturnal predators. In the daytime they are relatively safe in their labyrinthine tunnels, which they close by plugging the entrances with soil. By contrast the pocket mice and harvest mice, which typically run along the ground, seem to require grassy habitats which provide concealment and abundant seeds for nourishment.

Some animals avoid the major barriers of heat and dryness by living in the permanent waters of rivers, lakes, and marshes. The muskrat in a desert marsh not only has water to drink but has plants to eat and to use for building its shelter. The minks and the skunks that inhabit the shores of lakes and rivers have no particular specializations for life in the desert, since much of their food comes from animals that live in or near the water, including fish, frogs, crayfish, bird eggs, and insects. The toads and the tadpole shrimp, on the other hand, are specialized to benefit from torrential rains that fill temporary ponds. Here toads hatch their eggs, and the young toads mature and return to land and burrow into the soil to escape the desert's heat and dryness. The shrimp hatch from eggs that have lain dormant and viable despite the high temperature of the soil in the dried bottoms of their ponds. This generation leaves new eggs to hatch in the future—perhaps as long as five years hence.

The major problems for animals in the desert—adaptation to drought and regulation of body temperature—are solved in many ways. Some animals have physiological adaptations which enable them to withstand the desert environment. Certain desert insects are "wax proofed" so that their external surfaces do not lose water through evaporation at high temperatures. In contrast, some mammals need to evaporate moisture as a means of regulating their body temperatures and this they accomplish by means of sweat glands. Other mammals, such as the camel, can endure a body-weight loss of nearly 20 percent and then can restore the water loss at a single drinking. Still other desert animals—birds, for example—regulate their body temperatures by panting.

From the physiological point of view, the ears of jackrabbits are eminently successful structures for heat regulation. The thin ears, with only a sparse covering of hairs, reflect light and also transmit light so that less than half is absorbed. In the shade or darkness the rabbit loses body heat by vasodilation, or expansion of the blood vessels in the ears. In sunlight, where heat would be gained through the ears, the vessels are con-

Rock squirrels and ground squirrels of one kind or another live in all of our American deserts. They have a habit of popping into their burrows to release heat from their bodies when the desert temperature is high. They are prey for hawks, snakes, coyotes, and other mammals.

stricted and the blood carries less heat from the environment to the rabbit's body. It is possible that jackrabbits resting in shade also can radiate heat to the clear sky, since the radiation temperature of the sky is less than the surface temperature of the rabbit. At any rate, the vasomotor activity of rabbit ears constitutes a remarkable physiological adjustment given to few other animals.

Many desert animals make behavioral adjustments which enable them to endure or to avoid the harshness of the desert. In warm deserts numerous snakes live in holes in the ground during the day. Other snakes and some lizards bury themselves in sand to escape the heat. Some even have specialized scales that serve to keep the sand out of their eyes. The antelope ground squirrel, on the other hand, spends much time above ground during the day and accumulates heat under the desert sun. But before its body temperature becomes dangerously elevated, it retreats underground and radiates the heat to the cool walls of its burrow. Since most desert animals are small and are unable to endure the continued stress of high temperatures, we can readily understand why so many of them dart in and out of their burrows or remain underground for extended periods during the heat of the day.

The nocturnal burrowing animals, of course, avoid the high daytime temperatures by remaining in their burrows until nightfall. This nocturnal rhythm also results in moisture conservation, since the animals do not evaporate large volumes of moisture for body cooling. They must conserve moisture, because their diet of seeds offers a minimum of water. They seldom drink, but use metabolic water produced in their own bodies. Little of this water is used in excretion, since their urine and feces are highly concentrated.

Some of the seed-eating mice likewise live for considerable periods of time without drinking. I remember how, when I was a boy on our Nebraska farm, I used to amuse myself with the common house mice in our granary. They had enlarged a crack the length of the roof beneath the ridgepole. Their tails hung down from this crack, so I could lead them to a wide place, pull them out, and drop them into a wire cage. They lived in this cage without water for several weeks. The mice in the granary also ate wheat and corn grains for weeks when there was no rain or snow and no green vegetation. The nearest water was in a well some 200 yards distant. The mice did not leave their sanctuary in the granary to travel that far. As a boy I did not appreciate all the implications of the way these mice lived in a little biological desert of their own.

Now many reports of mouse survival on dry diets are available in the scientific literature. A study by Carl B. Koford of the water economy of native mice in the Peruvian coastal desert, for example, demonstrates that these mice can tolerate long periods of water deprivation, and at least 10 percent dehydration of their body water. During a sixteen-day deprivation caged mice lost weight for three days and then gained steadily on a diet of dry birdseed. They regained their weight in one day when given water. Koford also found that house mice which have become adapted to desert conditions can survive on a dry diet about as well as Peruvian desert mice can. He noted that gerbils, jerboas, kangaroo rats, and pocket mice are even more capable of survival under dry conditions, since they seldom drink even when water is available.

It is now known that some of the small desert mammals

adjust to dry environmental conditions by estivation, or summer dormancy. The Mohave ground squirrels (*Citellus mohavensis*) go into a "summer sleep" in which their body temperatures are nearly reduced to those of their burrows. Oxygen consumption also is markedly lowered. Arousal occurs spontaneously, or it can be elicited by external stimulation resulting in a quick change from deep torpor to normal metabolism and activity.

Medium-sized mammals that do not burrow, such as jackrabbits, exhibit numerous specializations for successful life in the desert. Although they do not drink, they feed at night on plants which contain considerable water, including the cacti and yuccas. They avoid direct rays of the sun by resting in deep shade, and their furry pelages insulate them from heat radiated from the environment.

Even though the camel is not now native to the American deserts, it is an animal worthy of contemplation because of its adaptations to arid environments. It is one of the most remarkable of the large mammals in its ability to meet the challenge of the desert. Since camels probably originated in America, they may have developed some of their adaptations in our ancient deserts. But a million years ago they migrated to the Old World, and in that length of time undoubtedly acquired more of their fabulous physiological and behavioral attributes.

The dromedary camel (*Camelus dromedarius*) has been well studied by scientists, and their findings have dispelled many misconceptions, especially the one that camels load up a storage tank with water before starting on a long journey.

Large size, for example, is of advantage to the camel. Unlike a small rodent, the camel can travel long distances to reach water. Its size also enables it to carry a pelage that shields it from the rays of the sun. The surface hairs on a camel may reach a temperature as high as 158° F., whereas the camel's internal temperature is approximately 100° F. A camel's internal temperature in the morning may be as low as 93° F. In the afternoon it may run a "fever" of 105.3° F. It conserves water by not sweating until this high temperature is reached. But high body temperature lessens the difference between the animal's body heat and the heat of the environment, and thereby lessens the heat absorbed by the body. At night the camel unloads its heat and thus exhibits a daily rhythm of internal temperature variation.

Poorly adapted man sweats and loses salt in an attempt to

maintain his body temperature at approximately 98.6° F. Drinking does not remedy his difficulty unless he also replaces his salt. A man can only drink a quart or less of water without getting waterlogged. But a man can carry his water with him, and given adequate food, can cope with most desert situations. Most of us, however, are not prepared to deal with the rigors of the desert by finding food and shelter there with only our own bodily resources. Only the plants and animals are adapted to confront the problems of survival in their allotted desert habitats.

The story of the interrelationships of plants and animals in the desert would be incomplete if the food chains were overlooked. When I see animals in the desert, I find it instructive to pry into their food sources and to trace their food chains back to their beginning. In the end, the ultimate food source will always be a plant or some product of vegetation.

In the desert, as elsewhere, plants are the mediators between the sun and all animal life. By their unique ability to photosynthesize their own food with the sun's energy they also supply food directly or indirectly to all the other inhabitants of the earth. Most plants are capable of making more food than is required for their own growth and reproduction. This surplus production is beneficial, since the majority of plants need the help of soil organisms, and even animals that eat them, if they are to survive.

The exchange of energy when plants are eaten by animals is not a one-way process. Insects, birds, and small mammals assist plants at pollination time and in seed dispersal. By selective feeding, animals reduce the numbers and vigor of some plants that could become destructively competitive with other plant species and thus upset the environmental relationships that allow a variety of both plants and animals to coexist.

Food chains start in many ways, and there is energy change between each of the links in the chains. When an animal dies, bacteria, insects, and scavenger animals begin the process of cycling the corpse into their own bodies or recycling it into nutrients that can be used by plants for their growth. Even the animal wastes from the scavengers are recycled into the environment. In similar manner, dead plants are returned to the soil by bacterial action or are incorporated into small animals such as termites, which in turn are eaten by ants, beetles, small snakes, and lizards. These animals then die to repeat the process or are eaten by still larger animals, until the ultimate predator, such as an eagle or coyote, ends the upward progression of the energy chain and then itself returns to the earth.

The coyote's link with the food chain is easy to see: he eats rabbits, mice, birds, and fruits and other plant parts. Similar foods are provender for the omnivorous raccoon-like coatimundi, which chews links out of many food chains involving insects, rodents, snakes, lizards, seeds, fruits, and bird eggs. But the process becomes more complex when one pries into the food-gathering and energy relationships of the creatures eaten by the coyote or coatimundi. These lesser living things also perform acts of violence on one another and on still smaller things farther down the food chain.

When I see a fox or a coyote, for example, the thought comes to mind that there goes maybe a thousand pounds of grass, or forbs, or shrubs, or seeds. You can figure this out for yourself. At 10 percent efficiency, ten pounds of plant material are required to make one pound of gopher, squirrel, or mouse flesh; ten pounds of rodent flesh are required to make one pound of hawk, owl, or coyote flesh. And if the final predator weighs ten pounds, then it represents half a ton of vegetable production. Of course, the ecological food chain is not always that simple.

Some mice, for instance, eat grasshoppers which have eaten grass; other mice eat scorpions which have eaten insects which have eaten grass, cactus, or leaves of shrubs; and coyotes eat fruits, grass, snakes, insects, eggs, and birds. So, part of the fascination of the desert comes from attempts to decipher the energy exchanges between its creatures and the ways in which they strike a balance of numbers so that all can continue to exist, not necessarily as individuals, but as species, each with its own niche or life style in its chosen habitat.

It is not my intention here to paint the desert as a harsh world

A chuckwalla basks in the sun after a meal of flowers and leaves.

of villainous creatures, a place of raw violence, or an arena for bloodshed and strife. Nature everywhere is harsh and raw in the whole web of life she has woven for existence on this planet. But nature also is attractive, and in the desert she exhibits beauty, mystery, diversity, and a cosmic story which man alone among all creatures may ultimately understand.

I prefer to think of the demise of each of nature's beings as a moment at the end of a short or a long life lived with creature enjoyment in a home made congenial by the presence of elements necessary for the universal processes of birth, growth, and love-making, and the enjoyment of food, sun, shade, and shelter. As I observe the desert creatures in their natural activities, I also enjoy the morning song of birds, the nimbleness of the jackrabbit being pursued by the desert fox, or the apparent comfort of the lizard basking in the sun. And behind this façade of familiar scenes and sensations I find additional pleasure in my attempt to interpret what I see in terms of the unifying principle of redistribution of energy as it comes from the desert sun.

Life in the desert is replete with many energy relationships we do not completely understand. We can speculate, however, that the woodpecker drilling holes for its nests in the saguaro cactus owes a certain debt to the temperature relations of the physical environment. The cactus, which is useful to the woodpecker, is sensitive to late spring freezes. But it grows on relatively barren, rocky slopes where much of the sun's radiant energy is conducted through and stored in the stony earth. At night the stored energy is radiated back to the body of the cactus and prevents its freezing. Thus the cactus, the woodpecker, and the insects it eats are interdependent and are integral parts of the local ecosystem and of the biosphere in which we all live.

As a part of the International Biological Program, a good number of ecologists now are working on the problem of deciphering the desert. This program, which involves biologists from more than fifty nations, each pursuing special interests, is concerned with every participant in the environment—from shadscale, and hawks, and weather, and soil organisms to water—in a programmed attempt to answer the question: How does the environment work? Let us hope they will discover, before it is too late, how each part characterizes and is essential to the whole natural world.

This island caused Captain John C. Frémont to give Pyramid Lake its name. The lake is noted for its giant trout and for the cui-ui, fish that have survived from prehistoric times. (Photo courtesy of Nevada State Fish and Game Commission)

CHAPTER 4

Desert Waters

The desert does have water. Without water there could be no life, in the desert or elsewhere. Plants grow only when a stream of water can pass from the soil through the roots and through the stems and leaves. Animals must have water for growth and other bodily processes. Without water neither plants nor animals could use the oxygen of the air, since oxygen must be in solution before it can participate in metabolic processes. In the desert, where water is in deficient supply, the problem of its availability and use is paramount among all other needs for survival of living things.

The waters of the desert are not only those we see in ponds and lakes and streams but are the waters of the atmosphere, the soil, and the rocks of the earth itself. Water, the only mineral that exists in solid, liquid, or gaseous form in the temperature range of our living environment, exerts its influence on the desert in all its forms. As a gas, it affects humidity and condenses to form dew, which is absorbed or imbibed by many lowly forms of life. As a solid, it forms ice, which fractures the rocks of mountains and heaves the soil. As a liquid, it builds the world of plants and animals, and composes the bulk of their body materials. As a liquid, it also creates the watery environment of springs, ponds, lakes, streams, and rivers. But these physical bodies of water did not always exist in the desert.

In the beginning the land where our desert now lies was covered with water. In the most ancient geological times the region was at least twice covered by the sea. For more than 300 million years of the Paleozoic era warm shallow seas covered parts of the western half of the continent (during the Ordovician period warm climates existed even in the Arctic). In this era the first fishes were established, the first amphibians appeared, sharks were numerous, and mammal-like reptiles and insects arose. In the following Mesozoic era—the Age of Reptiles—dinosaurs, modern birds, and seed plants evolved. Shallow seas still remained over parts of western United States, and chalk and shale were deposited as the Rocky Mountains were formed in the Cretaceous period.

These land forms were altered by erosion in the Tertiary period, beginning some 60 million years ago. Much volcanic activity accompanied the rise of the Sierra Nevada and Cascade mountains. The continued rise of mountains in western North America, including the upthrust of the San Gabriel, the San Bernardino, and the San Jacinto mountains, and the long parallel ranges of the Great Basin, transformed the older topography into essentially the landscape we know today.

Before the modern desert appeared, however, a time of great glaciation occurred in the Pleistocene epoch. During the four glacial periods of the Ice Age glaciers were not widespread in the mountains of the southern deserts, but rains and lakes increased as the glaciers advanced and decreased as they retreated. The falling waters of the Pleistocene lakes which stabilized for long periods of time and then continued to fall left a fascinating record of beaches and terraces along the mountain slopes.

One of the greatest of the Pleistocene waters was Lake Lahontan with its many bays and attenuations among the mountain ranges in west-central and northwest Nevada. This ancient lake was named after Baron Louis Armand La Hontan, a Frenchman who made early explorations in western America. There has been much speculation about the history and life of this old lake. Tufa (a calcium carbonate deposit) specimens collected chiefly from the vicinity of the present Pyramid Lake and analyzed for carbon-14 values indicate a high-water period from 25,000 to about 14,000 years ago. (Possibly a high-water period for both Lake Lahontan and Lake Bonneville occurred close to 11,000 years ago.) The recession of the lake left three major terraces, exposed former islands as isolated rock masses, and produced barren desert basins.

Biologically, the demise of this inland sea has posed many puzzles for ornithologists, mammalogists, and ichthyologists.

Endemic species or varieties—those limited to certain localities and found nowhere else—include insects, birds, rodents, and larger mammals, probably developed under unique ecological conditions following the recession of the lake. Some, such as the cui-ui or lake sucker of Pyramid Lake and the Amargosa pupfish in Saratoga Spring in Death Valley, are remnants of formerly widely distributed fishes.

Students of fishes believe it probable that a third Pleistocene lake in Oregon may have been continuous with Lake Lahontan in Nevada, since some of the larger fishes of the modern remnant lakes are identical, but different from those in the remnant waters of ancient Lake Bonneville. It has also been suggested that the kit fox, long-tailed pocket mouse, dark kangaroo mouse, Ord kangaroo rat, and botta pocket gopher may be remnants of formerly widely distributed mammals.

Contemporaneous with Lake Lahontan, Lake Bonneville stood some 1,000 feet higher than its present remnant, Great Salt Lake. During the pluvial, or rainy, period some 35,000 years ago this great inland sea in western Utah covered about 20,000 square miles and overflowed into the Columbia River drainage through Red Rock Pass. At its height it was fed by the abundant rains and the melting glaciers of the Wasatch Range that now borders the desert extending westward from Ogden. Salt Lake City, and Provo, Utah. In the time of Lake Bonneville, Lake Chewaucan covered the basins of Abert and Summer lakes in Oregon.

The demise of the great inland seas occurred in stages, with their levels fluctuating according to the rainy periods. Lakes Lahontan and Bonneville stood highest during the Bonneville Pluvial. Bonneville Lake has been given the name Stansbury Lake during the interpluvial low that dropped its level some 700 feet. During the Provo Pluvial the lake rose again to a level of some 625 feet. Then a long dry period lasted for some 4,000 years. The waters evaporated, their saline content increased, and over thousands of square miles marshes dried and desert appeared. Although the climate apparently has not changed significantly in the last 10,000 years, during that time the lakes again partially filled and fluctuated in level, and some disappeared. It was in this period that our heritage of modern desert waters was developed.

The traces left by the shifting climates, the fluctuating water levels, and the geological evidence of past erosion are there for us to see in the land forms of the desert. The terraces formed during long periods of lake stability are especially evident along the Wasatch Mountain front. Other ancient shorelines may be seen around Pyramid Lake in Nevada, in Searles Basin in California, and above dozens of other salty basins in the desert. At some of the higher levels of the ancient lakes, waves cut caves along their shores. These caves gave shelter to early man, and artifacts found there now tell us something of his history and

Out of the Great Basin sagebrush desert more than 100 mountain chains rise to altitudes of 6,000 to 10,000 feet. From their melting snows come the waters that make rivers in the desert or periodically flood the dry lakes in the basins between the mountain chains.

of the story of the great Ice Age animals that roamed the land when the climate was moist and vegetation grew luxuriantly.

Geologists have worked out the story of many of the ancient rivers that fed the prehistoric lakes. The mighty Columbia (which existed before the mountains were formed) and its tributaries at the northern edge of the cold Great Basin Desert flowed for aeons, draining the highlands and mountains of Canada, Washington, and Idaho, and some of the deserts of Oregon. The Colorado River, rising in the Rocky Mountains and flowing through the Grand Canyon to the Gulf of California, has remained a permanent stream through the desert for time without end. During the ages it has shifted its course with the invasion of the sea, and in recent time has formed the Salton Sea.

If one has the time and inclination, a fascinating story of ancient rivers can be read by exploring the borders and hinterlands of ancient lakes, basins, and their shorelines on encircling mountains. Much of this has been done by the geographers and geologists. But an actual journey, aided by maps and travel guides, is an inspiring trip that imprints the physical processes of the desert forever in one's mind. A lifetime is all too short for one person to trace the history of more than a few of the vanished desert waters. But even limited exploration can give an understanding of the desert obtainable from no book, lecture, or pictorial study.

If we turn to the history of a famous river, the Humboldt in Nevada, we find that it once supplied an important part of the water of Pleistocene Lake Lahontan. Now the river is a sluggish stream which drops about 1,100 feet between Elko and Lovelock, Nevada. It flows through a gorge of late Tertiary rocks about thirty miles below Elko and then winds around the other major uplifts in the Great Basin to disappear in a desert sink. The once-mighty ancestor of the Humboldt originally may have drained to the Pacific Ocean by way of the Feather River in California.

Because of my interest in the cui-ui, the fabulous sucker of Pyramid Lake, I have sadly traced the Truckee River from Lake Tahoe in the eastern Sierra Nevada to its outlet in Pyramid Lake. The Truckee was once a mighty stream whose turbulent waters cut down through the fault-block Virginia Range from Vista to Wadsworth. For millennia the cui-ui and the giant native trout ascended its rushing waters during the spawning season. Now the Canada geese still find sanctuary in the remaining stream in the very center of Reno. But the cui-ui and the trout come no more, since power and irrigation dams have diverted the river and reduced it to a mere trickle beyond Wadsworth.

In geologic times many other rivers flowed into troughs and basins to create lakes, some of which overflowed to form other lakes in lower valleys. The Owens River and the Mohave River thus formed chains of lakes. Searles Lake, for example, once overflowed into the Panamint Trough and from there into Death Valley to form the ancient Lake Manly and the present Lake Rogers. The Amargosa River, which formerly joined with the Mohave River, still sheds water into Death Valley when cloudbursts cause temporary floods.

A fascinating variety of biological communities occur along the edges of desert rivers. The lower Colorado River, for example, exhibits wide variation in streamside habitats that reflect the vagaries of the river itself in times of flood and drought. On the silt deposited by floods the reed *Phragmites communis* grows in dense jungles. From Needles to the mouth of the river, before farmers and irrigationists claimed the land, black willow and Fremont's cottonwood formed forests of trees three feet or more in diameter where summer flood water reached levels of twelve feet. In stretches where trees still remain, desert pallid bats, mule deer, hispid cottonrats, foxes, skunks, snakes, and a host of birds find congenial shelter and a variety of food. Common in the willow-cottonwood area are Cooper's hawks, ladder-backed woodpeckers, and redwing blackbirds. In summer nesting species include white-winged and mourning doves, yellow warblers, summer tanagers, and black-chinned hummingbirds.

Where floodplain sloughs are absent and the river is more deeply entrenched the vegetation zones change with increasing elevation above the high-water mark. Above the willow zone colonies of arroweed (*Pluchea sericea*) grow in dense thickets and provide acceptable habitats for deer mice, wood rats, skunks, and song sparrows. The slender arrowweed once provided arrow shafts and material for baskets and animal cages used by the Indians. Today its pale purple flowers may be seen along streams from California to Texas.

At increasing elevation above the floodplain mesquite groves border the arroweed communities and sometimes form a mosaic with saltbush. Here Arizona cottontails and Merriam's kangaroo rats abound. On rocky slopes and benches, brittlebrush (*Encelia farinosa*) is common and gives sanctuary to a variety of animals including antelope ground squirrels, spiny pocket mice, and wood rats.

Brittlebrush, or incienso, is an interesting bush in its own right. The gray-green leaves turn white at maturity and are shed when drought comes. The thick bluish stems then act as water-storage organs. Edmund C. Jaeger notes in *Desert Wild Flowers* that resin crystals exuded by the woody stems were burned as incense by the early padres and that the Indians rubbed it on their bodies for relief of pain.

For adventuresome and healthy people, exploration of streams and rivers from their sources to their mouths can be unforgettable experiences. Even visits to local stretches of stream channels at different elevations can increase one's understanding of the transition from mountains to desert. For example, in the Ruby Range, one of the most prominent massifs in the Great Basin between the Wasatch Mountains of Utah and the Sierra Nevada, you can start among 10,000-foot mountains and snow-fed lakes at the foot of cirques gouged out by ancient glaciers and descend from marshy meadows on timbered trails. Upper timberline is marked by alpine fir and limber pine. Aspen groves line the streams in valley bottoms, and then you come to mountain mahogany, juniper, and pinyon-pine groves as the lower slopes become drier. Wildlife in these zones includes mule deer, mountain lions, marmots, beavers, chipmunks, and many birds. Finally, you come to the ubiquitous sagebrush extending to the far horizons of the Great Basin.

A desert river with spectacular features is the Crooked River, which you cross on the bridge north of Bend, Oregon, on U.S. 97. The box canyon with vertical walls is 300 feet deep, and you can look *down* on violet-green swallows catching insects on the wing. But the "Island," a remnant of a great lava flow, standing at the junction of the Deschutes, Metolius, and Crooked rivers, is nearly 1,000 feet high. Beyond, the mountain rim of the Cascades rises to nearly 10,000 feet.

This is one of my favorite exploring grounds. You can stand in the sagebrush desert—where coyotes and jackrabbits bound away at your presence, and where lizards attend the large mounds of the harvester ant—and see where the old river has

Snow geese migrate across the eastern Oregon and Nevada deserts and find shelter and food in the marshes, ponds, and lakes.

slashed down through volcanic tuffs, lavas, and softer formations to expose past geologic history. The ancient Crooked River must have been a mighty stream to battle the valley-filling lavas and molten rock that came from giant Mt. Newberry and other vents in the earth's crust.

At Smith Rock, east of Highway 97, lava around 6,000 years ago blockaded the river and formed a huge lake which spread eastward where the city of Prineville now stands. But the river prevailed, cutting a spectacular gorge through the desert, rich in plant and animal life. Here many habitats are offered by valley fills, ancient terraces, steep canyon walls, and rocky talus slopes.

One of the rugged wild waters of the desert, seldom explored except by adventurers and river-runners, is the Owyhee River. Its source is in the remote mountains at the southeast corner of Oregon, where antelope, deer, owls, hawks, eagles, and a multitude of other wild creatures live virtually unmolested by man. In the Trout Creek Mountains in this area I once counted more than a thousand sage grouse in less than five miles of travel. In the Pueblo Mountains to the southwest, chukar partridges crept through the sagebrush in flocks of fifty or more, almost undisturbed by my presence, since many of them had not been harassed by hunters. From this kind of country, and from its tributaries, the Owyhee gathers water which pours through a gorge of stone for 250 miles across the Owyhee Desert to join the Snake River south of Ontario, Oregon.

Much of the river is now the Owyhee Reservoir, which provides opportunity for exploration of the canyon by boat. But the rugged and enriching way to see its battlements and the desert life in the gorge above the reservoir is to make the passage with boats or kayaks, life jackets, and skin divers' wet suits. There are peaceful stretches in the river, but the rapids are wild and dangerous.

The caves along the shores contain Indian artifacts. Beavers swim in the quiet stretches, otters play in the rapids, and deer race along the benches or plunge into the river and swim to the opposite shore. White-throated swifts and swallows flirt along the cliff faces while eagles soar high among the battlements. Geese raise their goslings here, and rabbits, foxes, coyotes, and rodents make their homes in the sagebrush-covered slopes beneath the rimrock. This is a place where the grandeur and the spirit of the desert still endure.

The fine silt and clay particles brought down by water from the mountains dry and crack in desert lake bottoms under the summer sun.

Although the Great Basin and Mohave deserts are arid lands they contain a surprising number of lakes. Some of these are permanent bodies of water; others are intermittently dry, or recede to marshlands in periods of deficient rainfall in the surrounding mountains. In prehistoric times the area now occupied by the western deserts was a veritable mosaic of lakes following the recession of Lake Lahontan and Lake Bonneville. Only remnants of these inland seas remain, and many of the floors of the desert valleys are level salt-encrusted flats, or playas.

Only three major remnants of Lake Bonneville remain in Utah: Great Salt Lake, Utah Lake, and Sevier Lake. Utah Lake receives its water from the Wasatch Mountains by way of the Provo River. It overflows through the Jordan River to Great Salt Lake. In its fresh water are fish related to those in Pyramid Lake, Nevada, and Klamath Lake in Oregon, indicating a much wider distribution of suckers and other species in the ancient past. Sevier Lake is no longer perennial, owing to heavy use of its water for irrigation.

The Lahontan Basin, primarily in Nevada, contains at least two dozen lakes and playas that have been named. These include Pyramid Lake, Lake Winnemucca (named after the Paiute Indian chief), the playa or marsh at Carson Sink (at the mouth of the Humboldt River), Desert Valley, Teels Marsh, Coal Valley, and Walker Lake.

Lakes of the Basin and Range Province in Oregon include Klamath Lake, Summer Lake, Abert Lake, and Goose Lake. The big mullet or sucker fish of Klamath Lake, related to the suckers of Pyramid Lake, have been the subject of newspaper stories for years. These fish, often exceeding twenty pounds, are of vacuum-cleaner design, acting as vegetarian cleaners of the lake bottom. When the mullet congregate in the waters of Sucker and Barkley springs to spawn, anglers assemble with a motley array of "sophisticated" tackle, including clubs, pitchforks, and treble hooks on heavy twine with nuts and bolts for weight. The fish do not strike at lures and have to be snagged, which is legal since they are not classed as game fish. Some people eat these fish, and old-timers used to catch them to render for oil.

Three interesting lakes in the Oregon desert are Malheur, Mud, and Harney. Much of the area around these lakes lies in the Malheur National Wildlife Refuge. The waters of Malheur Lake range from 500 to 50,000 acres, depending on drought and rainfall; they come from the Silvies River, which originates in the Blue Mountains, and from the Donner and Blitzen, which originates in the giant fault-block Steens Mountain. The Donner and Blitzen provides excellent trout fishing, but one sometimes is inclined to use its name profanely, in the German sense, because of the rattlesnakes along its shores. These reptiles also are numerous west of Steens Mountain; Clark Holscher and I once counted forty-three rattlesnakes *on the road* in thirty-nine miles between French Glen (the town made famous by Pete French, the cattle king) and the little hamlet of Fields, Oregon. Later I became a charter member of the French Glen Rattlesnake Eaters' Association.

Despite the rattlesnakes, Malheur Lake country is a splendid region, for few areas support a greater variety of wildlife than this desert oasis. In good years legions of migratory birds arrive in March and April. Sandhill cranes perform their strange dances and nest in the area. Song birds frequent the willows and cattail swamps. In the marshes are great blue herons, snowy egrets, grebes, and black terns. And on the sagebrush-covered uplands are sage grouse, mountain quail, Hungarian partridge, California quail, and ring-necked pheasants.

Mammals also find congenial surroundings in the Malheur country. Muskrats build houses which are used as nesting platforms by Canada geese. Mule deer raise their fawns in the Blitzen Valley and on the slopes of Steens Mountain and come down to winter in the sagebrush-juniper zones. Pronghorns are present the year round, and mink, raccoons, skunks, and rodents are among the fifty-one species of mammals recorded for the area.

For escape from urbanism, Pyramid Lake has been one of my favorite spots for many years. This unique body of water is one of the nation's treasures, a heritage that may vanish if pirating of the waters from its principal source, the Truckee River, is allowed to continue—even California has proposed to pirate the water through an interstate compact. This would further impoverish the Paiute Indians who depend on its recreational resources, and destroy the giant race of Pyramid Lake Lahontan cutthroat trout, a species of landlocked salmon. Gone also would be the already-endangered cui-ui.

I first saw and fished for the cui-ui—pronounced "kee wee," "kwee-wee," or, as the Indians say, "koo-ee-wee" (*Chasmistes cujus*)—some twenty years ago. Glen Fulscher at the University

The cui-ui sucker, more widely distributed in prehistoric times, now survives only in Pyramid Lake, Nevada. It may become extinct if additional irrigation water is withdrawn from the Truckee River and the lake continues to dry up. This one was caught by the author before fishing by white men was prohibited.

of Nevada called me long-distance to say that the cui-ui were running. I traveled 1,000 miles from Nebraska to see them. After I left Reno and Sparks, and followed the road north to the west shore of Pyramid Lake, I found there were no slot machines, crap tables, or kino games—only the desert.

At the mouth of the Truckee the water was too shallow for the spawning run and the fish were clustered near the shore, circling in vain for passage into the fresh water that had flowed into their domain for thousands of years. But spawning was in progress in the inflowing river water above the sand bars. With spinning gear one could simply cast a bare treble hook into a water-boil made by the congregating fish, reel in rapidly, and hope to snag a monster by accident. Usually the hook caught the fish in the back and slightly ahead of the tail. Then a considerable struggle ensued as the fish torpedoed toward deep water.

There is no limit to the number of cui-ui the Indians can take, since they own the fish. But whites in former years were restricted to five (and, later, three) per day for a tribal fee of one dollar per day or three dollars per calendar year. Some of the residents of Reno would drop the first fish caught into a shallow lagoon, a few yards back of the lake shore. Then as subsequent fish were caught they were compared for size with those in the lagoon, and the smaller ones were thrown back into the lake. This process of exchange allowed the fishermen to build up the size of their "keeper" fish, make numerous catches, and still have only three fish in possession. But because of wanton waste of fish which were caught and simply discarded, white men are no longer permitted to fish for cui-ui in Pyramid Lake.

Disputes between the Indians and white men have been all too common in this region, although the first contacts were peaceful enough. John C. Frémont and his men visited the Paiutes here in January 1844. The tufa island off the southeastern shore reminded him of the great pyramid Cheops, and hence he originated the name Pyramid Lake. At that time the Indians presented him with some of the native trout, which grew to a record weight of sixty-five pounds. The political history of the lake and of the Indian reservation since then has been one of wars with the whites, long controversy with the government over jurisdiction of the reservation, and pirating of the waters of the Truckee River, causing the lake to decrease in depth and extent.

Among the interesting geological features of the area are the terraces and bars formed by prehistoric Lake Lahontan. Pinnacles formed by tufa and a white margin above the water line, created by algae in the presence of the calcium in tufa, mark the promontories and Anaho Island. This island is the nesting ground for thousands of California gulls and for white pelicans so numerous they resemble great snow fields when they stand side by side on the sand flats.

In addition to the natural lakes of the desert, spectacular reservoirs have been created in recent years by Hoover Dam, which backs up the waters of the Colorado River for more than 100 miles in Lake Mead, and by Davis Dam, which created Lake Mohave. The fish fauna of these reservoirs is, of course, different from the original river populations, since largemouth bass, black bass, sunfish, crappie, carp, and Mississippi threadfin shad have been introduced. Whether artificial stocking of game fish will be effective remains to be seen.

An even more remarkable number of fish have been introduced into the Salton Sea in an attempt to establish a sports fishery. More than thirty species were introduced between 1929 and 1956. The fish planters must have been enthusiastic and hopeful, since they introduced species ranging from striped bass, anchovy, bonefish, halibut, corbina, spotfin mojirra, grunion, diamond turbot, opaleye, bairdiella, and mudsucker to Pacific thread herring. Many of the plants made during and after 1950 were of the "shotgun" type, since there was no way to predict what fishes would be successful. Less than a dozen species have survived.

The Salton Sea is about 235 feet below sea level and lies in the Salton Trough, which was in existence in the late Tertiary period, when it was inundated by the Gulf of California. The gulf waters receded from the Trough about the beginning of Quaternary time one million years ago, possibly as the result of delta formation by the Colorado River. Geologists differ regarding the formation of an ancient lake, Lake Cahuilla, now called Lake LeConte, which existed in the Salton Sink. This lake may have disappeared in relatively recent times, since Indian artifacts and legends indicate that the water was lowered by gradual evaporation.

The present Salton Sea originated after the beginning of irrigation into the southern end of the Sink (the Imperial Valley). In 1901 water was first brought in via the Alamo channel, and

Some species of pupfish are found only in a single spring or water hole in the desert. Others live in the Salton Sea in California and in the drainage of the Colorado and Gila rivers in Arizona.

by 1904 some 600 miles of canals from a head near Yuma were serving 150,000 acres. In the winter of 1904–1905 the Colorado and Gila rivers flooded and cut through the headworks, and a summer flood in 1905 poured into the Salton Sink. The Sea, as described by W. P. Blake in 1916, was some 45 miles long, 17 miles wide at the maximum, and 83 feet deep. Since the beginning the sea has fluctuated in level but has been predicted to stabilize at a surface elevation of −235 feet.

The desert pupfish (*Cyprinodon macularis*) is the only native fish in the Salton Sea. It is a chubby species, usually not over two inches long. It differs from the introduced mosquito fish, which is uniformly tan with tiny black spots. Male pupfish in summer have blue backs and golden bellies; in winter the colors often fade to brown or olive on the back and white on the under surface. This species of desert pupfish ranges from the Gila and Lower Colorado rivers to eastern Baja California and the Sonoyta River of northern Sonora, Mexico.

Since the Salton Sea is a difficult environment because of salinity, deficiency of dissolved oxygen, and unusual chemical composition, it provides an interesting example of ecological adaptation and food-chain development. Among the introduced invertebrates were crabs, squid, shrimp, mussels, clams, polychaete worms, snails, and limpets. Some of these were introduced unintentionally along with fish transplants, by boats, and, probably, by birds. Gulls, for example, discovered the Salton Sea within a year or two and came from as far away as Texas.

The introduced zooplankton included rotifers, copepods, an annelid worm, and a barnacle (*Balanus amphitrite*). These animals, along with small floating plants (phytoplankton), provided food for the more developed species, so that ecological niches were filled and a viable food cycle was established. However, nature still is not in balance in the Salton Sea, and how it will end, in the presence of changing salinity and changing chemical composition of the water is anybody's guess. The water may continue to evaporate and become so salty that plants and fish will not be able to exist, especially if irrigationists do not permit it to be replenished.

Some of the greatest riddles in nature appear in the little waters of the desert: springs, ponds, pools, and diminutive streams. Since the conditions in many of these waters are unique, the plants and animals they contain also are unusual in their adaptations for life. Some of the desert fish and insects in water-filled caves, springs, and salty creeks are relicts of populations that were widespread in more humid times.

The pupfish are among the best examples of surviving remnants from prehistoric waters. These small fish live in restricted communities in Arizona, Nevada, and California. The devil pupfish (*Cyprinodon diabolis*) exists in only one place in the world, in Devil's Hole, Ash Meadows, Nevada (a part of Death Valley National Monument). It has been estimated that the entire population consists of only 300 fish. They spend most of their time feeding on algae on a rock ledge that varies from a few inches to three feet in depth. When disturbed, they vanish in water which reaches a depth of thirty feet.

The Nevada pupfish (*Cyprinodon nevadensis*) is more widespread. It occurs in the Amargosa drainage, from Ash Meadows, Nye County, Nevada, to Saratoga Springs, Death Valley, California. Ira LaRivers, in *Fishes and Fisheries of Nevada,* calls *Cyprinodon nevadensis* the Amargosa pupfish. He also describes two varieties of *nevadensis*—the Lovell Spring Amargosa pupfish, and the Big Spring Amargosa pupfish. Similar kinds of pupfish occur in the Gila River, Arizona, and in Quitobaquito Springs in Organ-Pipe Cactus National Monument.

In spite of their uniqueness, relatively little is known of the life histories of pupfish. Apparently they breed the year round, since fish of all sizes can be seen throughout the seasons. Their food probably consists mostly of algae, since little animal matter seems to be available in their environments. The warm saline water seems to suit them. I have seen thousands of them darting about in the inch-deep water under the broiling sun in Salt Creek, near Stovepipe Wells in Death Valley.

Endemic animals—those confined to a limited dwelling place —are found in most deserts of the world. Some are fantastically restricted. At least ten fish, for example, are endemic in springs that rise from the desert floor in the Cuatro Cienegas basin of Coahuila. In this same basin twelve endemic species of snails occur. But an even more bizarre situation is exemplified by an endemic catfish (*Clarias cavernicola*) in the Kalahari Desert. This fish lives in a dark sink and feeds on the excreta of baboons living in a dry cave above the sink. If the baboons were to disappear, presumably the fish would disappear too.

Potholes and puddles in the American desert are so evanescent that one might assume they support no living things at all. But in temporary waters, especially those formed by flooding, Aedes mosquitoes, copepodids, tadpoles, brine shrimp, fairy shrimp, and tadpole shrimp appear as if by magic. They emerge from eggs laid by their parents, which in turn have emerged from the earth, or they hatch from cysts long dormant in the dry mud of their desert depressions. Some hurry into their life cycles to produce new breeding males and females, sometimes within four or five days, before the water evaporates. Others, such as *Triops,* the tadpole shrimp, require fifteen to twenty days to attain full size. These animals resemble tiny horseshoe crabs of the sea beach.

Few animals are better adapted for life in arid lands than *Triops.* Their eggs lie for years in the dried mud or dust, where they may be exposed to temperatures up to 80° C. In laboratory experiments D. B. Carlisle found that eggs of *Triops,* similar to those found in American deserts, collected in the desert near Khartoum, capital of the Republic of the Sudan, can withstand temperatures within 1° C. of the local boiling point of water. Although they are not subject to such a high temperature in nature, they apparently require exposure to temperatures exceeding 50° C. and a long period of desiccation before hatching. All species of *Triops,* however, do not live in the desert. Some are found in the tropics, and they are common in temporary ponds on the Great Plains. In California they sometimes become serious pests in rice fields, where they eat the young leaves.

The coming of rain and the accumulation of temporary waters quickens the lives of many creatures usually not seen in the desert. Even in ephemeral pools a food chain develops, beginning with bacteria and algae. The spores of these microscopic plants germinate within hours, and multiplication results in billions of new plants. Almost simultaneously minute animals such as copepods increase by the million, using the bacteria and algae for food.

Meanwhile, toads have laid their eggs. These hatch in three days to a week in the warm water, and the tadpoles feed on algae and even mud, which contains organic substance and nourishment. Shrimp and water-inhabiting insects also appear in increasing numbers and become prey for larger insects, adult toads, and salamanders. These in turn attract snakes, birds, skunks, and raccoons. The brief existence of the temporary pond thus transforms a barren area into a microcosm involving many plants and animals at many levels of nutrition and energy exchange.

The miracle is that so many sparks of life are kindled into the flame of growth, reproduction, predation, and coexistence within a few days or weeks. Then they die and leave a legacy of nutrients for the next flooding. Meanwhile, their spores, eggs, and cysts rest through the months or years of heat and dryness until the rains come again.

Evening primroses make white flower gardens in the desert after the seasonal rains have fallen.

CHAPTER 5

The Variety of the Desert

For those who have not learned to read the desert landscape it is a place of monotony where the soil bakes under the relentless sun and the night is dark. But the desert is far from monotonous when you are conscious of its daily changes, from sunset to dawn to noon, or from the cold of winter to the profusion of spring, and the unique adjustments of living creatures to the tempo of the seasons.

The fascination of the desert derives from a richer variation of land forms, plant and animal life, daily rhythms, and seasonal changes than the more favored terrains that most of us know. The very rawness of the landscape exposes the face of the earth and bears witness to the forces of nature that produce its shapes and forms. Nowhere can you better see and comprehend the physical changes wrought on the crust of our restless planet than in the desert.

If you travel extensively over the North American deserts and observe the variety of adaptations of living things to specific habitats, the dynamic nature of the desert becomes more meaningful. The interrelationships between plants, animals, soil, weather, and physiography increase your appreciation of the diversity, complexity, and intrinsic beauty of arid lands. When you observe the variety of desert environments, the bizarreness of creatures that live in specific places seems to disappear.

You need not travel endless miles to see the desert's variety. Its daily rhythm brings hourly changes in color, temperature, and voices of the day or night, and in the tempo of life itself. Early morning is the time to arise and become attuned to the spell of the desert. As the faint light of dawn appears, deer are still on the move, and coyotes are still prowling for the last morsel of food. After the false dawn the cadence of the western meadowlark melodiously pierces the translucent air.

If you travel widely, you can see great contrasts between the cold and the hot deserts. In the northern deserts, even in March when snow persists in drifts on the leeward sides of hills and lies deep in the gullies, the booming of the sage grouse announces the display of the cocks in advance of the breeding season. *Aquila,* the golden eagle, then leaves his perch on a distant escarpment with the hope of snatching an unwary grouse. He meets occasionally with competition, since the marsh hawk also is a harrier of birds, which it catches on the ground instead of pursuing on the wing. The eagles, hawks, and falcons, however, depend mostly on other prey such as rabbits, ground squirrels, and

An animal story in sand. A rabbit has passed during the night, and a bird has searched the worm and insect tracks for prey.

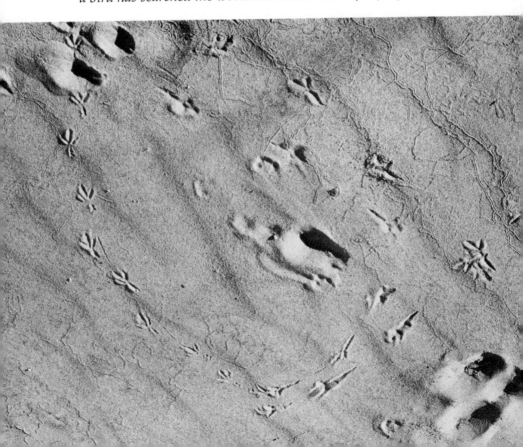

<u>**WEED**</u>

☑ **DATED (hard current science – 5 yrs)**
__**Doesn't SUPPORT CURRICULUM**
__ **Tatterd/Torn/Worn from old age (Falling apart)**
__**Tattered/Torn/Worn from use (Pages are dog eared, loose binding)**
__ **A Newer edition of this book exists**

Title: The Desert World

MW

prairie dogs. Later in the season snakes, immature birds, grass-hoppers, and other insects are added to their bill of fare.

In southern deserts, as the sun dominates the eastern horizon and the heat begins to rise, the cactus wren, big as a robin, bursts into song from his cholla perch, while curve-billed thrashers return time and again to rest atop their favorite saguaros. Chattering coveys of quail flow across the desert floor, bringing to mind closely packed mobs of sanderlings advancing and retreating with the ebb and flow of the ocean waves. Doves coo in a background accompaniment from their perches in paloverde trees along the sand washes. As the sun warms the rocks, lizards emerge, and the roadrunner dashes here and there, looking for an early-morning meal.

If you are in a sandy desert, early morning is the time to look for evidence of animal activity during the previous night. I once strolled down a desert road north of the Santa Rita Mountains in Arizona and in less than a mile counted more than a hundred snake tracks in the dust. Some of these were so narrow they seemed to have been made by large worms. One, possibly made by a large kingsnake, was more than an inch wide. The prize was the half-chevron-like marks left by a sidewinder that had crossed the road and disappeared in a rodent burrow beneath a creosote bush. The snakes had been active during the night; yet, in walking about the desert for three days I never saw a snake in the daytime.

Attempts at identification of animal tracks and "calling cards" left by animals in the desert are always instructive, since they provide clues to the local inhabitants and their activities. Mice leave dainty prints in the dust around their burrows. Kangaroo rats sometimes drag their tails and leave tiny furrows before they leap to a distant spot. A sparring match between a pair of these sprightly beasts leaves a veritable maze of tail marks and footprints.

The hoof marks of deer, mountain sheep, and peccaries, and the prints of coyotes, bobcats, and rabbits, of course, are more easily identified than those of smaller animals. The droppings of various animals are further evidence of their presence.

The best way to identify many of the marks made by desert animals in the sand or dust is to observe the animals in action. Some of the lizards make distinctive patterns as they run swiftly over fine sand. Quail, doves, killdeer, ducks, and other birds that come to water holes to drink leave characteristic marks in soft mud, as do prowling raccoons and foraging muskrats. Desert-tortoise tracks are distinctive because of the impressions made by their claws and flat feet attached to elephantoid legs. Sand at the rear of the tracks usually is pushed into little mounds and thus indicates the direction of travel. I have learned to associate other animal tracks with their makers by catching them and allowing them to walk, hop, or run on sand or in dust. Thus I have come to know the marks made by scorpions, centipedes, tarantulas, Eleodes beetles, toads, whiptail lizards, and grasshoppers.

Midday, especially in the southern deserts, is siesta time both for humans and for most of the animals. When the sun reaches its greatest height, the humidity drops and the heat increases. Then rabbits sit in their forms, ants retire to their underground chambers, and birds still their voices. But the buzzard still wheels in the sky, riding the updrafts and scanning the earth for animals that have died.

And other creatures may be abroad. Recently I sat eating my lunch beneath an ironwood tree in the Diablo Mountains in southern Arizona. The dense gray-green evergreen foliage gave some protection from the desert heat. The rocks beyond the shade were hot to my hand, yet a lizard rested on one for many minutes, apparently enjoying the radiant energy from the sun and the stone. For half an hour a large wasp fascinated me by digging a hole in the hard-packed soil. When her burrow was finished, she brought a spider and placed it in the tomb. Presumably she laid an egg on it. Then she closed the hole and spent many minutes covering the spot with tiny pebbles carried in her mandibles. When the job was done, I could see no evidence that the soil had been disturbed.

In late afternoon the ants appear once more, running rapidly because of the stimulating warmth of the earth. The lizards are as active as ever, and insects buzz around plants that are in bloom. Birds appear in increasing numbers with the approach of sunset. Then as the cool of evening precedes the darkness, the whippoorwill calls, the stridulation of katydids begins, and the voices of the night are heard. Night-flying insects and desert bats appear. There is much for the bats to eat; in the Mohave Desert I once counted nineteen kinds of moths attracted to the wall of my pickup-camper by the bright light of my lantern.

The night itself provides variety in the desert. The stars appear to be suspended at different depths in the blackness of heaven. As the dippers swing around the pole star, Orion, pursuer of the Pleiades, strides down the western sky to the dark mountains, followed by Sirius, the "Dog Star," brightest one in the sky. If the time is spring, and heavy rains have fallen recently, the stillness of the night is shattered by the toad congress assembled in pond water flooded from the distant mountains.

You need not be a scientist to appreciate geological and climatic diversity in the desert. The major relief features are always prominent: mountains, cliffs, escarpments, plateaus, basins, troughs, and plains. You can stand almost anywhere in the desert and see mountains, but their aspect varies from one region to another. Many of these are sharp-crested narrow masses, some of which extend north and south for many miles. The summits of many ranges in the southern deserts are sawtoothed, and their slopes are deeply notched by canyons and drainages that come down toward the basins and plains.

The topography of the Mohave Desert in California, for example, is extremely varied. Elevations vary from 282 feet below sea level in Death Valley to more than 10,000 feet in the surrounding mountains. Interior mountain ranges in the Great Basin reach elevations of 7,500 feet or more, with valley fills around 2,500 to 4,000 feet. Fault blocks of igneous, sedimentary, and metamorphic rocks are dissected by long drainages that end in barren dry lake beds. Volcanic cones, domes, craters, and lava flows add local character to the broad landscape.

Thousands of square miles of desert landscape are the product of relatively recent folding and faulting of the earth's crust. Movement of the earth's crust, for example, caused the downfaulting of the Gulf of California and the Salton Basin. The rocks of the Sierra Madre to the east were uplifted and then sculptured by stream erosion. The Chihuahuan Desert, part of which extends into southern Arizona, southern New Mexico, and western Texas, features lava flows, lost rivers, ancient beaches, and spectacular sand dunes.

The Painted Desert is a scenic plateau located mainly in northern Arizona and southeastern Utah. In this wonderland of colors fossil trees can be seen in the Petrified Forest National Monument. Also in the Painted Desert is Rainbow Bridge National Monument. These are local wonders, but the overall beauty

Alluvial fans and boulder pavements in Death Valley reveal the power of flood waters that move soil and stones from the mountains into the desert.

of the rugged plateau lies in the red, brown, orange, yellow, and gray bands of sandstones and lavas colored by iron, manganese, and other minerals.

The numbers of subordinate relief features in the desert are legion. In rocky areas exposed bedrock has been sculptured by water erosion; massive stones have been shaped into domes and elephantine forms by sand abrasion, and undercutting of less resistant layers has produced mushroom-shaped figures and has left balanced rocks on spires and pinnacles. Some of the giant caverns and overhangs of cliffs, formed by erosion in the geologic past, were inhabited by men from 500 to 20,000 years ago.

If you look thoughtfully at the desert landscape, the way in which many of its characteristic local land forms have developed becomes readily apparent. When you look to the mountains, you see alluvial fans made of material washed out of the mouths of canyons. You see where eroding streams have cut through the fans or have broken into braided channels. In many places "sheet floods" from the arroyos, or stream courses that begin in desert mountains, spread out and drop their debris to form bajadas, or sloping plains. The bases of the plains extend to the bottoms of the basins which are the floodplains, or desert playas. In flood time large rocks are deposited at the canyon mouths, coarse gravel is carried farther downslope, and sand, silt, and dissolved salts are carried to the floodplain. This gradation of valley fill produces different habitats for plants and animals.

Although sand dunes occupy only small portions of the North American deserts, they are among the most dynamic elements of the landscape. Dunes are mostly ancient in origin, but many are impressively active now. There are many types of dunes, and some are complex in structure and activity. Wind, of course, sets them in motion and reshapes them with its vagaries of speed and direction. Dunes frequently develop in a series of parallel ridges. Others are narrow linear ridges of sand that move lengthwise. Crescent-shaped dunes have long gentle slopes on the windward side and steep slopes on the leeward side in the direction of dune movement.

Dune colors vary according to the rocks from which their

The White Sands near Alamogordo, New Mexico, consist of almost pure gypsum. Specialized plants grow best in the swales between the dunes, but a few grow upward through the shifting sand.

sands are derived. Sands of some of the Utah desert dunes are pink and light red. The yellowish Algodones Dunes near Yuma, Arizona, are derived in part from Tertiary sandstones. The White Sands near Alamogordo, New Mexico, consist of pure gypsum and in bright sunlight are the most dazzling dunes on earth. But all dunes are fascinating because of their kaleidoscopic changes in hues and colors under the varying light of day, at sundown, and in the moonlight.

The wonderland of the White Sands in New Mexico consists of rounded hills of gypsum brought in by the wind from Lake Lucero, which receives gypsum with the waters that flow from the surrounding mountains. Gypsum also is brought up from beneath the dunes by capillary attraction. Plants grow with difficulty in the White Sands, which are deficient in potassium and phosphorus. The well-adapted ones originate in depressions between the dunes and resist burial in the moving gypsum by rapid stem growth and by production of adventitious roots near the surface of the rising dune.

Plants that survive the shifting dunes by extending their root systems include the soaptree yucca (*Yucca elata*), joint fir (*Ephedra torreyana*), skunkbrush sumac (*Rhus trilobata*), and Rio Grande cottonwood (*Populus wislizeni*). Hoary rosemarymint (*Poliomintha incana*) maintains itself by producing long prostrate stems on stabilized surfaces. Animals of the dunes, including the coyote, the rabbit, the bleached earless lizard, and the white Apache pocket mouse, are light-colored or almost white in comparison with their brown-colored relatives in the surrounding desert.

In marked contrast with the ceaseless wandering of the dunes is the rock glaze known as "desert varnish," which apparently persists for centuries on pebbles, stones, and cliff faces. This stain, which decorates canyon walls like tapestry in varied patterns, is formed by oxides of iron and manganese. Its origin is not clear. Edmund C. Jaeger in *The California Deserts* notes that lichens secrete acids which dissolve rock minerals that are deposited as oxides on the rock surfaces when the lichens die. On the other hand, Charles B. Hunt in *Physiography of the United States* writes that the oxides may have leached from the rocks or been brought from a distance by water. He notes that desert varnish stained the rocks before some of the cliff dwellings were built, at least five hundred years ago. He also suggests that most desert varnish may be an ancient deposit made during a wetter climate than now prevails in the desert.

The present climate of the desert is characterized by great variation from north to south. In the sagebrush deserts of Wyoming and the Great Basin cold winters are the rule, and blinding blizzards and drifting snow deal death to creatures that find neither food nor shelter. The storms of the northern deserts occur even in late spring. But suddenly the northward-marching sun brings heat to the soil and renewal of plant and animal activity in harmony with the late spring rains and the scattered summer showers.

In the southern deserts heat and drought are more pronounced. Annual rainfall generally is less than eight inches, and evaporation rates are high. In the interior of the desert in southeastern California, precipitation is only three to five inches at the lower elevations. Daytime temperatures of 100° F. sometimes occur for 100 days in a row in Death Valley and near the Salton Sea. The highest temperature ever recorded in Death Valley was 134° F. Evaporation from lakes varies from five to seven feet during the year.

Rainfall in the western Sonoran Desert averages less than eight inches annually, but this is only an average. Several years may pass with little recorded rain. In some places in Sonora and Sinaloa snow never falls, but two rainy seasons occur. Extensive storms bring winter rains from November to March. Summer rains occur as scattered showers from July to September. Cloudbursts occur locally and produce floods that scour the channels of arroyos miles away where no rain is falling.

Winds blow strongly in the desert. Travelers on U.S. Highway 30 often encounter "ground blizzards," even on clear days, that obscure the pavement with drifting snow and make the desert a featureless white expanse dangerous to man and beast. In April and May thundering winds coming through the mountain passes from the Pacific Ocean create violent sandstorms. These persist for hours or days in the Colorado Desert and along the Salton Sea. The winds blow so strongly in the Imperial Valley that one sometimes has to stop driving until the sand and dust momentarily subside before crossing the open spaces between the vineyards. Even then, pebbles and sand grains are likely to blast windshields and etch the paint on automobiles.

Less exasperating and more picturesque are the dust devils,

Sotol resembles the agaves and yuccas, but its smaller flowers are borne in a dense spike and its leaves are not sharp-pointed.

tornillos, or whirlwinds that appear in the desert valleys on calm summer days. These whirling columns of warm air rise to heights of a thousand feet or more and move slowly across the land picking up sticks, stones, and dust in the manner of miniature tornadoes. In Pine Valley in western Utah I have counted as many as ten of these whirlwinds spinning across the desert at the same time. Once, near Point of Rocks in southwestern Wyoming, I saw a large dust devil pick up a band of sage grouse and whirl them violently around until they emerged from their dizzy ride a hundred feet or more above the ground. These whirlwinds are also instrumental in the distribution of the seeds of many desert plants.

The desert has many environments where plants and animals associate in distinct communities. Some of these communities are limited to only a few acres; others extend for many miles and form zones. The boundaries of these zones are set by climate, soil, moisture, and other environmental factors.

The *ecotones*, or transition areas between zones, frequently are irregular due to topographic and geologic variation and their consequent effects on microenvironment. The transition from one zone to another may be almost imperceptible where the dominant plants of one zone gradually decrease in abundance while the dominants of the adjoining zone increase in abundance over great distances. A striking ecotone is that of the creosote bush growing in open groves of Joshua trees. The Joshua trees in turn merge with the pine-juniper zone on Mohavean mountain ranges where woodland grows at higher elevations.

The sagebrush zone is one of the representative plant communities on thousands of square miles in the Great Basin. This zone stretches over great valleys and rounded hills far north to the valleys of the Columbia River and its tributaries. It covers hundreds of square miles on the Snake River plains in Idaho. In Wyoming it reaches eastward beyond the Continental Divide and gradually merges with the midcontinental prairie which once flourished eastward to Ohio and Pennsylvania.

The shadscale zone, representative of cold northern deserts, occurs locally in the Red Desert in Wyoming. It is best developed on the wide bajadas of southwestern Nevada and in the Lahontan Basin of western Nevada. The aspect of this desert zone is one of low, widely spaced, more or less spiny, grayish shrubs with small leaves. Where small environmental differences occur in soil, salt content, and soil moisture, the vegetation is a mosaic induced by local abundance of shrubs such as winterfat, Nevada joint fir (*Ephedra nevadensis*), bud sagebrush (*Artemisia spinescens*), and spiny hop-sage (*Grayia spinosa*). Grasses such as galleta, Indian ricegrass, and desert needlegrass also add variety to the vegetation.

The third great zone of the Great Basin is the creosote bush community. This zone covers almost all of the Mohave and Colorado deserts. Here, if the rains are right, carpets of flowering annuals cover the spaces between the shrubs from February to April. The wild flowers usually present include the colorful sand verbenas, with their agreeable fragrance; the giant four-o'clocks, which form large mats on the desert floor; the evening primroses, sweet-scented and of numerous kinds; the little gold-poppies (*Eschscholtzia minutiflora*); and their large cousins, the California prickly poppies (*Argemone platyceras*), which grow in large patches in the Mohave Desert. The numerous species of gilia with their bright-colored flowers are conspicuous when they are profusely in bloom. Notably absent are most of the cacti and the trees characteristic of the succulent desert in Arizona and New Mexico.

Two strikingly different vegetation zones appear in the Arizona portion of the Sonoran Desert. The microphyllous desert, characterized by plants with small leaves, supports an abundance of woody plants, hardy and drought-resistant and capable of living with only four or five inches of annual rainfall. One of the abundant shrubs in the desert basins, along with the creosote bush, is the burroweed (*Franseria dumosa*), marked by white-barked stems and ash-colored leaves. Other abundant plants, especially on stony bajadas and along arroyos, are the paloverde (*Cercidium floridum*), mesquite (*Prosopis juliflora*), desert iron-wood (*Olneya tesota*), and the handsome gray-green smoke tree (*Dalea spinosa*). Cacti in the microphyllous desert zone are not abundant.

The succulent or crassicaulescent desert, characterized by plants with thick coarse stems, supports a great variety of trees and shrubs, and large numbers and species of cacti. Cylindrical and flat-stemmed opuntias are especially numerous. Paloverdes grow here, along with ocotillo and mescat (*Acacia constricta*), a pretty shrub when the orange-yellow balls of fragrant flowers appear. Cat's-claw (*Acacia greggii*) often forms thickets along streams and washes. It is an exceptionally spiny shrub or small tree that well deserves its local name, "wait-a-minute." Rabbits and other small mammals find a haven among its thorny lower branches.

The Chihuahuan Desert, extending far southward on the Mexican Highlands, is a region of small cacti. Its vegetation also includes numerous species of yucca and agave. Woody legumes are abundant. Tarbush (*Flourensia cernua*), for example, grows on dry sandy or adobe plains, mesas, and low foothills in association with creosote bush, mesquite, burro grass, and tobosa grass, The resinous thick leaves have a peppery taste and are not relished by grazing mammals.

Living space for a host of animals is provided by the enormous variety of plants in the desert, the many zones in which they grow, and the multitudes of microhabitats produced by gradations of soil, temperature, altitude, and moisture. Each plant, for example, has its own insect enemies, pollinators, and other associates. Since plant food is the basic material on which all animals subsist, animal variety is closely correlated with plant variety.

Insects are abundant in the American deserts. Spiders, scorpions, snakes, toads, birds, and fish derive much of their food from insects that eat leaves, roots, and stems or gather nectar from flowers. Desert food chains also begin with plants eaten by a wide variety of grazing animals, including the desert tortoise, the chuckwalla lizard, mice, rats, antelope, deer, and desert bighorn sheep. Many of these depend upon specific kinds or groups of plants. Their variety, in part, is a product of the variety of plant life in the desert.

The diversity of habitats in the desert provides living spaces for various specialized animals. Some of these live in caves, in drip pools in the rocks, and under shaded cap rocks in canyons. These habitats provide less variable climates than those in the open desert and furnish retreats for pack rats, hibernating bats, and specialized insects. Pupfish are limited to a few water holes or salty streams where they have survived since Pleistocene times. Other specialized animals are the tiny shrimp that hatch from eggs that have been buried for a quarter of a century in the salty earth.

Most of us are unaware of the many animals that are active at night in the desert, or burrow into the ground, or spend parts of their lives in estivation or hibernation during unfavorable seasons. The mice, kangaroo rats, some of the lizards and snakes, and even the desert tortoise dig burrows in which they escape the heat of the sun. Toads, frogs, and salamanders sleep as much as three-fourths of the year until a cloudburst fills the desert ponds with water where they lay eggs, which hatch into young who grow to adulthood and then in their turn bury themselves in the protecting soil.

Birds, by their numbers and diversity, make the desert a fasci-

When a saguaro dies, the riblike skeleton is exposed. Eventually it falls and is eaten by termites and wood-boring insects.

nating place for intense observation and study. The yearlong residents such as the sage grouse, magpies, and quail stir the imagination when one sees how they stay in business through the seasons in the northern deserts. In the southern deserts a multitude of resident and migratory birds express their individualities by occupying tiny separate worlds in microenvironments.

The bird tenants of the saguaro, for instance, are notably individualistic in their requirements for living quarters and food supplies. They and other animals are linked in a chain of dependence on the cactus and on one another. The Gila woodpecker and Mearn's gilded flicker chisel nesting holes in the saguaro. Without these holes, which the woodpecker and flicker eventually abandon, the Arizona crested flycatcher, the Mexican screech owl, and the elf owl would have no place to nest. Mice, rats, lizards, spiders, and insects also use the holes for shelter and escape from enemies. And when a saguaro dies, its woody skeleton provides food for termites and wood-boring insects.

In localities where a variety of habitats are present as many as two hundred species of birds may appear within the year. Some of these, such as the hooded oriole, the redwing and yellow-headed blackbirds, and the vermilion flycatcher, are colorful almost beyond description. Your first sight of the phainopepla, with his aristocratic black crest above flaming red eyes, is an event worthy of record. In contrast, the drabness of the curve-billed thrasher makes little impression until you hear his glorious song. Again in contrast, the pyrrhuloxia sits silently in his thorn grove, but his rose-red crest, face, and breast, and yellow parrot-like bill set him apart as another memorable bird. If you have the time, patience, and inquisitiveness to learn the family ways of these and a hundred other birds, and to fathom their adaptations to their chosen habitats, then the desert becomes a place of magnetism that draws you back again and again to learn more of its mysteries.

The spring and fall migrations of thousands of waterfowl bring great variations to the lakes and marshes in the desert. Many of these lakes, such as Malheur and Harney in eastern Oregon, are of the playa type with shallow water and widely fluctuating shore-lines. Ducks stop in these places in the spring and fall; many remain after the spring to raise broods in July and August. Canada geese nest in the meadows in May and June. In the summer long-billed curlews, western grebes, black terns, ring-billed gulls, willets, and avocets are attractions for the bird enthusiast.

On the delta where Bear River empties into Great Salt Lake in northern Utah many shorebirds hunt insects while wading in the shallow water. The black-necked stilt with its black and white body and long reddish legs is one of the distinctive shorebirds, along with the dowitcher, godwit, phalarope, willet, yellowlegs, and sandpiper. Nesting on the islands in Great Salt Lake and in Pyramid Lake in Nevada are thousands of California gulls and white pelicans. One of the salt-tolerant plants on alkali flats around these lakes is the glasswort (*Salicornia rubra*) which provides good food for waterfowl in autumn. This one plant, among many, illustrates the contribution of habitat variety to the lives of many of the desert's creatures.

The ocotillo produces flaming red flowers at the ends of the branches
in spring. Several crops of small green leaves may be produced in
a year of intermittent rainfall. The stems are armed with strong
spines.

CHAPTER 6

Plants of the Desert

For most of us, on our initial visit to the desert, the plants are strange and many of them are actually weird. Their strangeness and the spectacular beauty of many of their flowers impel at least some of us to learn their names. If we wish to feel at home in the desert, it is not enough to say that a plant is a cactus, or a sagebrush, or an evening primrose. There are many kinds of cacti, sagebrushes, and primroses, and each kind has its unique life cycle and adaptation to the desert environment. When one becomes familiar with the names of even a few dozen plant species, how they keep company with other plants, and how they seem to prefer different soils and topographic locations, then the vegetation of the desert becomes meaningful.

Identification of many of the common desert plants is not difficult. Lucky is the man who meets a friend or a native who can accurately name a fair number of the species in the locality where he lives. For the great majority of us, however, the picture books and paperback guides sold at newstands, in bookstores, and in nature museums are legitimate aids. Booklets such as *Flowers of the Southwest Deserts,* by Natt N. Dodge, describe and illustrate common desert plants and give background information about the habits of plants and their uses by men and animals. If a devil's-claw (*Proboscidea parviflora*) pod should happen to hook about your fetlock, this book will tell you how the mother plant looks and how it scatters its seeds. Look for other books and booklets if you wish to know about plants in specific localities, whether they be Death Valley, Anza Borrego, California, or Big Bend, Texas.

People who are familiar with plant manuals can "run down" the species through the keys and then check the description of the plant in the text. This is the best method for plant identification, since it requires attention to flower color, plant structure, and differences between the plant in hand and those of closely related species. This personal and unique experience with each new plant is analogous to solving a puzzle. When the puzzle picture is complete, the name of the plant usually is firmly imprinted in memory.

Diligent observation within an hour of wandering over the desert can turn up an amazing number of plant species. Close observation of shapes, forms, and structural characteristics of desert plants is necessary if you wish to distinguish closely related plants from one another. Merely looking at the plant from a distance is not enough. In this regard, I remember a stroll through the Red Desert in Wyoming with a rancher while my

Big sagebrush (Artemisia tridentata) *covers thousands of square miles in the Great Basin Desert. Grasses and forbs between the shrubs are few in number, owing to decades of heavy grazing by livestock.*

colleagues and I were making a botanical survey. This man informed me that, although he had lived all his life in the desert, he had never learned the names of more than a dozen plants growing on his ranch. Our search turned up eleven different kinds of grasses, more than thirty kinds of forbs, or broad-leaved herbs, and eighteen species of shrubs. He was astounded when we collected seven species of sagebrush within a radius of half a mile.

The only kind of sagebrush he had ever recognized was the ubiquitous big sagebrush (*Artemisia tridentata*), so characteristic of the Great Basin and millions of acres of other arid lands in the West. But he was quick to note, when he learned the names of other species, that big sagebrush grew in a variety of habitats, whereas silver sagebrush (*A. cana*) on his ranch was common only along creek banks and on moist soils. He also learned that the low-spreading, spiny bud sagebrush (*A. spinescens*) flourished on alkali flats and in valleys, and that the dwarf cushion-like brown sage (*A. pedatifida*) grew on rocky slopes and stony hilltops. He saw how it differed from all the other sagebrushes when I pointed out that its leaves resembled tiny bird feet.

The cacti, especially in the warm southwestern deserts, comprise a more numerous clan than the sagebrushes. If you really want to enjoy the cacti, it is not enough to know that they have succulent stems which enable them to store water, that most cacti are leafless, that some have woody cylinders enclosing the pulpy pith, and that they possess spines or bristles which grow from areoles, or small areas on the stem. Cactus flowers have many sepals, petals, and large numbers of stamens. The highly colored petals and contrasting stamens make the flowers among the most beautiful in the plant world.

If you plan to identify cacti with a key in one of the manuals, you will have to look for such attributes as flat stems or ribbed stems, areoles with or without tiny barbed bristles, curved or hooked spines, flowers and fruit on new or old stems, and dryness or fleshiness of the fruit at maturity. And this is only the beginning, since these features serve mainly to separate the genera of cacti. Keys to the species will lead you into a fascinating study of spines, tubercles on the stems, color of petals, number of stem joints, height of the plant, and whether it creeps, sprawls on the ground, grows in a clump, or is a tree from ten to fifty feet or more in height.

The plant world of the desert, of course, consists of more than cacti and sagebrushes. The perennial species number into the thousands. The forbs and grasses become seasonably conspicuous, especially when they are green and in vigorous growth. Frequently their showy flowers add patches of brilliant color to the landscape. The flower gardens that cover the desert far and wide, however, appear only when millions of annuals simultaneously produce their blooms in rhythm with rains that break the desert drought.

Shrubs and trees add a rich variety to the desert year. Some are conspicuous because of their brightly colored bark. A number of trees bloom brilliantly in midsummer when other plants are dry and gray. Still others, such as the rabbitbrushes, bloom in profusion only in autumn. And many of the watercourses and dune edges are bordered by mesquite trees, paloverdes, and other members of the pea family. Smoke trees, fan palms, desert willows, cottonwoods, hackberries, and elephant trees add to the floral assemblage of the desert.

The desert forbs are so numerous that not even a botanist can name them all at sight. For the North American deserts it has been estimated that 12,000 or more species represent the non-woody flora. The number of species found in an area varies according to the geographic locality, the kind of soil, the climate, and the degree of grazing by livestock.

Although shrubby vegetation contributes from 60 to 90 percent of the ground cover on most deserts, forbs are always present, and their floral beauty dominates the landscape for a few short weeks if rain comes in quantity in early spring. After good rainfall distribution in the northern sagebrush deserts I always look forward to the blooming of evening primroses with showy white flowers, sand verbenas with funnelform perianths and viscid stems, and bitterroots with rose-colored or white flowers arising from thick fleshy roots. The globe mallows, with their large grenadine-red corollas, are among the loveliest flowers of the desert and are found from Montana and Idaho south to Mexico. Balsamroots, if they have not been grazed heavily by sheep, sometimes litter the upper slopes of the desert border with their silvery leaves and sunflower-like yellow flowers.

Sagebrush deserts sometimes are dotted with the elegant mariposa lily (*Calochortus elegans*), whose nodding or erect flowers have white petals tinged with purple. Its relative, the sego lily (*C. nuttallii*), which has a green or purple stripe down the middle of each petal, grows over a wider territory, from Oregon to California and east to South Dakota and New Mexico. A show of wild beauty also occurs when the dwarf sunflowers (*Wyethia amplexicaulis*) suffuse the dry hills and slopes with their deep-yellow or cream-colored flowers.

Not so conspicuous, unless you view them from near at hand, are the phloxes. The desert phloxes tend to be somewhat woody, and the short and much-branched shoots produce a pulvinate, or pincushion, growth form. Some have white woolly stems and leaves. The corollas, with long slender tubes flaring into a circular limb, are white, pink, or sky-blue.

On desert ranges heavily grazed by livestock herbaceous vegetation is frequently scarce. In the shadscale community in Nevada, for example, large areas support only a few scattered perennials and ephemeral annuals in spring. Desert mallow (*Sphaeralcea ambigua*) sometimes is the principal forb among scattered tufts of Indian ricegrass, galleta, and desert needlegrass (*Stipa speciosa*).

In lightly grazed areas various small delicate herbs appear in company with the mallows and grasses. Among these are the buckwheats, purple-rooted forget-me-not (*Crypthantha micrantha*), glyptopleura (*Glyptopleura marginata*), which is related to the dandelions, and desert trumpet (*Eriogonum inflatum*), a unique plant with inflated internodes which make the stems appear to have bladders.

The floral season in the warm southern deserts is marked by a magical display of showy blossoms when winter and spring rains are plentiful and well distributed. The Mohave aster (*Aster abatus*) sometimes sets the desert aglow with multitudes of pale violet or lavender flowers. The many kinds of evening primroses with their flowers form pink or snowy blankets over the dunes and desert hills.

The list of desert forbs, including perennials and showy annuals, appears to be endless, especially if you attempt to assemble a representative collection of them. Several years ago I measured an acre in the high desert northeast of San Bernadino, California, and set about pressing specimens of each flowering plant in that area. According to my notebook I had pressed forty-nine species when a mighty wind-devil or desert whirligig caught my drying blotters up in its swirling vortex and scattered them beyond recall. But at least I had a record of species numbers and the prodigality of nature when the desert is in bloom.

We ordinarily do not think of grasses as being important components of desert vegetation, especially if we mentally picture the poverty-stricken sands of Arabia or northern Africa, where excessive grazing has been the rule for thousands of years. Our American deserts, however, support a great variety of grasses, possibly several hundred species, and formerly these produced extensive cover over thousands of square miles.

Historical records, based on accounts of vegetation in Utah at the time of Mormon settlement, indicate that grasses were abundant even on the poorer soils. Meadows produced excellent forage crops, and in many valleys, now covered with sagebrush, there was a luxuriant growth of sedges, tules, and willows. Captain Howard Stansbury, who surveyed the country around Great Salt Lake in 1849–1850, found "Cache Valley . . . covered with a profusion of rich green grass." Northwest of Promontory, where the golden spike for the railroad was driven, he found "tolerably good bunch grass." For Stansbury Island, which has been denuded of grass for many years, he reported, ". . . the grasses are rich and abundant, and the range for cattle the best I have seen in the country."

The paucity of grasses and forbs over wide areas of desert is due in large part to the effects of past overgrazing. Exclosures, or fenced areas where livestock are not allowed to graze, established by various state and federal agencies in Oregon, California, Arizona, and New Mexico, have permitted remarkable recovery of desert grasses. From these and other studies it is obvious that the desert can sustain grasses if only they are given an opportunity to grow.

Grasses are especially numerous in the broad transition zones between prairies and deserts. You can see these transitions while traveling westward through Wyoming or southward from Washington into the Great Basin. In Arizona and New Mexico the grass-desert transition is one of the attractive types at the eastern margin of the cactus country. It includes a perplexing variety of species. The gramas are abundant, especially black grama (*Bouteloua eriopoda*), rothrock grama (*B. rothrockii*), and hairy grama (*B. hirsuta*). At one time rothrock grama made pure stands of grass in the upper borders of the cactus and desert-shrub belts. Curly mesquite (*Hilaria berlangeri*) is a common grass of the foothills, and tobosa (*H. mutica*) occupies heavy alluvial soils and makes thick mats of twisted stems and a dense sod.

Thousands of acres of grasslands in Arizona have been invaded in recent times by velvet mesquite (*Prosopis julifera* var. *velutina*). The spread of this plant has been aided by reduction of grass competition through overgrazing and by increased seed dispersal by domestic livestock, which transport thousands of seeds in their travels.

The persistence of grasses in the desert is somewhat of a minor miracle when we consider the droughts, grazing mammals, and chewing insects they have to endure. They persist because of their morphological structure, growth habits, and longevity. Buds that produce new stems and leaves grow near the ground and hence are not liable to injury by large herbivores. Leaves grow from their bases so that removal of their tips does not stop regrowth. Many of the grasses also are able to persist for half a century by renewal of the root systems as old roots die. And in addition to reproduction by seeds, many grasses renew themselves or spread to new territory by means of runners that creep above ground (stolons) or stems that grow horizontally below ground (rhizomes).

If you wish to see an example of the reproductive processes of grass, look for the little bunchgrass called fluffgrass (*Tridens pulchellus*) anywhere from Texas to Nevada and southern California to southern Mexico. In maturity its little silvery tufts look like cotton balls on the black desert pavement; sometimes they are so numerous that they cover the ground, giving the appearance of frost. In fact, this little plant is called "frost grass" by some people. The panicle of flowers is compacted into a head of woolly spikelets, which produce the frostlike appearance. The culms, or creeping stems, produce fascicles of narrow leaves. These bend over to the ground, take root, and produce other culms, which are capable of repeating the process.

The desert abounds in shrubs. Not only do they grow around desert borders, where they form buffer zones between the lowlands and the tree-covered slopes of the foothills and mountains, but they dominate much of the desert itself. In endless variety over the desert as a whole, and in vast assemblages of single species on favorable terrain, they produce pigmy forests of sagebrush, creosote bush, or greasewood; or they form mounds or widely separated "pin-cushion" mats of species such as Gardner saltbush (*Atriplex gardneri*) or fringed sagebrush (*Artemisia frigida*).

Most of the desert shrubs are long-lived. Their deep root systems, which in many species penetrate to the water table, enable them to persist through long droughts. Also, shrubs compete with one another, so the established bushes become widely spaced, each with its own territory for moisture supply. Some shrubs compete with other plants by excreting toxic substances into the soil or by dropping leaves containing materials that inhibit germination and growth of herbaceous plant seeds and seedlings. Other shrubs, however, provide shade for grasses and forbs and protection from grazing animals.

In the absence of shrubs much of the desert fauna would cease to exist. Sagebrush, for example, is one of the important species in the diets of antelope and deer. It is life itself to the sage grouse, which eats the leaves, builds its nest in the bushy cover, and finds concealment for itself and its chicks when bird and mammal predators are abroad.

Rabbits and mice eat the seeds, leaves, and bark of shrubs when more succulent plants are dormant in winter and in times of drought. Birds and lizards find concealment, shelter, and insect food in the shrubby cover of what otherwise would be a barren expanse of sandy and rocky land. The insects that live in and on shrubs help pollinate the forbs that bloom when the rains come in late spring and early summer. Then in autumn, when the herbs have ceased to flourish, the rabbitbrushes bloom and furnish pollen and nectar for other insects, which in turn contribute to the diet of desert birds, mammals, reptiles, toads, and fish.

The sagebrushes are among the most abundant and widely distributed of desert shrubs, especially in the northern regions. A. A. Beetle estimates that the eleven species and five subspecies of the taxonomic section *Tridentatae* of the genus *Artemisia* occur in varying amounts over about 422,000 square miles in the eleven western states. Big sagebrush—locally known as black sage, purple sage, or just plain sagebrush—probably occurs over an area of 150,000 square miles.

Big sagebrush is one of the larger shrubs of the genus. It often attains a height of six to eight feet. Each leaf has three teeth at the apex. But this is not sufficient to distinguish it from other species with three-toothed or three-parted leaves, such as Bigelow sagebrush (*Artemisia bigelovii*), black sagebrush (*A. nova*), or three-tip sagebrush (*A. tripartita*). Identification of individual species requires attention to such attributes as shape and color of leaves, presence or absence of hairy coverings on the leaves, and characteristics of the inflorescence.

Numerous species of plants normally are associated with big sagebrush. In the desert it grows in mixture with various salt-bushes, bitterbrush, Indian ricegrass, galleta, and wheatgrasses. In central and eastern Wyoming the herbaceous understory consists of blue grama and other short grasses where the desert shrubland merges with the midcontinental prairie. In the foothill zone bordering the desert in the Intermountain region, sagebrush alternates with oak or pinyon-juniper stands, or is intermingled with them. In the same zone a shrub community consisting of sagebrush, rabbitbrush, Brigham tea, service berry, and needle-grass is common. On Grand Mesa in western Colorado you can stand in sagebrush near Land's End and look down into the Gunnison–Colorado River Valley, 5,000 feet below, and see the land sprinkled with greasewood, shadscale, and other desert shrubs.

Fringed sagebrush (*Artemisia frigida*) is an interesting plant because of its wide distribution, clustered foliage, aromatic foliage, and usefulness as an indicator of livestock range condition. It is a half-shrub, a term used to describe perennial plants with woody bases from which semiherbaceous annual stems arise. Each year a new set of stems grows from the persistent woody base, forming a small shrub six to twenty-four inches high. The stems are densely gray or silvery-hairy, as are the clusters of leaves. The half-inch-long leaves are divided twice or three times into linear leaflets, a characteristic alluded to in the name "fringed." In late summer flower heads consisting of many yellow flowers growing in small spherical clusters develop along the upper portions of the annual stems. The flowers near the tips of the stems are practically stalkless, while those lower down are nodding or drooping on short stalks or branches.

Fringed sagebrush grows from the arid deserts of Mexico through most of the western United States to the frozen regions of Alaska and Siberia. It also grows in Europe. J. Macoun, a botanical explorer, recognized it as an indicator of range abuse in 1875 in British Columbia. When grasses are thinned by heavy grazing, fringed sagebrush becomes more abundant; when it in turn is overgrazed, it assumes a mat form. A profusion of fringed sagebrush is an indicator of the misjudgment and mismanagement that started in many places with the beginning of the livestock industry in the West.

The widely distributed black greasewood (*Sarcobatus vermiculatus*) is sometimes mistaken for the larger species of sagebrush. Also known by the Spanish name "chico," greasewood grows to heights of two to ten feet on very alkaline soils. The rigid branches and twigs are thornlike at the tips and make penetration of thickets difficult for large animals and man. The fleshy leaves are cool to the touch and appear to be round in cross section. They are about a sixteenth of an inch broad and from half an inch to one and a half inches long. The flowers are unisexual; male and female flowers are separate, but both occur on the same plant.

A highly prized browse plant of the deserts and semiarid West is fourwing saltbush (*Atriplex canescens*). In the Southwest it is called "chamiso," or "chamisa." It is often erroneously called "shadscale" and even "sagebrush." Being a member of the goosefoot family, it is closely related to Russian thistle, some of the so-called pigweeds, and common winterfat (*Eurotia lanata*). Its most striking features, other than the grayish-white mealy covering on the leaves, are the fruits which bear enlarged bracts resembling net-veined wings half an inch in diameter.

The shrubs of the warm deserts are a varied group, with many forms and adaptations to hot dry weather, stony soils, shifting sands, grazing mammals, and insect depredations. Creosote bush (*Larrea divaricata*) is one of the widespread shrubs the traveler sees over endless miles in the Sonoran Desert. The plants appear to be evenly spaced, and the evergreen, heavily scented, resinous leaves impart a dark color to the landscape. The bushes are highly flammable and produce a penetrating creosote-like odor when burned. In the Mohave Desert I always watch for the coachwhip snakes which like to climb into these shrubs and poke their heads out two or three feet above ground.

The elongated, daggerlike, or bayonet-shaped leaves of the yuccas sometimes confuse newcomers, since they superficially resemble several other plants in the southwest deserts. The broad-leaved yuccas, of lesser size than the Joshua trees (*Yucca brevifolia*) in the Mohave Desert, can be distinguished from similar plants by examining their flowers, inflorescences, and leaves. The yuccas have bell-like blossoms borne in huge clusters and leaves that produce long fibers, much used by Indians in former times for weaving cloth and other articles.

The century plant (*Agave palmeri*), which superficially resembles some of the yuccas, produces a plumelike flower stalk capable of growing as much as a foot or more a day. The plant flowers only once, when it is seven to twenty years old. The smaller species of agave, called lechuguillas, are characteristic plants in the Chihuahuan Desert.

A group of plants called bear grass, sacahuista, or basket grass, of the genus *Nolina*, have narrow leaves that give the clumps the appearance of long-leaved grasses. The tiny flowers are borne in plumelike inflorescences. The sotol (*Dasylirion wheeleri*) of the Arizona desert resembles the agaves and yuccas,

Yuccas provide food, shelter, and nesting places for birds, reptiles, insects, and small mammals in the southwestern deserts.

The agave, or century plant, blooms once, in seven to twenty years, and then the plant dies. The leaves are like sharp-pointed bayonets. The leaf fibers are used in the manufacture of rope.

but the leaves with barbs on the edges usually are split at the ends instead of being sharp-pointed. The tiny flowers are of two sexes and are borne in large terminal panicles on separate plants; those on the staminate or male plants form dense catkin-like spikes.

The joint firs are widely distributed and interesting shrubs of the desert. They are known by various names, including Mormontea and shrubby horsetail. Nevada joint fir (*Ephedra nevadensis*), found from Utah to California, Sonora, and Chihuahua, is a practically leafless, opposite-branched shrub with numerous

The agave in bloom. The flower stalks of some species grow from twelve to eighteen inches per day.

The joint firs, or ephedras, have long jointed stems which drop their scalelike leaves early in life. The male flowers are borne in numerous small cones. Desert people boil the stems to make a palatable tea, which is reputed to have medicinal properties.

rushlike twigs. The male and female greenish-yellow flowers are borne on separate plants. Five or six species occur on arid lands in the West. The large canatilla (*E. antisyphilitica*) grows nine or ten feet tall. The Indians for centuries prepared a drink from the dried leaves and twigs, and the plants have long been reputed to have medicinal value, especially for the treatment of urethritis. The scientific evidence for this, however, is not conclusive.

Thorniness is one of the keys to the survival of desert shrubs; large grazing mammals avoid most of them in preference to more succulent forage. The nature of some of these shrubs, many of which lack functional leaves, may be surmised from their names: crucifixion thorn (*Holacantha emori*); all-thorn (*Koeberlinia spinosa*), also known as "corona de Cristo"; canotia (*Canotia holacantha*), called Mohave-thorn and tree of Christ; and "wait-a-minute" (*Mimosa biuncifera*), a shrub of the pea family with roselike thorns recurved at the tips. In spite of the prickles of this last-named species, livestock, deer, and goats graze it, and bees visit it for nectar.

Ocotillo (*Fouquieria splendens*) always intrigues the first-time visitor to the desert. It is one of the most distinctive of shrubs and one of the thorniest. The short woody crown produces a cluster of spreading branches that grow to a height of twelve to twenty feet. The plant is leafless through much of the year, but spring or summer rains initiate a crop of green leaves which turn red as drought follows the rainy period. The leaf petioles remain on the stems as slender spines after the leaf blades drop. On older parts of the stems the leaves consist only of blades in the axils of previously formed spines. Five or six crops of leaves are possible within a year if the distribution of rainy periods is favorable.

The scarlet or salmon-colored tubular flowers of the ocotillo are produced in terminal racemes after the end of the winter rainy season. In the desert sun the flower clusters resemble bright flames at the ends of the spreading stems. They make the plants especially conspicuous when viewed against the dark background of volcanic soils and rocks that occur in the midst of endless miles of creosote bushes. Ocotillo, however, is most abundant on rocky slopes and on compact soils, where sheet flooding does not wash out its spreading shallow root system.

Ocotillo flower clusters resemble red flames at the ends of branches. Deer eat these flowers when they appear in April and May.

*The ribs of the saguaro expand and contract with moisture or drought.
Insects and birds leave scars on the trunks of the aging cacti.*

All through the desert and far beyond its borders, cactus
occurs individually, in thickets, and in forests. Only three states
in the United States have no native species of cactus, but they
have been planted widely in these states. Of the more than 1,000
species originally confined to the Americas, many now grow
throughout the world, from Africa to Asia to Australia.

The cacti come in many sizes, but the symbol of them all,
and of the Sonoran Desert, is the giant cactus, or saguaro
(*Cereus giganteus*). This is the one people look for when they
come to Arizona or travel southward into Mexico. Its massive,

spiny green trunk one to two feet in diameter, with two to ten or more stout upward curved branches, may reach a height of fifty feet or more. A few years ago the champion at Saguaro National Monument was fifty-two feet tall, had fifty-two arms, an estimated weight of ten tons, and an age of perhaps 235 years.

The saguaro is so large and has so many animal associates that I like to think of it as a microcosm—a little ecosystem in the desert. Once the saguaro has attained maturity it becomes relatively self-sufficient, although it is not indestructible—winds can blow it down, diseases can conquer it, and rodents can eat its offspring. But its influence extends far beyond the long shadow it casts in the desert sunset.

The jackrabbit that grazes far away during the hours of dusk and dawn seeks the shade of the saguaro trunk in the furnace heat of day. The Gila woodpecker and the golden flicker excavate their nesting holes in the fleshy trunk after their young have flown. Before the next nesting season the cactus seals the flask-shaped cavity with dry callus tissue, which remains for years and ultimately provides nesting room for elf owls, flycatchers, mice, and rats. These creatures, not being bound to the cactus, forage in territories far and near, and thus transmit nutrients and energy back and forth across the desert.

The saguaro furnishes food directly and indirectly to many creatures. The white flowers in late spring attract moths and other insects, and are ultimately followed by juicy sweet fruits, green outside and red inside. Birds and mammals prize these as food, and the black seeds are eaten by mice and other rodents. In the pleats of the stem are many insects which are eaten by spiders, which are eaten by lizards and birds, which are eaten by larger lizards, birds, and snakes. Little of the energy thus transferred is lost in the world of the saguaro, since the materials cycled in this environment are not washed into rivers and lost to the sea.

In contrast with their mighty parents, saguaro seedlings lead a precarious existence. Of all the seeds produced by these cacti probably only one of each thousand remains after birds, rodents, and insects have taken their toll. When a seed is spared, it must receive moisture to germinate, and its seedling must survive drought, erosion, and frost. Then it must escape predation by jackrabbits, desert cottontails, wood rats, ground squirrels, cactus mice, and insects. A single larva of the granulate cutworm

(*Feltia subterranea*), for example, has been observed to consume all of the fleshy parts of twenty-eight seedlings of saguaro and organ-pipe cactus in seventy-two hours. Some of the plants were nine weeks old and had stems four to six millimeters in diameter.

Life for the saguaro is most likely to continue if it starts in the protection of a desert tree, a shrub, or the crevice of a stony hillside. Ultimately, when its shallow roots spread as much as fifty feet in every direction and the thick waterproof outer layer is established on its stem, it becomes master of its domain, and no other perennial plant is likely to invade its immediate territory.

Cholla cacti are the untouchables of the plant world. The easily detached branches fall to the ground, take root, and produce new plants.

Other treelike cacti abound in the Sonoran Desert. Organ-pipe cactus (*Lemaireocereus thurberi*) is notable for its numerous cylindrical branches, five to eight inches in diameter with twelve to nineteen vertical ribs, which rise from the ground in such a way as to suggest the pipes of a mighty church organ. This cactus is found in Arizona, Sonora, and Baja California. Also found with the organ-pipe but rare in the United States is the old man cactus, or senita (*Lophocereus schottii*). The branches have five to seven prominent ribs, and their upper parts bear long bristles, resembling gray hair or a beard—hence the plant's name. Specimens may be seen very close to the Mexican border in Organ-Pipe Cactus National Monument.

Of all the jointed cacti, jumping cholla (*Opuntia fulgida*) seems to fascinate people most. The name cholla (pronounced *chaw-ya*) is not forgotten by anyone who has the misfortune to fall into or roughly touch one of these sharp-spined horrors. Legend has it that the armed joints jump out and attach themselves to passersby. The joints, when brushed by the side of a horse, detach from the plant, and instead of falling to the ground roll down under the horse's belly, making it a pincushion of spines. If a joint attaches to your pants leg and you attempt to kick it off, likely as not it will roll up your leg and give you a great deal of pain, as well as a tedious job of extracting spines. The white to pink flowers streaked with lavender and the large pear-shaped fruits which hang down in branched chains make this one of the most distinctive of cacti.

There are other chollas equally troublesome if they touch the hides of human beings. The teddy-bear cholla (*Opuntia bigelovii*) looks cuddlesome since its spines are so numerous that they obscure the branch from which they grow. Buckhorn chollas (*O. acanthocarpa*) are large shrubs or tree chollas with less spiny branches, which bear a fancied resemblance to deer antlers when viewed from a distance.

Prickly pears are the flat-branched opuntias found throughout the Southwest and in many other areas. There is not space here to list all the other kinds of cacti in the desert. Some are large and some are small. The interested traveler, with the aid of a guidebook, should be able to identify the common ones, including barrel cactus, beavertail cactus, hedgehog cactus, and fishhook or pincushion cactus. Some of the small species have the most attractive flowers of all the plants that grow in the desert.

*Beavertail cactus is common in the California deserts. It is one
of the prickly-pear cacti, species of which are found in almost
every state in the nation. There are no spines on the flat blue-green
stems.*

Trees are usually present all around the desert on mountain
slopes, on high mesas, and in the grassland transitions in the
Southwest. Junipers and pinyon pines are common above the
sagebrush zone, and although these are not true desert plants,
they are equipped to endure the stress of semiarid environments.
Trees are common along watercourses, even in the driest deserts,
and if they can reach groundwater with their roots, they grow
on floodplains, ancient lake basins, and sand dunes.

In the northern sagebrush deserts stream courses often are
marked by willows and cottonwoods where stream terraces and
hillside springs provide permanent moisture for woody plants.
Cottonwoods were welcomed by the early explorers in the desert,

since they marked the location of water holes and fuel for camp-fires. Fremont cottonwood (*Populus fremontii*) is the tall one you see in southwestern Utah, southern New Mexico, Nevada, California, Sonora, and Chihuahua. On my former trips to Pyramid Lake I frequently sought the shade of these trees in the heat of the day. John C. Frémont made the first note of these magnificent trees on January 6, 1844, near Pyramid Lake.

The trees of the cold deserts develop root systems that reach down to perennial water. Consequently they do not cast their leaves at the first sign of drought. Nor do they store water in succulent stems as do the cacti. And they do not produce spines to protect them against thirsty animals. But as you go southward in the desert, it is instructive to note the increasing variety of trees with drought-resisting and drought-enduring devices and processes. Among these are water-storage tissues, shallow but widespreading root systems, twisting of leaves in the heat of day to reduce transpiration, leaf-dropping in dry seasons, and substitution of green stems for leaves which are likely to evaporate excessive quantities of water. The forty-foot taproot of the mesquite, of course, explains why it can remain green when other plants become desiccated.

The persistence of some of the desert trees in seemingly impossible habitats seems to be beyond understanding until we examine their structural characteristics and their adaptations to seasonal environmental factors. Many trees flourish with leaves of the smallest possible size, which they immediately shed when moisture supplies become minimal. A goodly number make their food in chlorophyll-bearing branches and twigs which present relatively small surface areas to the sun and winds. The desert smoke tree (*Dalea spinosa*), for example, stands nearly leafless throughout the year. It puts out a few leaves in summer and a profusion of bluish-violet flowers when the fierce desert heat is at its highest. The young twigs are covered with a silvery gray pubescence, and the zigzag growth of the thorny boughs avoids any development of symmetry. At night the reflection of the moon on the silvery twigs produces ghostly apparitions along the sandy washes to which these trees are mostly confined.

Desert ironwood (*Olneya tesota*) is a tree you will remember if you ever try to cut its wood with a saw or any other hand tool. I tried my axe, which was not too sharp, on the trunk of one in southwestern Arizona, and it made no impression on the wood. Shaving the wood with my knife was impossible. But in spite of its hardness boring beetles can chew the wood, and the mistletoe invades its tissues, produces large swellings a foot or more in diameter on the trunk, and ultimately kills the tree. The berries of the mistletoe are eaten by the phainopepla. When the living seeds are voided on another tree, the mistletoe repeats its cycle of parasitism.

The profusion of indigo flowers produced by the ironwood in summer adds a subtle fragrance to the desert air. The red sap sometimes exuded by the tree attracts bees, hummingbirds, and ants. The leaf-cutting ants (*Atta desertorum*) also clip the leaves and carry them to their underground fungus gardens. Altogether, the ironwood tree merits examination and understanding of its place in the desert cycle of energy exchange.

Tree members of the pea family are well represented in the warm southern deserts. The New Mexican locust (*Robinia neomexicana*) is a spiny little tree with fragrant lavender or purplish blossoms grouped in clusters that remind me of the wisterias on the stone walls in Rome. The desert cat's-claw (*Acacia greggii*), with its compound leaves, ferocious armament of thorns, tufts of golden stamens in the yellow-petaled flowers, and contorted pods containing polished seeds, is a tree to remember —and avoid. The thorns are cruel to humans. But game birds, rabbits, and rodents use the tree for sanctuary from predators, and the verdin builds its nest in the safety of its branches.

The green-barked paloverde trees stand along the desert washes like twiggy leafless willows. You can see them in a wide variety of places from southern and western Arizona to southern California, in Sonora and Sinaloa, Mexico, and in northeastern Baja California. The blue paloverde (*Cercidium floridum*) is the most striking of the species. It is a tree of green switches, leafless excepting a short time in the spring when the inconspicuous compound leaves appear. But these are obscured by the flaming yellow flowers that adorn the tree with a "shower of gold." The yellow paloverde is smaller; its stout twigs are pale yellow-green, and its flowers are pale yellow instead of golden, in contrast with its larger relative. The paloverde trees are intolerant of frost and hence are confined to the warm southern deserts.

In addition to these trees, the legumes are represented by other tree-sized or shrub-sized species, especially honey mesquite (*Prosopis glandulosa*), velvet mesquite (*P. velutina*), common mesquite (*P. juliflora*), and the screwbean (*Strombocarpa odorata*).

The desert palm (*Washingtonia filifera*) is a rare species in its wild habitat. It is a picturesque plant in the canyons of the San Bernardino Mountains, in the secluded gorges on the eastern face of the Coast Ranges, and in the protection of mountain walls in Baja California. Groves of these trees can be seen in Thousand Palms Canyon north of Indio, and in Palm Canyon a few miles from Palm Springs. The canyon walls of their chosen sites shade them from the desert sun for a few hours daily, and the seepage from springs provides the water necessary for their existence.

The majesty and strangeness of the desert palm has resulted in its cultivation in nondesert places, including Florida, Hawaii, and Algeria. Growth comes only from the great bud at the tip of the trunk, and from this bud comes the crown of fan-shaped leaves with their sharp-tipped, lancelike divisions. As the bud grows skyward, producing new leaves, the old leaves die and bend downward against the stem; they remain as a thatch enclosing the stem like a pants leg, or, as the Hawaiians visualize it, like a Hula skirt. If this gray thatch, which harmonizes with the weathered background of the desert, is not burned by vandals it provides retreat for lizards, insects, and birds.

It is possible that the Indians planted desert palms in favorable habitats beyond the original range of the trees long before they were noted by Father Juan Crespi on March 29, 1769, when members of the Portolá expedition observed the species northwest of Callicola, Baja California. Padre Junipero Serra saw it in May of that same year in the same place. It is obvious then that the Franciscan missionaries did not introduce the desert palm from the Old World. Instead, it is a true native of our own deserts.

Silhouetted against the sunset sky, the strangeness of the Joshua tree (*Yucca brevifolia*) is not to be forgotten. The trunk is thatched with stiff gray dead leaves. The burly distorted branches are giant pincushions of leaves, sharp as daggers, with saw-toothed edges. When blooming occurs in March or April, the cream-white flowers appear in clusters eight to fourteen inches long at the tips of the branches, which sometimes reach forty feet into the air.

The flowers of the Joshua tree, in common with those of other yuccas, are linked in partnership with the female yucca moth,

The Joshua tree is the character plant of the Mohave Desert. Many birds, lizards, insects, and rodents are closely associated with this tree yucca. The night lizard completely depends on it for shelter and for the insects and larvae that live in or on the tree.

which lays her eggs in the ovaries and seems to pollinate the flowers deliberately. The insect larvae do not eat all the seeds, and without the pollination the yucca could not reproduce.

Joshua trees and their fallen branches are sanctuaries for a menagerie of creatures ranging from the desert night lizard (which seldom ventures away from the thatch of leaves) to flickers, woodpeckers, titmice, flycatchers, wood rats, mice, snakes, ants, and termites. No one knows how long a Joshua tree lives, but a hundred years may be a conservative estimate. Joshua trees have been present in the desert for ages. Their leaves have been found in the fossilized dung of the extinct giant ground sloth. Formerly the trees occurred over a wider area than their present range in the Mohave Desert and in Nevada, Utah, and Arizona. The best place for seeing them is in Joshua Tree National Monument, where many square miles of beautiful high desert country are preserved and can be reached from the towns of Joshua Tree or Twentynine Palms.

The cirio, or boogum tree (*Idria columnaris*), possibly is the most striking woody plant in the flora of the North American continent. The trunk, which reaches a basal diameter of eighteen to twenty inches and a height of sixty feet or more, resembles a slender upside-down carrot. It tapers from the base to an elongated tip of fairly uniform diameter. Short branches extend horizontally from the smooth gray trunk; these bear leaves, but they never produce flowers. The yellow tubular flowers growing on slender stalks at the tip of the tree are one indication that the cirio is related to the ocotillo.

The cirio is native in the Sonoran Desert. It gives individuality to the desert, along with the elephant tree (*Bursera microphylla*), by its bizarre appearance and its production of leaves during the winter rains. When the trunk is cut open, it reveals a greatly enlarged succulent pith. The cirio occurs in greatest abundance throughout the central third of Baja California and grows in a small area on the Sonoran coast near Puerto Libertad. These unique trees keep company with the giant cardón (*Pachycereus pringlei*), which rises to a height of sixty feet and is undoubtedly the largest cactus in the world.

The great opportunists of the desert are the annual plants which come into showy beauty, complete their life cycles in a few weeks, and then are gone for the remainder of the year. As Forrest Shreve (1951) has noted:

The desert environment offers particular advantages to the short-lived plant. The restriction of its vegetative activity to brief moist periods almost completely relieves the ephemeral plant from the difficulties of water supply which beset the perennial. By speed of germination, rapidity of growth, and early flowering and maturity during favorable periods the ephemeral escapes the most potent one of the conditions controlling the life and ecological behavior of desert plants. Also the large expanses of bare ground assure ephemerals ample space and little competition with established plants.

The wealth of blossoms covering the earth after an abundance of rain is almost beyond comprehension. In spite of all the scavenging by birds, ants, and other animals, myriads of seeds buried in the sand or covered with leaf litter from shrubs and trees germinate in fantastic numbers. I once counted more than 9,000 Russian thistle seedlings on a square meter in the Utah desert south of the Vermillion Cliffs. This hardly compares with the estimate by Lloyd Tevis, Jr., that woolly plantain (*Plantago insularis* var. *fastigiata*) produced 309,900 seeds per square meter, or 1,254,165,300 per acre.

Harvester ants (*Veromessor pergandei*) have a field day harvesting these seeds and storing them in their deep underground granaries as insurance against leaner days to follow. Tevis found these ants foraging as far as 150 feet from their nest. When the temperature was 33° C., they ran across the desert sand at eight feet per minute. From April to June 91.9 percent of the food they collected was seeds; insects, flowers, and miscellany made up the remainder.

Much as we may derive aesthetic pleasure from shows of flower color when square miles of desert are covered with the white of evening primroses, the blue of lupines, or the yellow of "desert sunflowers," the landscape can be even more meaning-

Acton encelia is only one of the many "desert sunflowers" that bloom profusely in the late spring or early summer. This one, from Death Valley, has sulfur-yellow flowers and gray-green leaves.

ful if we remember that many animals are attuned to this sudden luxuriance. These animals in turn are depended on by a multitude of other animals which must live beyond the day of senescence and death of all the ephemeral plants.

Many insects, particularly some species of bees and wasps, appear to correlate their appearance with the blooming of the annuals. Some of the wasps specialize on spiders that specialize on certain insects that specialize on certain flowers. The life cycles of these insects continue through egg, larval, or other stages, and are subject to other predators, including mammals, reptiles, and birds. Consequently, the lizard that is eaten by a roadrunner in July may have grown large on insects that gathered nectar from flowers in June that came from seeds germinated in April. The same temperature and moisture factors that triggered the germination of the annuals also quickened the eggs of their pollinating insects.

The desert annuals are even more meaningful if we consider some of their physical attributes and physiological adaptations. Most of them are not woody, spiny, hairy, or distasteful to animals, as are many of the shrubs, cacti, and some of the grasses. They lack bulbs, or succulent stems for water storage, and they compete wildly with their own kind for moisture. Time for them is of the essence, and their gaudy flowers are there mainly to attract insects quickly so pollination can be accomplished and a new crop of seeds matured before the burning sun withers their bodies back to earth.

Some of the annuals are blessed with germination polymorphism, a big word for having two kinds of seeds. This is an aspect of the opportunism of annuals. If all the seeds of a species germinated at once and drought killed all the seedlings, the species could be wiped out in a single season. But this is not the case; some plants produce two kinds of seeds, those that can germinate quickly and those that delay germination, even when moisture is abundant. A built-in safety factor insures that trivial rains will not activate the seeds to growth. When rain is sufficient to insure completion of the life cycle, temperature and length of day also must be right. Some species confine their appearance to warm periods and others start growth during cold rainy periods. Some grow only after the summer rains. Many are "winter annuals" that start growth in late autumn and produce flowers in the following spring.

Pronghorns are still common in parts of the Oregon and Nevada deserts. Both sexes have horns which are composed of fused hairs covering a bony core. The hairs of the rump patch, when erected, make a flash of white which serves as a danger signal to other pronghorns.

CHAPTER 7

Mammals of the Desert

In Oregon there is an ancient deer trail that passes through a cleft in the rocks on a small mesa a few miles east of Lava Butte and runs southeast through the pine woods toward the desert around Fort Rock. For millennia the mule deer have followed this path each autumn to their winter range, where bitterbrush and sagebrush provide forage even when snow covers the lesser plants of the desert. Prehistoric men undoubtedly hunted deer, antelope, and buffalo along this trail and lived in caves eroded by the waves of ancient Lake Chewaucan.

Among these caverns Fort Rock Cave, along with numerous other caves of the old lake country in the Great Basin, gives us an insight into the lives of desert men and the animals they knew during Folsom times. Deep in the litter of Fort Rock Cave the bones of animals, along with scrapers, knives, arrowheads, and other obsidian tools, were unearthed in 1938. Also discovered were sagebrush-bark sandals bearing the mud of a vanished lake where the ancient men had fished, hunted water birds, and ambushed mammals as they came to drink.

During the 9,000 years since these sandals were made, the waters dried and the desert emerged. Mammals adapted to an arid climate replaced the ancient ones that once flourished on lush prairies and verdant meadows. Elephants were among the ancient ones. Bison once roamed in herds, as did the bison that moved across the eastern prairies in more recent times. And before them, Pleistocene fossils indicate the presence of mammoths, camels, peccaries, glyptodons, and tortoises.

In Gypsum Cave, east of Las Vegas, Nevada, the skull of a

ground sloth (*Nothrotherium shastense*), sloth dung, and hair were uncovered along with two atlatl dart fragments. Men were contemporaneous with this ancient sloth, as was the horse, which vanished and did not appear again until Spanish explorers brought the modern horse to the Southwest soon after the time of Columbus.

A few years ago my two sons and I camped overnight near Fort Rock Cave to capture some of the spirit of the area, to think about the past, and to consider how the ancient mammals were replaced by the creatures left to us now and to the future. As night came on, the pleasant acrid smoke from our sagebrush campfire symbolized a million sagebrush fires of the past that had been kindled by family groups of the Desert Culture for 10,000 years before "civilization" came to the land. As Orion and his dog marched down the western sky and disappeared behind the Cascades, our dialogue recalled the pictographs we had seen earlier that day when we passed over Picture Rock Pass between Silver Lake and Summer Lake, where John C. Frémont camped in 1843.

In a hundred places in our travels through the desert we had seen pictographs, made by painting with red or yellow natural earths. Also we had seen petroglyphs, made by chipping or scraping the desert varnish from stained rocks. These rock writings may have had religious or other symbolism for prehistoric Indians, but whatever their purpose they depicted reptiles, fish, and mammals present at the time of the painting or carving. Of these, the mountain sheep, an elusive and wary animal, was pictured in countless numbers. These sheep must have been important in the economy of the hunters and a test of their skill with atlatl and bow and arrow. Now there were no mountain sheep on the rocky hillsides or under the canyon rims in all that country where we were spending the night.

In the failing twilight we did see the jackrabbits bounding along the cow paths radiating from a distant water well. Then the yipping coyote chorus reminded us that some of the sagacious mammals have survived even in the face of man's persecution. Later a mumbling porcupine roused us from sleep. The rasping of his teeth on the salty edge of our grub box caused us to haze him away from camp and into the desert shrubs.

In this night we realized that there were no bears, dire wolves, bison, camels, saber-toothed cats, or other mighty beasts around us. Even the giant mylodon, a Pleistocene sloth with enormous claws that were used to drag down trees and dig roots, had been dead for some 11,000 years. The only creatures left were the deer, rabbits, bobcats, panthers, coyotes, foxes, badgers, skunks, and pack rats, and a multitude of mice, ground squirrels, chipmunks, and pocket gophers.

Some scientists believe that the extinction of the great animals resulted from "Pleistocene overkill" by prehistoric hunters, who ringed the sluggish beasts with fire when increasing heat and aridity caused them to concentrate near the ever-more limited watercourses and the shores of vanishing lakes. Men with their spears and bows may have had a part in this extinction, but the destruction of the original Eden of forests and marshes and plains also was caused by climatic and physiographic changes. In the desert that came out of this change, the heirs to the land are the animals we now know. Their adaptations and ways of living are part of the fascinating story of the interrelations between all living things in the desert.

The problems of existence are marvelously exhibited by the numerous species of rodents found in almost every habitat in the desert. Most of these small mammals have secretive nocturnal habits, and hence the casual observer is seldom aware of their numbers, their impact on plant and animal life, or their contribution to the desert food chain.

Some of the wild mice are specialists in their choice of food and in their ability to persist among enemies by jumping, by camouflage, and by rapid reproduction. Many of the desert rodents—especially the pocket gophers, badgers, ground squirrels, and prairie dogs—are accomplished diggers. Their contributions to the desert environment include cultivation of the soil, building homes useful for other animals, controlling insect populations, and providing food for animals larger than themselves.

The wood rats, also known as pack rats or trade rats, are the "ghosts" of the desert. Although related to the mice and the Old World rats, they are not true rats. They are mammals of the genus *Neotoma*—soft-furred, bright-eyed, mischievous creatures that rattle stove pipes at night in the attics of abandoned cabins, cut the buckles from your boots left by the campfire, exchange pebbles for your watch, and drop slices of bread all the way

Jackrabbits are among the commonest mammals in the desert. They escape some of the desert heat by resting in the shade of shrubs or the trunks of large cacti.

between your grub box and their nests made of cactus joints or sticks of wood in the nearby rocks. I know of a pack rat that took the booties from the feet of a baby sleeping in his cradle in a camp in Oregon. And there is a report of a wood rat storing a cache of dynamite in a miner's cook stove.

This propensity for collecting and trading all kinds of objects —including sticks, stones, dung, cactus, bark chips, shiny metal, and dried grass—has never been explained. But the process involves an enormous amount of labor, and much of it seems to be a method of working off excess energy. In western Nevada I once found a dozen or more joint-fir shrubs whose lower branches were neatly loaded with stones the size of walnuts. Each branch supported at least a pound of stones balanced in rows from the base of the shrub outward for a distance of one to two feet. The pack rat, or rats, must have spent many nights at this task. And for what purpose?

The huge trash pile that serves as their nest, and which is cemented together with feces and urine, does serve as an effective sanctuary for old and young. A coyote or other large predator is not apt to tear the place apart. And the rubbish pile is so huge and well insulated that cold can not penetrate to the young wood rats, even when they are born in early March.

Of all the desert rodents, mice are the most numerous. If we contemplate the problems of existence in nature, it soon becomes apparent that small creatures must be more numerous than the larger ones that eat them. If there were only one mouse for each coyote, or weasel, or hawk, or owl, there soon would be no mice, or coyotes, or hawks, or owls. But since there are flesh-eating animals in the desert, and since each transfer of food from green plants to small animals to larger animals is done with 10 percent efficiency or less, it follows that smaller creatures must be numerous to maintain themselves and their predators.

There are many kinds of mice, and their habits and different specializations nicely illustrate the environmental complexity of the desert. The most plentiful and beautiful are the mice of the genus *Peromyscus*. Their bright beady eyes, silky gray bodies shading to white on the belly, large ears, sensitive spreading whiskers, and gentle dispositions appeal to almost every one who sees them around campfires at night, in brush heaps, and in abandoned miners' cabins.

The genus includes many species, among them the canyon mouse (*Peromyscus crinitis*), cactus mouse (*P. eremicus*), brush mouse (*P. boylii*), pinyon mouse (*P. truei*), and white-footed mouse (*P. leucopus*). One of the most common and widely distributed species is the deer mouse (*P. maniculatus*), of which many forms have been recognized by scientists. Gerrit S. Miller, Jr., and Remington Kellogg, in their *List of North American Recent Mammals*, give type localities and ranges for sixty-two forms of this species, many of which are locally distributed and adapted to restricted environmental conditions. Many of these forms have no common names, but some of their scientific names indicate a characteristic of the animal itself or where it is found: *Peromyscus maniculatus sonoriensis*, in Sonora, Mexico; *P. m. magdalenae*, on Magdelena Island off the west coast of southern Baja California; or *P. m. artemisiae*, living among the sagebrushes.

The spiny pocket mice of the genus *Perognathus* are a group with fur-lined cheek pouches, spiny hairs on the rump, naked soles on the hind feet, and long tails bearing a tassel at the end. These friendly creatures are present in many habitats in the desert. Common species include the Great Basin pocket mouse (*P. parvus*), the Arizona pocket mouse (*P. amplus*), and the Apache pocket mouse (*P. apache*). The silky pocket mouse (*P. flavus*) is four inches or less in length, including the tail, and is possibly the smallest rodent in North America. All of the pocket mice can jump many times their own length.

The grasshopper mice are not as numerous as the other genera of mice in the desert. They burrow under bushes or sometimes live in holes abandoned by prairie dogs and ground squirrels. These are small short-tailed mammals that live on insects, particularly grasshoppers. They are also called scorpion mice, owing to their fondness for scorpions. When eating insects they hold them in their front paws and go to work on them head first. The northern grasshopper mouse (*Onychomys leucogaster*) ranges from Minnesota and Kansas west to the Cascades, to the Pacific coast of southern California, and southward to the table-lands of Mexico.

As many as nine kinds of rodents may live more or less in harmony on one acre. In a study made in Arizona to investigate the ecological patterns of kangaroo rats and desert mice, Michael L. Rosenzweig and Jerald Winakur found that some species of pocket mice are associated with denseness of vegetation, in contrast to kangaroo rats, which associate with sparseness of vegetation. Thus the two do not compete in the same micro-habitats. The investigators also found that some mice associated with bushes, while others selected their territory according to soil surface, height, and different densities of vegetation. And when rodent species coexisted in similar microhabitats, each possessed specialized features different from those of all others.

The specializations of mice take many forms. The Apache pocket mouse (*Perognathus apache gypsi*) is almost snow-white and lives only on the white gypsum sands southwest of Alamogordo, New Mexico. The little pocket mouse (*Perognathus longimembris*), one of the smallest of North American rodents, has a high metabolic rate and must have a constant supply of food to maintain its body heat. It stores some food, but it becomes torpid and estivates when temperatures are high in summer. It hibernates when temperatures are low in winter. These quiescent periods, however, are not as predictable as the seasonal hibernations of chipmunks and ground squirrels. Some mice eat seeds almost exclusively and are capable of existing without drinking water. Others are carnivorous and eat worms, insects, and scorpions. Some have favorite foods: the dark kangaroo mouse (*Microdipodops megacephalus*), for example, prefers the seeds of the desert star (*Mentzelia albicaulis*).

The success or failure of rodent reproduction is correlated with rainfall and the production of winter annual plants. In a study of various species of kangaroo rats and mice on Jackass Flats, Nye County, Nevada, Janice C. Beatley found that rodent numbers increased when rain caused autumn germination and winter growth of annuals. When rain failed to come and winter annuals were scarce, rodents did not reproduce in the spring. The data suggested that dietary water and vitamins in the winter vegetation are requirements in the physiology of reproduction of long-tailed burrowing rodents.

Unfortunately, the complex interrelationships of rodents, plants, and predators have not been studied extensively. The rodents are of special importance because of their numbers. The order Rodentia comprises about half of all the mammalian species found in the desert. The gnawing, seed collecting, digging, insect-destroying, and reproductive activities of rodents all play a part in the development and maintenance of the patterns of desert communities.

Of all the mammals that inhabit the desert the hares and cottontails are most likely to be recognized by the casual visitor. The jackrabbit bounding away among the sagebrush clumps or over the cactus beds, zigzagging every two or three seconds, and then sitting upright for a moment, is easily seen and recognized. Even in flight, his long ears immediately identify him.

The jackrabbit is primarily a nocturnal creature. In the hours between dusk and dawn he nibbles a lot of green plants. Desert ranchers prefer to have these plants used by their sheep or cattle. But the jackrabbit's nibbling affects vegetation even in areas where livestock are not grazed. In spring he is enamored with grasses and forbs, and eats so much that the number of fecal pellets dropped by a single rabbit has been estimated at 531 per day. Many of these pellets are dropped while the jackrabbit eats. When he nips off all the stems of a clump of rabbitbrush, it is possible to judge his size by measuring the distance from the bush to the circle of pellets left behind. This clipping of shrubs and eating of brush increases in summer and autumn, when more succulent vegetation has dried under the desert sun.

Jackrabbits are strictly herbivorous and obtain their water from the plants they eat. This explains why they are seen many miles from the nearest ponds or streams. In times of drought they eat the bark of shrubs, and in extremely dry periods they eat the succulent stems of cactus. The swordlike leaves of yuccas sometimes are clipped at the base so that the yucca stems bear a superficial resemblance to ripe pineapples.

Jackrabbits and cottontails belong to the order Lagomorpha and have two pairs of incisors—unlike rodents, which have only one pair. The two pairs of teeth are arranged in tandem—one set grows behind the other. The family Leporidae includes the genera *Sylvilagus* (cottontails and rabbits) and *Lepus* (hares or jackrabbits). The cottontails, brush rabbits, and pigmy rabbits are born naked with eyes closed and stay for a time in a fur-lined nest in a depression or in a hole in the ground. The young of jackrabbits are born fully furred with eyes open and are able to move about at an early age.

The jackrabbits, which are related to the Arctic hare and the snowshoe rabbits, are large mammals that weigh as much as ten pounds and measure as much as two feet in length. The ears of the white-tailed jackrabbit (*Lepus townsendii*) are 4.5 to 5 inches long and are about 18 percent of the animal's length. The black-tailed jackrabbit (*L. californicus*) has ears about 20 percent of its length. The antelope jackrabbit (*L. alleni*), common in the deserts of southern Arizona and Mexico, has ears equal to nearly 24 percent of its length.

There has been much speculation about the ears of jackrabbits. It has been suggested that the large thin ears aid in dissipation of body heat; at least, it is true that jackrabbit ears appear to be longer in hot southern regions than in cold northern areas. But the sensitive long ears also are a part of the animal's equipment for avoiding enemies, of which it has many: coyotes, foxes, bob-cats, eagles, hawks, and the caracara, which lives by persistent hunting in the southern deserts. The ears of the jackrabbit, his bulging eyes which command the horizon in every direction, and his speed are his equipment for survival.

The antelope jackrabbit, like others of his clan, is endowed with tremendous speed, especially on the takeoff from his resting place beneath a spiny shrub or from a depression among clumps of grass. One moment he is stock still; an instant later he is bounding across the desert like a wraith from the depths of the earth. The white hairs on his rump and sides come erect, and a flash of white appears first on one side and then on the other. It has been suggested that the jackrabbit flashes his location to a pursuing predator, then turns right or left without further signal, and thus confuses his enemy while disappearing in the ashy grayness of the desert.

Jackrabbits have other mysterious ways. In the desert and on the western prairies they make paths which sometimes extend for a mile or more. These trails may be six inches or more in width and resemble miniature cow paths. They are kept free of plant growth and are used nightly by the jackrabbits, which sometimes travel in groups of two, three, or four in tandem. At intervals, cross trails connect with the main trails, both of which are used by jackrabbits, cottontails, coyotes, skunks, and badgers. These trails lead to feeding grounds and also are used for escape when coyotes follow the jackrabbits in furious pursuit.

Several years ago I helped fence an acre of ground with netted wire in order to observe the growth of grasses and shrubs when they were protected from grazing by rabbits. The wire happened to cross an established trail. Soon a large dent appeared in the netted wire where the trail was blocked by the fence. I repeatedly found coyote hair on the wire but never found the hair or remains of a jackrabbit that had bounced off the fence. The jackrabbits ultimately changed their trail so that it paralleled the fence and then continued through an adjoining plot fenced with barbed wire to exclude cattle but not rabbits. Within a year the new trail through the livestock-excluded area was as conspicuous as a cow path. We never knew how many coyotes in pursuit of jackrabbits banged their heads against the wire, but as the years passed the dent in the fence grew deeper and deeper.

The jackrabbit's life is not entirely an exercise in eluding enemies. Most of its days are spent in rest in the shade of a protective shrub, in the shadow of a giant saguaro, or in a form nibbled out of a clump of grass. At night much time is spent foraging from plant to plant or from shrubs which are eaten as high as the animal can reach. Also, considerable time is spent in leisurely travel along the innumerable rabbit paths.

One mystery concerns the legendary dance of the hares. Years ago Ernest Thompson Seton described the dance of the snowshoe rabbits in the Bitterroot Mountains in Idaho. He had placed a young rabbit under a box, and the tattoo of its feet apparently attracted other rabbits from the woods. They came in increasing numbers until at last ten sat in plain view gazing at the bright light of Seton's lantern beyond the camp fire. The nearest ones sat close together, while others danced about and chased one another in large circles. Seton wrote: "It is the only time when I found the snowshore hares gathered for a social purpose, and is the only approach to a game that I ever heard of among them."

But in 1967 Ronald E. Smith described an assembly of jackrabbits in a Kansas prairie-dog town. He wrote:

> In early morning six to ten jackrabbits would congregate at various seemingly established places near the edge of dogtown and engage in a sort of play activity; while four to eight rabbits sat in a circle, two others would run around the circle, one following the other by about ten feet, and these two would "take their places" in the circle and two others would take off. All the while guttural sounds would be audible from the group of rabbits. During such activity, prairie dogs would sit on their mounds and watch. This happened two or three times a week in summer and the prairie dogs seemingly always remained curious about it, just as I did.

Are jackrabbits really sociable? No one knows. Once after sundown I drove into my camp in the Oregon desert north of Gray Butte, which is near the town of Prineville, and saw more than a dozen jackrabbits congregated in a clearing used in early spring by sage grouse for their booming-ground. They were loosely grouped near the center of the stage, and in the glow of my automobile headlights I detected the pink reflections from the eyes of other jackrabbits in the sagebrush. Perhaps more succulent forage attracted them to that clearing. Or, since it was the mating season, a number of males may have collected around a few females. Or maybe rival males had come together on the booming-ground to do battle with feet and claws. But this is only speculation; little is known about the mating habits, the early days of the young, or the social habits of adult jackrabbits, since people do not watch rabbits as they watch birds.

More secretive but less mysterious than the jackrabbits are the cottontails. The desert cottontail (*Sylvilagus auduboni*) is an animal of the brushy borders of riverbeds, of rocky canyons, and of cactus patches where succulent food is available and escape cover is near at hand. Cottontails are mostly nocturnal and spend their days in grassy forms or in burrows dug by other animals. Nuttall's cottontail (*Sylvilagus nuttallii*) is slightly smaller than the desert cottontail and has ears that are densely hairy inside, whereas its desert cousin has short sparse hairs on the inner surfaces of the ears.

Nuttall's cottontail is common in sagebrush areas and is also found in the pinyon-juniper woodlands bordering the desert. The pigmy rabbit (*Sylvilagus idahoensis*) is much smaller than the other cottontails and is marked by buff-to-cinnamon-brown fur and a white spot on either side of the nostrils. It inhabits sagebrush and rabbitbrush communities at the upper edges of the desert.

Cottontails manage life in the desert by finding safe shelter among rocks, in prairie-dog towns, and in holes dug by badgers, large kangaroo rats, and ground squirrels. They forage mostly at dusk and during the night, and stay close to brush or holes in the ground for escape from their innumerable enemies. These include coyotes, foxes, badgers, weasels, snakes, eagles, hawks, and owls. Their home ranges are small, and an individual rabbit may spend its entire life within an acre or two. Cottontails nicely exemplify the effect of environment on animal life: where food, shelter, and protection from enemies are available, the rabbits are abundant; where the desert is open and retreat from enemies is difficult, they are scarce or absent.

Mammal predators have always been numerous in the desert. Most of these carnivores, which stand near the top of the food chain, are secretive creatures and are seldom seen by humans. Twice in my lifetime I have had the memorable experience of seeing a mountain lion in the wild. One of these was under the Tonto Rim in Arizona, a place made famous by Zane Grey in his novel of that name. The lion was pursuing a deer in long graceful leaps up a saguaro-covered slope. The deer escaped, and the lion then walked slowly over a rocky ridge and disappeared. The other lion was dislodged by hunters near Eagleville, California, on the east slope of the Warner Mountains. It, too, bounded over a rocky ridge and was lost to sight.

Man's hand has been raised against many of the predators because the larger ones sometimes kill livestock; others dig holes into which horses step and injure themselves; and some are merely disliked because of legendary misunderstanding or folklore. Just recently the ecological place of predators has received consideration. Now they are being recognized as important factors in environmental management. In addition, the desert world would not be the desert without its predators.

Near-extirpation of the coyotes, for example, has resulted in local increases in rabbits and damage to forage plants valuable for livestock. Coyote destruction has also been followed by increases in the numbers of ground squirrels, mice, and rats that threaten the seedling crops of saguaros. Thus, indirectly with traps, guns, and poisons a few men can destroy a cactus forest that multitudes of other people like to visit, study, and enjoy.

In spite of persecution, the coyote (*Canis latrans*) still yaps weirdly under the moon and the stars. He persists because he is an opportunist and a shrewd customer. He takes food as it comes, whether it be rodents, rabbits, snakes, grasshoppers, lizards, frogs, fish, grass, or watermelons. He is alert, adaptable, and quick to learn. When men found that he could solve the secret of buried steel traps, trip them, and steal the bait, then synthetic scents, cyanide guns, and powerful poisons were introduced by the professional destroyers of wildlife. But still the coyote sings his song in remote parts of the desert, telling his fellows, "Here I am, and this is my hunting territory for tonight."

The bushy-tailed doglike coyote is established over a geographical range that includes the midwestern prairies, the Canadian wild lands, the mountains of the West, and the deserts from Wyoming and Idaho to Mexico. I have seen coyotes digging for gophers in the snow on Grand Mesa in western Colorado at an elevation of 10,000 feet. And I have watched them chase jackrabbits near Badwater in Death Valley far below sea level. It seems that wherever the coyote's territory is he covers it tirelessly in search of food, even if the nightly journey requires twenty or thirty miles of travel.

Coyotes prefer dens that have been excavated by badgers or other digging animals. But they themselves dig holes in the sands of creeks and riverbeds as the water level drops below the surface.

These pits, which are dug deeper and deeper during droughts, often supply life-giving drink to birds, small mammals, and insects. Even though the coyote catches and eats some of these, he contributes to the survival of those that remain.

Other secretive, nocturnal, doglike mammals of the desert are the foxes. The gray fox (*Urocyon cinereoargenteus*), with its large bushy tail marked with a broad black streak and a black tip, is a silent creature and an accomplished catcher of mice, ground squirrels, pack rats, lizards, and cottontails. It also includes fruits, nuts, and birds in its diet. Its den is a sheltered place in the rocks or in a shallow hole in the earth.

The rarely seen kit fox (*Vulpes macrotis*), the smallest of the clan, with its sandy-yellow coat and very large ears, is a gentle and inquisitive creature. In the early hours of night one may see kit foxes in the campfire light on sandy areas in the desert where kangaroo rats abound. They are seen occasionally in the campground at the edge of the sand dunes near Stove Pipe Wells in Death Valley, California. Even if you do not see them there, you can find their catlike foot prints in early morning before they are smoothed away by the drifting sand.

Several species of skunks inhabit the desert. The striped skunk (*Mephitis mephitis*) is quite common. Count it a desert adventure if at dusk or dawn you see a female and her brood of five to nine kittens waddling in line like a mother duck and her ducklings. They will not be much disturbed by your presence, but the white-plumed graceful tail at full mast will be sufficient warning for you to keep your distance.

The little spotted skunk (*Spilogale putorius*), about the size of a half-grown kitten, is much more active than the striped skunk. Its combination of white stripes and spots and its white-tipped tail are distinctive. When pressed closely by a possible enemy, it not only erects the hairs on its tail, but pats the ground with its front feet. If danger appears imminent, the little skunk may make a handstand on its forefeet and lift its body, hind legs, and tail in the air in preparation for a spray job that will nauseate and repel most animals and man. In times of food scarcity, however, coyotes, mountain lions, badgers, bobcats, horned owls, and eagles endure the stench to obtain a needed meal.

The spotted skunk also is called a polecat and a civet cat. It is not a cat, nor is it a civet; instead, it and the other skunks belong to the family Mustelidae and are related to the weasels, minks, badgers, and otters. In the Southwest it is called the hydrophobia skunk, since its bite is reputed to cause hydrophobia, a malady one can get if bitten by dogs, foxes, and many other tame and wild creatures.

The fear of hydrophobia probably gave rise to the idea of the "skunk tub," a canvas structure that was open at the top and shaped like a bathtub. Propped up with sticks, it was supposed to protect a cowboy in his sleeping bag from skunks, scorpions, snakes, centipedes, and other night-wandering desert horrors. Since the thing was open to the stars, I once asked Lee Kirby, then supervisor of the Tonto National Forest in Arizona, what the cowboys did when rain came and the tub filled with water. He replied, "When it rains on the Tonto, it is so welcome that everyone goes to town and gets drunk."

Another skunk found in the southwestern border country, in Mexico, and in South America, is the hog-nosed skunk (*Conepatus mesoleucus*). The upper half of this skunk's body, and its tail, are pure white. Its claws are heavy and well adapted for digging, and its bare snout is built for rooting like a hog. Its habits and food preferences are similar to those of the striped skunk and the spotted skunk.

The skunks are omnivorous and in some respects are the garbage cans of the desert. Anything is accepted if it is edible, including fruit, young birds, eggs, insects, berries, prickly-pear fruits, grubs, worms, and meat both fresh and malodorous. Turtle eggs buried in the sand near riverbanks are dug up, and any kind of carrion, including dead fish, dead snakes, and dead ducks, are provender in times of stress. In the warmer months, however, the bulk of the skunk's diet consists of mice, pocket gophers, moles, chipmunks, ground-nesting birds, and cottontails.

One could imagine that with such a wide choice of food and with so few enemies the desert might be filled with skunks. But the skunk must compete with other animals equally adept at foraging; and his single litter of five to nine kittens a year, some of which are caught by owls and other predators, just manages to balance the skunk population. Other creatures survive and thrive because the skunk takes only its share of the desert bounty.

There are numerous mammals you may or may not see on a casual visit to the desert. Some of these, such as the bats, are as abundant in some places as the mice. But since they are animals of the night, and since they spend their days in caverns and dark holes, few people see them or have any idea of the quantity of insects eaten by these flying mammals. Visitors to Carlsbad Caverns National Park, where about fifteen species of bats are found, become aware of their numbers as they watch the great swarms emerge for the nightly flights each summer evening.

One of the common bats in these hordes, and in the Southwest, is the Mexican freetailed bat (*Tadarida mexicana*). Another is the pallid bat (*Antrozous pallidus*), also called the large pale bat, which has light-brown wings and inch-long ears. It lives in caves and also in hollow trees and abandoned buildings. Another bat you may see in the desert canyons is the western pipistrelle or pigmy bat (*Pipistrellus hesperus*). It appears in early evening and is smaller than most other bats.

One mammal not ordinarily thought of as being a desert inhabitant is the porcupine (*Erethizon dorsatum*). The porcupine subspecies *cousei*, known as the Arizona porcupine, occurs in Arizona, New Mexico, Utah, northeastern Nevada, southwestern Texas, and Sonora, Mexico, close to the Gulf of California. The subspecies *epixanthum*, or California porcupine, is common in the western states.

I have seen many of these porcupines in the sagebrush desert in eastern Oregon. In autumn they migrate upward on the foothills and mountainsides, where ponderosa pines furnish bark for their winter food. Although the staple food of the porcupine is tree bark, many green succulent foods rich in vitamin A are eaten prior to the autumn breeding season. Hudson G. Reynolds once observed a porcupine near an ocotillo from which pieces of the stem had been peeled. Porcupines have been observed in many desert-shrub habitats, where they apparently eat paloverde, paloferre, and mesquite.

The widely distributed racoon (*Procyon lotor*), familiar to most people because of the black "mask" across its eyes and the black rings around its tail, can be found in the desert wherever there is water in streams, lakes, or marshes. The raccoon is an omnivirous mammal, and because of its inquisitive nature it is able to live off the country wherever it may be. It has two relatives that possibly exceed it in sheer snooping ability, efficiency in catching prey, and distinctive animal personality: the ringtail (*Bassariscus astutus*), sometimes called ring-tailed cat; and the coati (*Nasua narica*), also called coatimundi, and some unmen-

The coatimundi, or chula, frequents the borders of the Sonoran Desert. This inquisitive animal, a relative of the raccoon, runs in packs and is omnivorous.

tionable names in Spanish and English when it gets into a farmer's chicken coop.

You may never see a ringtail in the wild unless you accompany an experienced trapper or a hunter with a coon hound that has learned the ringtail's tricks. This little night marauder, about two and a half feet long, including the bushy tail with eight black rings that do not completely encircle the underside, ranges from Oregon through the Southwest, east to Texas, and southward through Mexico and Central America. It also has been found in the Red Desert in southwestern Wyoming.

The ringtail is a cute little animal with big dreamy eyes that resemble those of a lemur. Its tail serves as a rudder when the animal is catching its prey or jumping from branch to branch in a desert tree. If caught when young, it makes a gentle and affectionate pet. It readily learns tricks such as coming to dinner with its human friends, drinking beer, and squeezing through the bars of its cage to kill its owner's chickens at night (returning to be found in innocent sleep in early morning).

In the wild, the ringtail nightly explores the desert in quest of mice, lizards, birds, eggs, scorpions, small snakes, insects, and anything else it can kill. A chicken or even a wild turkey is none too large to serve as its prey. But mice are its specialty, and no cat can equal it in ridding a cabin of deer mice. For this reason, miners welcomed the little animals in pioneer days and called them miner's cats. The Mexicans use the Aztec name *cacomixtle*, which indicates that the ringtail has been known for centuries.

The other queer relative of the raccoon, the coatimundi, occasionally crosses the Mexican border into the southwestern states. Its generic Latin name, *Nasua*, means nose. The long snout appears to be almost prehensile, and it bears a keen sense of smell. This nose leads the prowling animal to food ranging from rodents, birds, snakes, centipedes, and scorpions to berries, ripe fruit, and chickens.

Coatis are well known in Mexico, where they are called *chulas*. Because of their peculiar characteristics they are also called lone cats, chula monkeys, and chula bears. They seem to have some of the attributes of all these animals: like bears and raccoons, they walk on plantigrade feet, with the whole lower surface of the foot on the ground; they carry a long banded tail aloft; they root somewhat after the manner of pigs; and they travel in bands like baboons and leave no small creature alive in the territory searched by their group.

The coati, arboreal by nature, prefers the bushy thickets and rocky areas at the upper edges of the desert in the Southwest.

This animal with the two-foot body and two-foot tail is quite capable of climbing high in pine trees and in paloverde and mesquite thickets to look for birds and their eggs. In Mexico it lives in the true desert, and unlike its nocturnal relative, the ringtail, it is active in daylight.

The desert has never had the productivity to support hordes of large mammals, such as the bison which once darkened the horizon in the midcontinental prairies. True, bison once lived in the desert, as did camels, which vanished in prehistoric times and then returned with man's help in the nineteenth century. Camels were introduced in Texas in 1856, and by 1860 were transporting grain and other commodities between Texas and California. The upheaval during the Civil War brought the doom of the camels, and many were left to wander away or be killed by the Apaches. The legend of camels still wandering in the Southwest persists, but only their ghosts now walk in the night shadows where deer, pronghorns, peccaries, and desert bighorn sheep still survive in restricted areas of their original range.

The desert bighorn or mountain sheep (*Ovis canadensis*) on their journey to North America may have passed the camels on their ancient trek to Asia, since both crossed the prehistoric bridge that once connected the two continents. Wild sheep probably originated near the Black Sea, and after drifting across Siberia and the western reaches of our continent adjusted to a remarkable diversity of habitats. The homes of the wild sheep range from the frozen peaks of the Alaskan mountains, where Dall's sheep (*Ovis dalli*) now survive, to the sun-scorched desert mountains of the Southwest and of northern Mexico, where the desert bighorns exceed even a camel in their ability to go without drinking for many days during the cooler part of the year.

The desert bighorns now are localized in the dry and barren desert mountains of their primitive range, which includes parts of western Texas, southern Utah, New Mexico, Arizona, southern Nevada, southeastern California, Baja California, and northwestern Mexico.

When the first white men explored the West, there may have been as many as two million bighorns. Francisco Coronado saw them in 1540 after he left the little town of Compostello, on the west coast of Mexico, on his exploration to the northeast. In later years many bighorns succumbed to the guns of hunters and adventurers. And competition for grazing from cattle, horses, and domestic sheep, as well as damage from their parasites, reduced the herds to remnants of their former numbers. In recent years fences, roads, recreational areas, and military establishments in the desert have usurped their habitats and reduced their numbers. Only recently have areas been established by the federal government and by some of the states for their preservation.

The bighorns are distinctive creatures. They are heavy-bodied sheep that stand approximately three feet at the shoulder and weigh from 120 to 170 pounds as adults. Both sexes have horns,

Desert bighorn sheep now live only in the wildest areas of the desert, since they have been extensively hunted in the past. Trophy rams have a horn curl of up to forty inches and a basal horn circumference of fifteen inches or more. (Photo by Ned Smith, courtesy of Arizona Game and Fish Department)

but the massive curling horns of the rams make them one of America's most coveted game trophies. Fighting between males is a ritualistic contest in which the combatants square off, lunge forward, and come together horn to horn at combined speeds estimated at forty miles or more per hour. Relatively few injuries result from these tilts. Ralph E. Welles and Florence B. Welles, in their detailed study *The Bighorn of Death Valley*, write: "There is a real question as to whether their dramatic butting bouts are fighting or are simple contests of skill and stamina with little real antagonism involved."

The daily and seasonal activities of bighorns contribute to their survival. They travel in bands, and one or more sheep are always on watch for enemies, including mountain lions, bobcats, and coyotes. When escape is necessary, they climb precipitous cliffs and ledges with deceptive ease. On their daily travels they eat a variety of plants, particularly grasses and the succulent parts of forbs and shrubs. Seasonal movements are primarily shifts in elevation in relation to availability of water and seasonal foods.

Although the sheep are seldom seen by people, signs of their presence are the beds they make by pawing depressions in the ground. Their droppings may be seen around bed grounds and water holes. These droppings resemble deer pellets, but usually the two animals do not occupy the same habitats. If you are lucky, you may see bighorns by the side of the road in Death Valley, in the far back-country of the Sierra de la Giganta of Baja California, and in Joshua Tree National Monument, California. The Desert Game Range in Nevada supports about 1,200 sheep. Bighorns also have been transplanted to Hart Mountain National Wildlife Refuge in southern Oregon. The restless nature of these animals, the unpredictability of their activities, and the reward of seeing a band of bighorns ranging in their natural environment make them interesting subjects for study by both the dedicated and the casual observer of wildlife.

Deer are among the larger mammals that are common around the borders of the desert when they come down from their summer ranges to spend the winter in relative freedom from deep snow. The annual fall migrations from the mountains of Colorado, Idaho, and Utah bring herds of thousands of mule deer into the sagebrush deserts. On winter trips east of the Cascades

The peccary, or javelina, is the "pig" of the desert. This animal runs in packs and is mainly a vegetarian, cactus being its principal food.

in Oregon I have counted more than 2,000 deer within sight of the road while I traveled less than twenty miles. These, however, are only transient visitors; their true home is in the high mountains from spring until late autumn.

There are deer that live the year round in the desert. A variety of mule deer known as the burro deer (*Odocoileus hemionus eremicus*) endures the intense summer heat of the Sonoran Desert. It is a pale-colored animal that lives on the cactus flats and hides under brush and trees bordering the dry desert washes. Another pale desert deer is the desert mule deer, or Crook's mule deer (*O. h. crooki*). The white-tailed deer (*O. virginianus couesi*) also is a desert dweller, ranging from southwestern New Mexico and southern Arizona through parts of Sonora and Chihuahua to western Zacatecas and northern Jalisco. These and other races of desert-dwelling deer alleviate the heat and drinking problem by seeking shade during the day, living near water supplies, and frequenting the desert mountains in summer high above desiccating heat and winds.

A desert animal that is tougher than the deer and able to survive where lesser beasts would perish is the collared peccary (*Tayassu tajacu*), also known as the javelina, musk hog, desert rooter, or cactus pig. The peccary is not a pig, but it has a snout, and it roots and grunts like a pig. The legends surrounding this animal have an aura of savagery: its knife-sharp tusks sprouting from an oversized head, its ferocious nature when cornered or wounded, and its ability to keep Mexican and South American hunters in trees until they drop from hunger and exhaustion—all of which have encouraged writers to publish a lot of "hog-wash" on the subject.

Young javelinas make good pets. They follow children around like family dogs in Mexico. But when they grow to full size, they may revert to their wild ways and become vicious fighters. In the open desert, however, if a band of javelinas runs at you, they probably are scurrying for cover, since they can smell you but are prevented by their poor eyesight from seeing and locating you.

The first javelina I ever saw was standing under a mesquite tree. The light-gray band across its shoulder did not match the shadows, and its motionless profile suddenly materialized into the piglike animal it is. For a moment it stood listening, and then with remarkable speed crossed a dry wash and faded into dense brush on the farther side. The next javelina I saw, a few years after the first, walked out of the cactus forest south of Tucson, Arizona, stood on the highway near my parked truck, grunted, and then trotted into the brush. Of course, my camera was out of reach in my camper.

Hunters consider the javelina a fine trophy, even though the little animal seldom weighs more than forty to sixty pounds. The hunters soon learn that javelinas are shy, elusive, and nimble of foot. They keep together in bands near tree-covered streamsides, in cactus forests, and on brush-covered hillsides.

Sometimes they live in caves, from which they wander considerable distances to forage. Their food includes cacti, fruits, roots, insects, lizards, snakes, acorns, mesquite beans, and almost any other edible thing they can catch or root out of the ground. They frequent streamsides if water is available. But apparently they can live without drinking, if they can get cacti, sotol, and other succulent plants. Count it your lucky day if you see one or a dozen of these rare, self-sufficient, and versatile animals.

The pinicate beetle stands on its head and emits a puff of gas which repels birds and other enemies.

CHAPTER 8

Insects and Other Arthropods

I have often wondered what would happen to the desert if all its insects suddenly ceased to exist. If the innumerable moths and other night-flying insects were instantly exterminated, the bats would be in for hard times. Joshua trees and their yucca relatives, which are pollinated by pronuba moths, would live out their lives and then be no more. The little horned toad that stations himself beside an anthill and gulps its residents soon would be hungry. The insect-eating lizards would fall upon lean days; even the plant-eating chuckwalla lizard would see his favorite insect-pollinated forbs decline in numbers and ultimately disappear. And if the lizards died out, some of the desert snakes, the coyotes, and the roadrunners would have to change their diets.

If one thinks a little more about the links between insects and insects, insects and plants, and insects and other animals, the relationships between living things provide fascinating material for speculation about life principles and processes in the desert. If there were no insects, the dragonfly would no longer hawk for mosquitoes, flies, and midges along the rivers and far inland over the desert. The mosquito and dragonfly larvae would provide no food for the minnows and larger fish in lakes and streams. And of greater importance, the mice, rabbits, antelope, and other grazing mammals would be confronted with a scarcity of annual and perennial forbs which depend on insect pollination for their continued existence.

In spite of their small size, insects are dominant animals in the desert world. One group alone, the grasshoppers, during population explosions can decimate plant life over hundreds of square miles and upset the food chain for multitudes of other animals including birds, reptiles, and even fish. The social insects—ants, termites, bees, and wasps—especially affect ecological processes. E. O. Wilson recently wrote:

> Ants and termites in particular weigh more and utilize larger amounts of energy than all the birds and reptiles combined, they turn more soil than all the earthworms, and they also serve as very important predators and degraders of cellulose. If some catastrophe removed all the highly social vertebrates, including man, the remainder of the natural global ecosystem would scarcely register the perturbation; but if the social insects were exterminated, the result would be a major reorganization of the land environment.

Many of the insects in the desert are beautiful, and all have strange and interesting lives. Certain moths have ears sensitive to sonar pulses of bats and take evasive action before the bats can detect them. The tarantula hawk (*Pepsis thisbe*), one of the largest of wasps, with brilliant orange wings and blue metallic body, is astounding in the strength that enables it to drag tarantulas to its nest. And the ant-lion larva, or doodlebug, waiting at the bottom of its sand funnel for an unwary ant or spider is one of nature's most patient creatures. Even if it waits for months before catching its prey, it does not starve. One that I kept in my study without giving it food was alive at the end of 228 days. Then it ate a spider which I dropped into its pit.

The insects most of us see in the desert are creatures of the daytime world. On warm summer days grasshoppers rise ahead of your footsteps in crackling flight or hide behind the stems of desert shrubs. Many of the grasshoppers roost in shrubs at night and graze on grasses and forbs during the day. Ants are almost universally present but are inclined to retire to their nests during the hottest hours of the day. If you doubt their presence, try turning over rocks—it is not unusual to find ants under more than 20 percent of the large stones in the desert pavement. The large thatching ants (*Formica rufa*), of course, are easily located by spotting their foot-high domes made of twigs and other debris. Harvester ants may be seen from March until November building their gravel mounds to heights of one to three feet and clearing the vegetation in circles up to thirty feet in diameter around their homes.

Among the conspicuous daytime insects are the butterflies, large wasps, and noise-making cicadas. The cicadas have specialized sound-making equipment consisting of drumlike cavities in the lower abdomen containing vibrating and resonating membranes. The whole mechanism is complex, and the intensity of the buzzing when the cicada "saws" its song is unforgettable.

If you are more than an occasional observer of butterflies, you will find many varieties of interest in the desert. But even the casual visitor may expect to see old friends such as the painted lady (*Vanessa cardui*), which occurs worldwide; the milkweed butterfly (*Danaus menippe*); and various species of swallowtails (*Papilio*). The anise swallowtail frequents prickly-pear cacti to obtain nectar when the flowers are in bloom. In the Mohave Desert you should look for the two-tailed swallowtail (*P. dannus*) when the milkweeds are in flower.

Great numbers of insect larvae are visible in the desert, if you search carefully for them. Most of us do not see them because they move slowly, or have protective coloration, or cling to the undersides of leaves. The tent caterpillars of the genus *Malacosoma*, however, are distressingly evident when they hatch from egg clusters laid by brown or gray moths and construct tentlike nests of silk on antelope bitterbrush and other shrubs. The black and hairy larvae, with a yellow stripe down the middle of the back, feed on leaves and return to their tent at night for shelter and for protection from enemies. They defoliate shrubs so completely that the plants frequently die.

The nighttime world of the desert insects seems to be dominated by moths, beetles, katydids, weevils, and bugs which suck blood from mammals or sap from plants. The moths which have spent the day hanging under leaves and branches now make their visits to the night-flowering plants. Many of the night flowers attract moths by their fragrance; others have white flowers—for example, the evening primroses, which are visited by the hawk moths with rapidly beating wings. Some of the moths are rather rare; one of these is the Zuni tiger-moth (*Arachnis zuni*), found on the tablelands of New Mexico and Arizona. In contrast, moths of the genus *Catocala*, with its numerous species, are exceedingly abundant. These moths, called underwings or afterwings, because the hind wings are distinctively colored, are noted for their protective coloration or mimicry of the backgrounds on which they rest. When sitting on bark or gray stones, with the brilliantly colored hind wings covered, they are almost invisible. Under the beam of a flashlight, however, their eyes glow like spots of fire.

In the all-encompassing silence of the desert night the buzzing of large moths and other flying insects becomes audible along with the squeaks of pursuing bats. From the shrubs and herbs on the desert floor, insect voices rise in volume as they communicate with one another by sounds distinctive for each species. The katydids, especially, are the songsters of the insect world. These members of the long-horned grasshopper family, with their long antennae and green wings, make sound by rasping a scraper on one wing against a file on the opposite wing. They stridulate with such complicated notes that many studies have been made of their songs with sound-recording instruments. Analysis of the songs shows they are complex systems of pulses and vibrations instead of the simple clicks, chirps, *chruu*'s, *tsip*'s, or *s-s-s-* sounds that come to our incompetent ears.

The skeletons of cacti and the fallen stems of shrubs and trees provide hiding places for lizards, snakes, and insects. This wood persists for a long time in the dry desert air unless it is destroyed by termites and beetles.

We never hear or see the great majority of insects in the desert because they live in hidden worlds or in underground nests, tunnels, or caverns of their own making. The adult lives of most insects are much shorter than the larval stages spent within plants, boring in wood, or hibernating in protective earthen cells. The innumerable ants spend much of their time below the surface of the soil. The termites, of which there are many in the desert, abhor light and the desiccating dryness. They are seen only when one digs them out of the earth or lifts dead branches of cacti, yuccas, trees, and shrubs that are being reduced to hollow skeletons by their busy mandibles.

Many insects live secretive early lives, appearing only as adults in countless millions at the proper season. The larvae of small ephydrid flies live in the alkaline waters of Great Salt Lake and saline ponds in such numbers that sometimes they are cast up on the shore by storm waves in windrows and heaps six inches deep. The adult flies swarm in clouds over the water at hatching time. Mosquitoes that buzz in the desert far from lakes, rivers, and ponds lay the eggs from which their larvae hatch in unexpected places, such as springs in shallow caves and seeps in gravel beds. A tree-hole mosquito deposits its eggs in rainwater collected in the flask-shaped nests excavated by woodpeckers in the giant saguaro cactus in the Sonoran Desert in Arizona.

Grasshoppers are among the dominant insects of the desert. In addition, they have a host of relatives and allies of strange appearance and sometimes pestiferous habits that bring grief and despair to farmers and ranchers by eating their crops. Most of us are familiar with grasshoppers, crickets, katydids—all are common members of a group called orthopteroid insects. Their other relatives include the fantastic walkingstick insects, with slender twiglike bodies; the earwigs, with horizontal moveable forceps at the rear end; the fiercely predacious praying mantids; and the roaches, some of which are so tiny that they live in ant nests. All of these insects have representatives in the desert and are among the most interesting of all the animals found in arid lands.

No one knows how many kinds of grasshoppers there are. Some are large, such as the two-to-three-inch-long lubber grasshoppers; others, such as the pigmy grasshoppers, are scarcely half an inch long. The desert long-horned grasshoppers are strange nocturnal insects found mostly on sagebrush and eriogonum plants, especially in the Mohave Desert. The Mormon cricket, neither a cricket nor a grasshopper, is a shield-backed katydid with short wings and an appetite that has brought economic ruin to thousands of people in the West.

Most of the grasshoppers are solitary animals. They live out their lives by feeding on selected plants, on vegetable debris, and even on cow manure. They avoid a legion of enemies—including birds, skunks, lizards, hungry little owls, grasshopper mice, and scorpions—by expert jumping, by camouflaging themselves in the dust and among stones, and by hiding behind stems or beneath leaves of shrubs and other desert plants. The female lays eggs by thrusting her abdomen into the soil. The "pod" of eggs remains in the ground and hatches during the following spring. The young, which resemble miniature adults, shed their skins five or six times as they grow larger and become adults.

Some of the grasshoppers multiply to form enormous hordes, especially if several favorable seasons occur in succession. They then become gregarious and migrate in swarms of countless billions. Plagues caused by the desert locust (*Schistocerca gregaria*) of Africa and Asia have been known since biblical times. The dramatic swarms of the Rocky Mountain locust (*Melanoplus spretus*) have not been seen in recent years in the United States, but various migratory grasshoppers are common on the western prairies and in our southwestern deserts.

Each of our major deserts contains dozens, if not hundreds, of species of grasshoppers. Many of these are common, some are rare and restricted in their geographic ranges, all have interesting habits, and some are beautiful and make prize items in insect collections. The furnace heat lubber (*Tytthotyle maculata*), for instance, lives on creosote bushes on the sun-baked slopes in Death Valley, California. Adults are present during the great heat of summer from April to September. The green-striped grasshopper (*Chortophaga viridifasciata*) is widespread in the desert; it makes a crackling sound in flight.

Many of the desert grasshoppers are colorful. The horse lubber (*Taeniopoda eques*), found on mesquite, burroweed, and other shrubs, is shining black above and has rose-red wings. Its brilliant colors make it a collector's item. This grasshopper is not as shy as other grasshoppers: when disturbed, it hisses and spreads its wings in a threatening manner. Oslar's grasshopper (*Lactista oslari*) has bright yellow on its wings. The creosote bush grasshopper (*Bootettix punctatus*) is green with pearly white, brown, and black markings. Other grasshoppers have spots of various colors on their wings and bodies. The Great Basin grasshopper (*Trimerotropis sparsa*) has hind tibia that vary from green to yellow to brown. The thighs of the hind legs of many grasshoppers are marked by bars arranged like chevrons.

An orthopteran that has always intrigued me, because of its distinctive habits and unusual appearance, is the Jerusalem cricket. I frequently find insects of this species on my visits to the Oregon sagebrush desert; however, they can be found in hot sandy deserts all the way to Mexico. They are not true crickets; instead, they belong to the subfamily Stenopelmatinae, a group of ground crickets with bulky black-banded abdomens, short legs, and large heads with widely spaced eyes. The male stridulates weakly by rubbing its rear legs against a spine on its abdomen; but the faint rasping sound is sufficient to attract a female—who may eat him after mating is accomplished.

The Jerusalem cricket is omnivorous. Seedling plants are choice food, but potatoes left in Oregon fields provide a starch diet. And if a dead mouse or insect, including another cricket, happens to lie around, the Jerusalem cricket changes to a protein diet. In fact, living crickets, because of their cannibalistic nature, stay healthy longer if they do not come into close contact with their own kind. Their numbers are held in check to some extent by tachina flies, which lay their eggs on the cricket. When the fly larvae mature inside the cricket, they cause its death. California gulls also avidly devour Jerusalem crickets, Mormon crickets, and grasshoppers by the millions when population explosions occur.

Walkingsticks are more abundant in the desert than most of us realize. Their profound modifications of shape and color, plus their habit of remaining motionless on grass stems and twigs of desert shrubs, make them invisible to all but the sharpest eyes. Their enormously elongated bodies and heads and long irregular legs make them resemble twigs, or thorns, or even the petioles of the green leaves to which they cling.

One of the Asian walkingsticks reaches a length of ten or twelve inches, and some tropical species are large enough to be roasted over a fire and eaten by natives. In comparison with these, our species are small. The gray walkingsticks (*Pseudo-sermyle straminea*), found on grass, rabbitbrush, burroweed, and sagebrush in our southwestern deserts, are from one and a half to three inches long. Like others of their kind, they are strictly vegetarian. The best way to find them is to search sagebrush and creosote bush stems and leaves with a flashlight at night when they are feeding actively.

While searching for walkingsticks you may find one of the desert mantids. These are distinctive insects, well known because of their peculiar forms, their spined or toothed legs that snap out to capture insects, their triangular heads that turn in all directions, and the superstitions about their prayerful appearance while at rest. They are indeed voracious eaters, and the hapless insect falling into their grasp is in a death trap. Many of the mantids are shaped and colored like the leaves or flowers on which they wait for insect prey. These unusual patterns undoubtedly provide protection against bird and insect predators as well as camouflage against, or even attraction for, prey insects. Even the male mantid is not safe from the female. Frequently he is eaten after or even during the process of mating.

Some mantids in the desert are found on grasses and forbs, and some species are partial to shrubs. The slim Mexican mantis (*Oligonicella mexicana*) may be found by careful examination of flowers of plants belonging to the composite or sunflower family. The minor ground mantis (*Litaneutra minor*) runs on the ground, as does Yersin's ground mantis (*Yersiniops sophronicum*). The latter can jump several inches—one indication of its relationship with the grasshoppers.

More ancient than the desert itself are the roaches, whose ancestors were mighty insects in the Carboniferous period some 300 million years ago. Roaches have traveled the world for centuries in ships, and the domesticated kinds in houses and kitchens have given the whole tribe a bad reputation. Their flattened bodies, long legs for running, and ability as scavengers have contributed to their survival through millions of years. The wild roaches are not all drab creatures. Many are brightly colored, and all have interesting and varied habits.

Desert roaches live in debris beneath cactus clumps, beneath the bark of dead trees, under rocks, and in the nests of wood rats. The Wheeler ant cockroach (*Attaphila fungicola*), only one-eighth of an inch long, lives with the leaf-cutting ants that cultivate fungus gardens deep in the desert soil. For some unknown reason the ants clip the antennae of the roaches but tolerate them, possibly because they are useful scavengers in the ant nest. The chemical trails made by the ants are followed by the wingless female roaches, who keep their maxillary palps in constant contact with the ants' paths.

Butterflies and moths are known by everyone. The incedible beauty of many of these insects, their extraordinary habits and behavior, and their relationships with other living things provide fascinating opportunities for study of dynamic natural history in the desert. If we probe beyond names and descriptions, we find a hidden world of relationships vastly more important than the mostly evanescent life phases of the adult butterflies and moths.

The largely unseen lives of the Lepidoptera enter strongly into the food web of the desert. The larvae of most species feed on plants and in turn are eaten by a great variety of predators, including other insects, rodents, and birds. These in turn are eaten by still larger animals at or near the top of the predator food chain. The larvae also are part of the parasite chain, since many serve as hosts for wasps and other insects that lay eggs on or in the bodies of the caterpillars. When moth or butterfly larvae feed on and kill cacti, shrubs, and trees, the dead plant material becomes provender for roaches, beetle larvae, grasshoppers, worms, and other animals. The very numbers of all these interrelated animals thus result in a large amount of energy flow.

The multitudinous means by which butterflies and moths accomplish their purposes provide sufficient excuse for the desert visitor to consider some of their ways of life. The major purpose of the winged adults, of course, is to perform the marriage rites. Elaborate devices and chemical secretions are used in the attraction of mates and in courtship. The male queen butterfly (*Danaus gilippus*), for example, possesses "hairpencils," or tufted stalks with glandular hairs, which produce an aphrodisiac for seduction of the female. The pheromone, or attracting substance, is sensed by the female when the secretion, borne in a kind of "dust," is placed on her antennae by the male.

Many of us are aware that most insect activity is strongly influenced by temperature, and in the desert there are broad temperature changes as day turns to night. Insects on the desert floor are less subject to these temperature ranges, since the soil, and plants to which insects cling, retain daytime heat for considerable periods after the sun has set. But great numbers of moths fly rapidly and hover with beating wings over flowers that remain open in the cool desert air.

In a laboratory study of sphinx moths (*Manduca sexta*), reared from eggs obtained from the Mohave Desert, Bernd Hein-

The pronuba moth pollinates yucca flowers to insure a seed crop that will provide food for her larvae. Without her the yucca could not produce seeds. (Photo by Albert Haanstad, courtesy of Denver Public Library, Conservation Library Center)

rich has given us an insight into how these insects can fly in a wide range of air temperatures. By means of thermocouples he found that the moths maintained thoracic temperatures within a degree of 42° C. while in flight over a range of air temperatures from about 17° C. to 32° C. He found that the moths underwent a warmup period of "wing-whirring" before flight, a process analogous to the engine warmup of a propeller airplane before it leaves the runway. He also found that the moths overheated when the dorsal vessel leading from the thorax to the abdomen was tied off. This indicated that normally the blood pumped to the abdomen cooled the insect, somewhat as a radiator cools the engine of an automobile. It may be an oversimplification to say that moths have thermostats for temperature control, but their flight machinery is admirably adapted for nocturnal activity in the desert.

The pronuba moth (*Tegeticula yuccasella*) offers the classic example of mutual adaptation between insect and plant in its association with the yucca. Charles V. Riley, a Missouri entomologist, made the original observation more than three-quarters of a century ago. The pronuba moth pollinates the yucca, apparently not by accident but by design. She gathers a ball of pollen from one flower and carries it to another flower. There she inserts a few eggs into the pistil and then climbs to the stigma. She not only places her ball of pollen on the stigma but rubs it in so that there will be no failure in fertilization or production of seeds for her infant larvae. The larvae never outnumber the seeds, so in the end the yucca and the moth both reproduce their kind. Without one or the other, both would perish, since no other insect can successfully pollinate the yucca.

The moths and the butterflies are charming, lovely creatures in their own right. Close examination reveals how they are specialized and differ from other insects. Their wings are covered with scales. The mouth parts are modified for sucking, although a few do not feed as adults, and the mouth parts in one family (Micropterygidae) are adapted for chewing. The proboscis, when present, is coiled like a watch spring. The eyes are large and compound, and, in addition, most moths have two ocelli, or simple eyes.

Moths and butterflies resemble each other in that both are caterpillars in the larval stage. Many of the larvae are brilliantly colored, and some are ferocious in appearance but harmless, with the exception of a few that have stinging body hairs. In general, butterflies are diurnal and moths are nocturnal. Most butterflies fold their wings upward while at rest; moths rest with their wings flat, and folded in such a way that their brilliant colors are invisible. Many moth larvae are expert spinners of silk and make elaborate cocoons. The pupae of most butterflies are called chrysalids and are suspended from leaves or twigs in various ways, or are held upright by silken girdles. The skippers, which are stout-bodied butterflies, differ from other butterflies in their wing veination. Skippers usually have antennae hooked or recurved at the tips, and their larvae have large heads and constricted necks. They are common in the southwestern deserts.

People who know the eastern swallowtail butterflies may see their relatives in the desert, since they are addicted to visiting flowers. Most of the species have tail-like projections on their hind wings. In the northern deserts, especially at higher elevations along the mountain borders, you may see the Old World swallowtail (*Papilio machaon*). In the Mohave Desert mountain ranges of southern California, two papilionid butterflies (*Papilio indra fordi* and *P. rudkini*) occur in the canyon bottoms. In years of normal rainfall the larvae of the former feed on panamint cymopteris, a member of the carrot family. The latter feed on thamnosa, a low aromatic shrub of the rue family. The larvae of these two butterflies reach population peaks following optimal rainfall; then they eat the two plants interchangeably and thus become competitive.

Common butterflies in the southwestern deserts include the anise swallowtail, the alfalfa yellow, and the rufescent patch (*Chlosyne lacinia crocale*), which is present from Texas to California. The milkweed butterfly (*Danaus menippe*) is common and noticeable because of its orange-brown wings with black borders. The pierid (*Pieris beckeri*) inhabits the deserts from eastern California to western Sonora.

A moth whose larva is more of a curiosity than the adult itself is the Mexican jumping bean moth (*Laspeyresia saltitans*). Each larva lives in a seed of sebastiana, a shrub related to the poinsettia, and consumes the kernel as it grows. When the seed is exposed to sunlight or heat, the larva snaps its body against the side of its container and with luck may land in shade. Here, away from the heat of the sun, the little caterpillar can spin its cocoon. It ultimately escapes through the circular hole it cut while still a small larva. The moth resembles the coddling moth of the eastern states.

The moth larvae that attack cactus are exceedingly numerous, and dozens of species have been described. Among the most interesting are the species of *Melitara,* whose female moths deposit their eggs in chains or sticks. These "eggsticks" may contain as many as 150 eggs. The cocoons spun by the larvae may be found in the debris at the base of cactus plants or in dried-out prickly-pear segments.

The larvae are great tunnelers. If you examine cacti closely, you can find moth larvae in practically every species. Even the mighty saguaro is not immune to attack. The barrel cactus (*Echinocactus acanthodes*) shows a yellowish appearance where the larvae of the moth *Cactobrosis fernaldialis* are at work: as they tunnel they discharge excrement through small holes in the stem. Ultimately the cactus rots inside, and the semiliquid pulp furnishes food for fly larvae and other scavenger larvae. Finally, the cactus is reduced to a dry hollow shell.

Beetles and bugs and ants are numerous in the desert. Many of the adult beetles are conspicuous because of their size, coloration, and penchant for walking or flying in the heat of the day. The bugs are less conspicuous, since many are colored to match the plants from which they suck juices or on which they wait for their prey.

The larvae of beetles and bugs are much more numerous than their parents. Most varieties are usually hidden from sight, eating inside plants or feeding on roots. Although many of the adult beetles have mouth parts fitted for chewing, gnawing wood, or sucking blood from prey, their impact on living things is small compared to the activities of their larvae, some of which live and eat for several years before reaching maturity.

The larvae and adults of boring beetles are especially efficient in reducing wood and dry plants to dust and returning plant material to the earth from which it came. Some beetle larvae, such as the mesquite girdler (*Oncideres pustulatus*) bore beneath bark of living trees. Others live in the dead trunks of palm trees and Joshua trees. A large number of beetle larvae bore in living cactus stems, while still others live in the debris beneath cactus clumps and in the root zone of desert grasses. Among the adults, a wealth of beetles occur in desert flowers, which they eat or use as a blind for hunting prey. Inadvertently they perform the useful service of pollination. Some of the weevils (a type of small beetle) bore into yuccas. Many of these crawl over the ground and are easily seen.

One of the beetles known to most travelers in the desert is the pinicate beetle (*Eleodes armata*), or "circus bug." There are many species of *Eleodes,* but the big black pinicate beetle that climbs the sand dunes in broad daylight or wanders into your camp at night, if disturbed, will thrust its abdomen into the air and stick its head down toward the ground. If handled roughly, it emits a black fluid with an offensive odor. Most beetles of this group, called darkling beetles, feed on dead plant materials, but they also accept green vegetation and are fond of fresh fruits from desert shrubs. Their grubs eat roots of plants, and pupation occurs in the soil.

Many ground beetles of the family Carabidae hunt for other insects and consume cutworms. Among the most interesting of these are the bombardier beetles of the genus *Brachinus.* Their method of defense is more efficient than the offensive odor produced by *Eleodes.* When disturbed they emit puffs of gas which are accompanied by an audible explosion. The beetle manages this effect by mixing in a spray an aqueous solution of hydroquinones and hydrogen peroxide with catalases and peroxidases to trigger an instantaneous and explosive set of events. The spray is not only repellent to many predators, but also is ejected at a temperature of 100° C. with a burning effect. The beetles can "shoot" as often as twenty-nine times in a row and can rotate their abdominal tips so as to hit their targets with unerring accuracy.

Tiger beetles, found on sandy areas in prairies, along beeches, and in the deserts, are bloodthirsty insects. The adults are fierce predators on other insects. Most adults are strikingly colored in hues of green, blue, purple, and iridescent bronze, with stripes or bars on their wings. Their keen eyesight makes them exasperating creatures to photograph in the wild, even with a telephoto lens. Even though they are not unduly afraid and fly only short distances when followed, they always face the photographer as soon as they alight, and fly again as the photographer approaches them.

The larvae of tiger beetles are quite as fierce as their parents.

They live in vertical tunnels in the soil and wait at the openings to snap up passing insects between strong mandibles. Their prey has little chance for escape, since the larvae have hooks on their backs anchoring them in their holes.

Although most of the bugs suck juices of plants or of other insects, the assassin bugs prefer the warm blood of mammals. The western cone-nose bug (*Triatoma protracta*) frequents pack-rat nests and acts as a carrier of a trypanosome disease of these rodents. The Mexican cone-nose bug (*T. phillosoma pallidipennis*) is an inch-long beast with a small head and an abdomen widened beyond the wings. It can suck blood from a human without causing pain or any other sensation. Unfortunately, in tropical America these bugs can spread a serious infection called Chagas' disease. Repeated bites by these insects, which also are called kissing bugs, can build up a sensitivity and cause severe reactions varying from papular lesions to large swollen areas several inches in diameter on the skin.

Many familiar and less noxious bugs abound in every habitat in the desert. In rivers and freshwater ponds waterboatmen occur along with the highly predacious back swimmers. Water striders make dimples in the surface film of water, and dragonfly larvae hunt for insects and even small fish below the water's surface. On forbs, shrubs, and trees stinkbugs exhibit interesting patterns of green, gray, brown, and variegated metallic markings that make it difficult to detect them against their backgrounds.

Preeminent among the social insects of the desert are the ants and termites. There also are many bees and wasps in the desert, and they enter strongly into the biological scheme by pollination of flowers and by parasitism of other insects. But with the exception of the large bumblebees and the honey bees, which were introduced from the Old World, most of the bees and wasps live solitary lives. In contrast, the termites and ants form colonies of a few dozens to thousands of individuals. Their complex social organization, mutual cooperation, and foraging ability make them particularly successful insects with important impacts on the biology of the desert.

The large mounds of the occidental harvester ant (*Pogonomyrmex occidentalis*) are conspicuous in the sagebrush deserts of Wyoming, Utah, Nevada, and much of Arizona and New

Mexico. A similar species (*P. owyheei*) builds mounds of sand, gravel, and lava particles in eastern Oregon, Washington, and Idaho. These cone-shaped hills reach a height of two feet and are surrounded by a cleared circle from five to thirty feet in diameter. The ants chew down grasses and weeds with the result that dead roots do not leave channels through which water can enter the nest.

The internal structure of the nest varies according to the soil, the needs of the ants with regard to climate, and the availability of seeds and other food. The entrance hole usually is somewhere on the south side of the mound, where the warmth of the sun is greatest, especially in early spring and late autumn. The entrance leads into a foyer from which tunnels spread to a multitude of chambers where the eggs, larvae, and pupae develop into mature ants. If temperature rises too high in the mound, these young ants are moved to other chambers or to lower levels. The queen usually resides in the center of the mound. In winter the colony moves to chambers below the frost level, where the ants remain quiescent and do not eat. The winged males and females fly from the mound in late summer, when they mate; and the queen digs a shallow cell in the earth where her new colony will develop.

The harvester ants are great collectors of seeds. These are carried into the mound, shelled, and stored in chambers and galleries near the periphery. Seeds of each species of plant are stored in separate granaries, probably because the ants specialize on certain kinds of seeds, each of which is available at a given time. The husks are carried out and dropped at the edge of the cleared circle. Kangaroo rats are adept at digging into the granaries and stealing the stored seeds.

Numerous other species of harvester ants live in the desert. The red harvester ant (*Pogonomyrmex barbatus*) ranges from southeastern Colorado and southwestern Kansas south to Texas, westward into New Mexico and Arizona, and far southward in Mexico. Its gravel mound usually is not as conspicuous as that of the occidental harvester; it may be a low, widespread pile of gravel with a small crater surrounding the entrance, or there may be practically no mound at all. The mound of the California harvester (*P. californicus*) commonly is a lopsided crater of sand. *P. maricopa*, a harvester with no accepted common name, makes multiple craters of sand that overlap at the edges. The

The author preparing to weigh the soil and gravel excavated by a harvester ant colony in the sagebrush desert near Squaw Butte, Oregon.

entrance holes are in the centers of the craters. Other members of the genus nest in cavities among stones or live beneath stones.

Another harvester ant, *Veromessor pergandei*, digs deep formicaries to escape the desert heat. This species lives in Death

Valley, California, and in the hot deserts in Mexico. The ants are inactive at temperatures below 40° F., and when daytime temperatures are high, they work early in the morning and late in the afternoon. Frequently they collect most of the seed supply of globe mallows, evening primroses, rabbitbrush, and other plants. This limits the numbers of seeds that can germinate and grow in succeeding years. But woolly plantain, which has been estimated to produce 1,254,165,300 seeds per acre in the Californian and Mexican deserts, has a surplus of seeds and is little affected by ants.

The dynamics of vegetation in relation to ants has been insufficiently studied, especially in the desert. Certainly ants are efficient soil builders. I have weighed some of the harvester-ant mounds in the Oregon sagebrush desert and estimate that they carry as much as four tons of soil to the surface per acre every five years. Ants are seed planters, flower pollinators, and possibly plant protectors. Ants attracted to the nectaries of acacias and other plants that produce honeydew possibly fight off caterpillars and destructive insects that might destroy the leaves. Ants also are efficient predators of other insects. However, they do not decimate the pollinating insects, since their population is in turn controlled by lizards, toads, birds, and even snakes. Thus the balance of desert creatures is maintained.

A remarkable association occurs between the blind snake (*Leptotyphlops dulcis*) and the small army ants (*Neivamyrex nigrescens*) in the southwestern deserts. These ants are much less spectacular than the army and legionary ants of Africa and South America that travel great distances in columns many ants wide and hundreds of feet long. Instead, the foraging workers of the southwestern army ants run in single file, mostly in search of insects, and they return to their nest at night.

The little blind snakes, five to eight inches long, rounded at each end, and slender as small earthworms, prey upon the army ants and their larvae. The snakes are attracted by secretions originating in the ants' heads that they deposit along their trails. In turn, the snakes produce a substance in the cloacal sac that repels both army ants and other insectivorous snakes. Since the blind snakes are so small, they undoubtedly need protection from larger predatory snakes.

The honey-pot ants, of which there are several species in the desert, have the astonishing ability to turn some of their young workers into living honey bags. One of these, *Myrmecocystus mexicanus*, lives in sandy or gravelly areas and makes an underground nest that may be only a few inches below ground level or may extend to a depth of fifteen feet. When honey is available from plant exudates or from the secretions of aphids, worker ants collect the liquid and by regurgitation transfer it to the young or callow ants. As their storage crops expand, their gasters swell until they are the size of peas. Being unable to walk, these storage ants, or repletes, hang from the ceilings of chambers in the nest. When food is scarce and drought is on the land, they release the honey to the other members of the colony.

Honey is stored in the repletes for long periods of time. At first the ants are amber-colored and almost transparent. As the honey ages it sometimes sours, and the ant's gaster darkens or appears to be black. When the honey is fresh in the ant's body, it is sweet and makes good eating. Knowledgeable honey hunters recognize the ant nests by the flattened disks or pebbly craters that surround the large-bore entrance. Craters made by the honey-pot ants (*Myrmecocystus mexicanus hortideorum*) are seen by visitors to the Garden of the Gods near Colorado Springs, Colorado. There the ants are a tourist attraction. They obtain their nectar from galls on oak trees.

The termites are among the most numerous, most fascinating, and biologically least known social insects of the desert. Their social nature makes them difficult to study in the laboratory, and their long-lived colonies make thorough investigation of their life histories a slow and difficult process. Furthermore, not many students of termites live in desert areas. Yet few insects play a more important part in the economy of nature.

In desert areas termites are somewhat the equivalent of earthworms in humid climates in their role of burrowing in the soil, making it pervious to water, and fertilizing it. Their eating of dead wood recycles organic matter that otherwise would remain bound in unusable form for decades. And the termites themselves provide food for predators, particularly the ants, which in turn cultivate the soil and cycle energy in the desert ecosystem.

Termites superficially resemble ants, and sometimes are called "white ants." But they are not ants. Ants belong to the order Hymenoptera, along with bees and wasps. Termites belong to the order Isoptera and are generally grouped into five families; one of these, the primitive Mastotermitidae, lives only in Australia. The other families are distributed worldwide. Termites may be distinguished from ants by their grayish-white bodies with thick waistlines (ants have red, yellow, black, brown, or green bodies with thin waistlines). The two pairs of wings of male and female ants are transparent and of unequal size; those of termites are whitish or opaque, and they are of equal size.

Termites are famous for damaging homes, for building spectacular mounds, and for the productivity of large sausage-shaped queens who lay thousands of eggs daily to maintain populations of millions in large termiteries. These characteristics hold true for many tropical species and for some native species in the United States. For example, a number of years ago, Charles Epler, the postmaster in my hometown in eastern Nebraska, was called home by his wife because one end of the piano in the living room had fallen partway into the basement. Termites had reduced the floor joists to mere wooden shells. However, not all termites possess a fauna of intestinal protozoa for converting cellulose to digestible material—in the United States only about 25 percent of the known species of termites possess such protozoa.

All of the approximately 2,200 species of termites live in unique family groups which include different morphological and functional forms, or "castes," consisting of workers, soldiers, and winged male and female reproductives. In the desert the winged kings and queens, or *alates*, usually fly in swarms after rain has fallen. Frequently they fly at night. In the food chain they become prey to birds, lizards, spiders, ants, dragon flies, skunks, and mice.

The flying termites drop their wings, usually after a short flight; some of the more primitive species make a series of flights. The *dealates*, as the kings and queens are called after their wings have dropped, form pairs before entering a nesting area. The male follows the female during the search for a suitable site, which may be a crack or hole in wood, or they may enter the ground. When a chamber or room large enough for both is prepared, then they mate. As the colony grows, they co-

The desert centipede reaches a length of six to eight inches. Its bite is painful but not dangerous. Centipedes dig tunnels in which they wait for passing insect prey. (Photo courtesy of George M. Bradt)

habit from time to time, and reinsemination of the female may occur over a period of years.

Various types of individuals are present in the termite colony. The developing young have the general appearance of adults and metamorphose through a larval or pupal stage. The workers generally are sterile, but in one group of species they are capable of molting into alates or soldiers. The soldiers are the defenders of the colony. Some groups have mandibulate soldiers, with large heads and pincerlike mandibles, and nasute soldiers with tubes that project forward from the head. From these tubes a thick secretion is excreted which is effective in repelling ants.

The desert damp-wood termite (*Paraneotermes simplicicornis*), found from California to Texas, is a subterranean species. From its runways it attacks decayed wood in the soil and also eats dead roots of grasses and forbs. It builds shelter tubes of

The vinegarroon, or "whip-scorpion," is not a scorpion and is harmless to humans. It gets its name from the acetic acid, or vinegar fog, it produces to repel enemies. The large claws are used to hold insects and other small prey. (Photo courtesy of George M. Bradt)

soil on the stems of shrubs and is known to damage living trees. This termite has higher moisture requirements than other desert-inhabiting species, and its construction of shelter tubes above ground undoubtedly protects it from desiccating heat and predators, especially ants.

The desert subterranean termite (*Heterotermes aureus*) is fairly common in the desert areas around Phoenix, Arizona. It also occurs in Baja California and in Mexico. It is a destructive species since it eats the wood of posts, telephone poles, and buildings. It mines dead cacti and other desert plants.

The common desert termite in California and Arizona is *Gnathamitermes perplexus*. The winged reproductives fly in the daytime, usually after rainfall. The colonies frequently are formed under rocks. Another member of the genus (*G. tubiformans*) builds covered earthen passageways aboveground over cow chips, and over weathered vegetation which they consume. They eat only the weathered surface of wood, unlike other termites, which burrow from within and reduce posts and dead tree stems to fragile shells.

An unusually large desert termite (*Zootermopsis laticeps*) lives in dead wood near stream beds and the edges of ponds. It is a damp-wood dweller and almost entirely consumes the logs in which it occurs. The workers are more than half an inch long, and the winged forms are approximately an inch in length. Their wings are heavily veined and about a quarter of an inch wide. The alates fly only at night during rainy periods; otherwise, little is known of the detailed biology of this species.

Scorpions, spiders, and centipedes, along with insects, belong to the large group called Arthropoda. Many of these relatives of insects seem to possess more than their share of spare legs. The spiders have eight legs, and the centipedes have several dozen. Most are capable of biting or stinging, although they seldom harm humans. But the fables and legends that have grown around such hairy "horrors" as the tarantulas have given these arthropods the undeserved reputation of being the demons of the desert. Actually, they are among the most interesting and useful of the desert's animals.

All the arthropods share two things in common: their skeletons are on the outside, and their muscles are on the inside; and they have jointed legs. But unlike most of the insects, the scorpions, spiders, centipedes, mites, and others do not have wings. Some of these animals, known as arachnids, have been around for a number of years. Among the first to appear in the geologic record were the scorpions, the fossils of which we find in Silurian and Devonian rocks, which are some 405 to 425 million years old.

Scorpions are easily recognized by their pedipalps, leglike organs with crablike claws which are used for holding prey. The abdomen is segmented and is terminated by a tail with a sting at the end. This tail is sometimes carried erect and can be whipped overhead to stab and immobilize the prey. Persons stung by scorpions may experience intense pain and discoloration of the tissues around the point of injury. Although more than twenty species of scorpions live in our southwestern deserts, only two are deadly species, liable to cause the death of children or persons in poor physical condition. These are the yellow slender-tailed scorpion (*Centruroides sculpturatus*) and the yellowish-tan scorpion (*C. gertschi*). The larger striped-tail scorpion (*Vejovis spinigeris*) and the desert hairy scorpion (*Hadrurus hirsutus*) sting with about the same effect as a wasp or hornet.

Some of the scorpions dig holes in the sand and leave a pile of soil outside the flattened tunnel entrance. If you close a scorpion's hole, it will open it again when it returns to the same den after its daily or nightly travels. Other scorpions hide beneath sticks and stones. On the east side of Mount Hood in Oregon I have found scorpions in the rotted wood of Douglas fir trees. In the desert area around Steens Mountain and in the Owyhee River country I have found three-inch scorpions by turning stones while on rock-hunting expeditions.

Scorpions are important links in the desert food chain in that they eat spiders, ants, grasshoppers, butterflies, moths, crickets, beetles, solpugids, and even mice. Occasionally they are cannibalistic. In turn, they are eaten by birds, snakes, lizards, coyotes, and scorpion mice. Scorpions do not actually eat their prey; instead, they pick the prey apart and suck the juices into their mouths.

The hunting habits of scorpions vary according to the species. A few walk or run over the desert in daytime. Most species do their foraging at night, and food finding may be a sedentary process. In a revealing study of the nocturnal activities of scorpions in the desert coastal areas at Puerto Penasco, Sonora, Mexico, Neil F. Hadley and Stanley C. Williams used ultraviolet light to detect the locations of scorpions marked with fluorescent paint for individual identification. The scorpions themselves fluoresce brightly in darkness when shortwave ultraviolet light shines upon them. Two species, *Vejovis confusus* and *V. mesaensis*, were less frequently seen aboveground as the evening progressed, and their surface activity also decreased under moonlight. *Centruroides sculpturatus* remained randomly active throughout the night. The vejovid scorpions did not stalk their prey as did the yellowish-tan scorpions; instead, they waited until an insect or other animal made actual contact. Then the scorpion immobilized its victim and began ingestion, which required from one to several hours.

The courtship dance of the scorpions is as unusual as is the appearance of the animals themselves. The male grasps the female's claws in his and walks backward or from side to side while she follows his lead. Sometimes their tails are held erect or entwined. The dance may last for several hours. At the end of the courtship the female lowers her body and the male deposits a spermatophore, or sac containing sperms, into her genital pore. The young are born alive and may climb on their mother's back to remain until the first molt is completed.

The whip-scorpions are fantastic creatures, much misunderstood and burdened with untrue legends and folklore. Another name for these creatures is vinegarroon, which is based on their ability to spray acetic acid with a strong odor of vinegar. The spray comes from small orifices at the base of the whiplike tail, which resembles a stiff thread extending from the abdomen. Some authors have stated that when the whip-scorpion is threatened by an enemy, it waves its tail rapidly to stir up the air and spread the stench of the acid spray all about.

Actually, the whip-scorpion is not a scorpion at all, and it can be held in one's hand without danger. In fact, it is an interesting subject to use in wildlife lectures to children and adults. It looks like a large bug with enormous swollen pincers, or pedipalps. The front pair of legs are not used for walking; instead, they are slender and are used as tactile organs. Since the animal is virtually blind, it uses these "feeler" legs to find its way around and to recognize prey. It feeds on grasshoppers, slugs, termites, and other insects. Although most whip-scorpions are timid, the large species, *Mastigoproctus giganteus*, is said to include small frogs and toads in its diet.

Another arthropod of the desert with an undeservedly bad reputation is the sun spider, solpugid, or "Child of the Earth" as the Mexicans call it. Although it has no poison, and eats scorpions, it is greatly feared because of its spiderlike appearance and formidable jaws, which form a four-parted beak used to cut up prey. Sun spiders are very active and are capable of running at high speed as they dash about in search of insects. Some of the large hairy species in foreign deserts have a leg span of five inches. They are accomplished predators of spiders, scorpions, and even small lizards.

The desert supports an unnumbered variety of other arthropods too numerous to describe in this book. Some are known in general by most people: the tarantulas, centipedes, millipedes, harvestmen, mites, and ticks. All have interesting habits. Life histories of many are unusual, spectacular, or poorly known. And each contributes to the biological functioning of the desert ecosystem by burrowing, seeking prey, or scavenging, or by being eaten by other animals.

In my years of wandering about the desert I have become aware of the prodigality of nature in her production of insects. I have made estimates of the biomass, or weight per unit area, of a few insects, particularly the harvester ants. On a single acre in the Oregon sagebrush desert near Squaw Butte I once counted forty-seven large anthills, and by excavating five of these I found approximately 20,000 ants per colony. The average ant weighed .0096 grams. From these data I computed a weight of nearly 13,000 pounds of ants per square mile. This was more than half the weight of cattle that could be grazed properly on a square mile in that locality.

In southern Idaho I estimated the number of aphids on big sagebrush plants by counting the aphids on twigs, the twigs on sagebrush plants, and the plants on an acre of ground. My count resulted in the astounding total of some 430 million aphids. These aphids were being tended by ants for their honeydew. Among these ants were several colonies of thatching ants of the genus *Formica*. It has been calculated that a large colony of these ants can make 300,000 foraging trips to collect as much as 350 grams of honeydew per day.

Those of you who have been to Carlsbad, New Mexico, and have seen the bats erupt from the dark hole in the earth like smoke from a volcano, have some idea of the prodigality of nature. The show may last for hours. Estimates of the numbers of bats have ranged as high as two million. No one has estimated the numbers of insects eaten, but studies of captive bats indicate consumption of one-third to one-half their weight in insects each night when their prey are abundant.

Irruptions of migratory insects occasionally result in numbers almost beyond comprehension. Flights of grasshoppers have been estimated to contain trillions of individual insects. In Utah I have seen Mormon crickets moving across paved roads so close together that automobile tires crushing their bodies left red strips on the pavement. These plagues of insects occur only sporadically, but they do indicate the potentiality for reproduction in the insect world.

Predators and parasites tend to keep most insects in balance with their food supply of pollen, nectar, leaves, stems, dried wood, and animal carrion. But even when they are in equilibrium with plants and other animals, they are exceedingly more numerous than the lizards, toads, birds, rodents, skunks, coyotes, and other animals that eat them. Without their life-giving substance in the animal food chain, and without their beneficial pollination of flowers, their seed-planting activities, and their partial control of plants that compete with other plants, the desert environment would not exist as we now know it.

The roadrunner, with its large bill, prominent crest, long tail, and appearance of starvation, is easily the most distinctive bird of the southwestern deserts. Lizards, small snakes, insects, and bird eggs are part of its diet.

CHAPTER 9

Birds of the Desert

One of the pleasing aspects of birds in the desert is that they are so visible. They use shrubs, cacti, and low trees for perching places. Unlike the birds of the prairie that sing on the wing, the singing birds of the desert distribute their melodious notes from the highest vantage points in the landscape—the desert plants. Thus, in establishing their territories they can be seen as well as heard by other birds. The less vociferous birds commonly inhabit the desert trees, especially along dry washes and riverbanks. And although they tend to be secretive creatures, the arborescent foliage seldom is dense enough to obscure them from the view of the careful watcher who looks for their movement among the branches or sees their brilliant plumage. The eagles, hawks, and buzzards wheeling in the sky, of course, are easily visible. On the ground, the fleeting glimpses of the roadrunner, flashing between creosote bushes while running parallel with your automobile on a dusty desert road, is always an occasion for amusement.

Hundreds of species of birds* frequent the desert, from the sagebrush zones in the north to the cactus-and-yucca-strewn slopes southward into Mexico. Among the desert birds are cardinals, towhees, longspurs, kingbirds, tanagers, quails, owls, nighthawks, crows, grouse, wrens, thrashers, and sparrows. Some of the birds, such as the magpies, are yearlong residents; on the

* The scientific names of birds are not given in this chapter, since the common names have been standardized in *The Check-list of North American Birds* prepared by the American Ornithologists' Union. This check-list and the better popular bird manuals give the scientific names of bird species along with the accepted common names.

171

The curve-billed thrasher frequents the saguaro forests and may be seen in many of the desert campgrounds, since it is not easily alarmed by the presence of people.

other hand, the hummingbirds, the American golden plover, some of the gulls, and a host of others are migratory birds or are transients found in the desert only in spring, fall, or winter.

A pleasing variety of birds usually occurs in each desert environment. In an Arizona desert canyon, for example, you can expect to see the Arizona hooded oriole, the white-winged dove, the gilded flicker, the yellow-breasted chat, the Abert towhee, the Beckwith wren, the Arizona pyrrhuloxia, and—if a stream of water runs in the canyon bottom—the Anthony green heron.

Part of the lure of the desert is the opportunity it affords for sighting one of the rare birds, especially the wanderers from Mexico. It is an occasion to be recorded if you see the coppery-tailed trogon, parrot-green above with a geranium-red belly and a white-banded breast, sojourning in the sycamore canyons. Since it has not been seen in the United States in recent years, you may have to go south of the Border to see the thick-billed parrot with its poppy-red head, stocky green body, and heavy black bill. With very good luck you may find Nuttall's poorwill —the ornithologist Edmund C. Jaeger found one clinging to a granite wall in winter hibernation in 1946; and more than two dozen, also in winter torpor, have since been recorded. In the northern deserts, around ponds, lakes, and forest groves, rare birds include the pectoral sandpiper, the ruddy duck, the catbird, and the slate-colored junco.

Much of this variety derives from the desert's innumerable environments. The seasons in the north are distinctive, and migration peaks of waterfowl and songbirds occur in spring and fall. Birds that nest in Alaska and Canada find winter on the desert more congenial than in the far northern climate. Migrants from the south find seasonal habitats near desert lakes, tree-lined rivers, shaded canyons, and insect-infested shrublands, and in the spiny protection of succulents in cactus land. The desert rim is especially acceptable to birds because here the transition between forested slopes and shrubby flats permits adaptation to a broad range of requirements for food and shelter.

Desert birds adapt to the perennial problems of little water and extreme temperatures in many ways. The insect eaters and the scavengers such as the vultures and magpies obtain needed moisture from the food they eat. Birds also conserve water in their bodies by producing concentrated droppings. The nocturnal birds fly when the temperature is relatively low and the humidity is high.

The body temperature of birds is high in comparison with temperatures of mammals. Many birds maintain a body heat of 106° F., which narrows the differential between their temperature and that of the diurnal environment. Consequently they are not liable to radiate excessive amounts of heat and thus require more food for metabolism. Since they possess no sweat glands, they control body temperature to some extent by panting. This is particularly noticeable among the pelicans on their breeding grounds on islands in desert lakes.

The small perching birds avoid the high temperatures of the desert floor by resting in trees or shrubs during the hottest part of the day. Other birds, such as Audubon warblers and ruby-crowned kinglets, migrate away from the desert during the season of greatest heat. The burrowing owls emulate the ground squirrels by entering tunnels and releasing heat to the cool earth. The low temperatures of northern deserts in winter can be endured by sage grouse and owls from the Arctic because they are insulated with thick layers of soft feathers. Birds not adapted to the bitter cold of northern winters simply migrate to warmer climes.

The small birds are the most numerous in the desert. These are the seed and insect eaters. Most of them are migratory, but a few, such as the quails and magpies, are yearlong residents.

The small birds are not scattered indiscriminately over the desert. Their food habits and nesting requirements relegate them to habitats favorable to each kind. Thus, at the desert edge of the Santa Catalinas, the Santa Ritas, and the Huachuca Mountains in Arizona we look for the bridled titmouse among the sycamores and oaks in the canyons. Here also are insectivorous night birds: elf owls, poorwills, and whippoorwills. Around the desert rim, where junipers, pinyon pines, and scrub oaks mark the border, Mexican juncos, red-faced warblers, and Coué's flycatchers occur.

The sparrows and towhees, which are widely distributed in the sage and brushy desert borders, possess stout beaks adapted for crushing seeds, which they gather almost entirely from the ground. The sage sparrow and Bell's sparrow, in the California Desert, gather seeds deposited by the wind at the bases of bushes. When storms drive them down from the mountains, Thurber juncos sometimes join the sparrows in the desert. Likewise the waxwings, which do not breed in the desert, appear when dried berries are plentiful.

In the vicinity of desert ponds habitats are sometimes compressed or telescoped, so that many kinds of birds occupy varied niches in a small territory. Recently, while eating my lunch at Quitobaquito Pond in Organ-Pipe Cactus National Monument, in Arizona, I saw thirteen species of birds in the diverse habitats around this beautiful oasis. A pair of coot cruised at the edge of the reeds near the shore, while a Gila woodpecker explored the bark of a cottonwood that shaded my luncheon spot. Across the pond vermillion flycatchers made flashing forays for flying insects and then returned to their perches forty feet above the water's surface in a large cottonwood tree. A furtive phainopepla, glossy black with a jaylike crest, silently made his rounds among the taller shrubs, while half a dozen white-crowned sparrows searched for seeds and insects in the ground layers of lesser shrubs. Beyond, in the parched chaparral, brown towhees uttered an occasional metallic note, but they did not sing. At Quito-baquito more than 175 species have been identified, including migrating waterfowl and other water birds.

Quail are numerous and are among the most beautiful birds in the desert. They are great runners and generally are reluctant to fly unless closely pursued. Even a trained dog finds it difficult to keep up with the scaled quail of the southwestern arid lands. This species is marked by light-colored feathers with dark margins, giving the appearance of iridescent fish scales. Unlike some of its relatives, the scaled quail sometimes lives far from a source of water. It eats a great many weed seeds but satisfies its need for water by supplementing its diet with insects, green leaves, buds, and berries.

The harlequin quail is a handsome bird of the border states and of Mexico. It tends to inhabit the oak canyons and the upper grassy slopes of desert mountains. The peculiar stripes on the bird's face, its pale crest of feathers, its brown-splotched back, and its speckled breast and belly set it apart from all other quail. Its habit of "freezing" until almost stepped on has resulted in the name "fool hen." The harlequin quail eats seeds, berries, acorns, green vegetable matter, and bulbs of plants which it digs from the soil.

Gambel's quail is a true denizen of the desert over a range extending from southern Utah, southern Nevada, and southwestern Colorado eastward to Texas, westward to California, and far south in Mexico. The male bird is a panorama of color, especially during the courting season, in springtime, when the desert blooms. He has a black head plume, curved forward, a black throat, and a black patch on his belly. His flanks and crown are russet, and his wings, tail, and back are gray.

Gambel's quail and its close relative, the California quail, live near water, which is required when their seasonal food is dry. They eat fewer seeds than other quail species and prefer tender shoots of forbs, willow buds, and various kinds of flowers. Among their many enemies are bobcats, foxes, coyotes, hawks, and owls. Skunks, ground squirrels, and snakes eat their eggs. But since

The white bars distinguish the white-winged dove from the other doves of the desert. These doves are numerous in Mexico, but many of them live in the southwestern deserts in summer.

the coveys fly quickly when disturbed, they escape many of their enemies.

Mourning doves occur in the vicinity of springs, ponds, and streams, since they require water along with their diet of seeds. They lose large amounts of water by panting when their temperature reaches 108° F. When drinking, a dove can replace 17 percent of its body weight by a single visit to a water hole.

Since water supplies are scarce in the desert, many doves nest around the desert rim in juniper and pine country, where streams and lakes provide a more dependable water supply. Many thousands of doves now breed in irrigated orchards and then migrate southward through the desert in autumn. In Oregon, east of the Cascades, they assemble in large flocks in September and forage in harvested grainfields. At night they roost in shrubs bordering small streams. They also make regular visits to desert wells and stock tanks where water overflows, but they obtain their food from the desert itself.

White-winged doves are conspicuous in the southern deserts. Their distinguishing mark is the white patch on the outer wing coverts and the white terminal patches on the tail. Like the mourning doves, they come regularly to water, sometimes in flocks of hundreds. When the saguaro seeds are ripe, they dig into the red fruits with their bills. During the breeding season they call from the mesquite groves with a harsh sound, not at all like the soulful *coo*'s of the mourning dove.

Among the small doves of the group is the Inca dove, resident from southern California to western Texas. Its feathers give it a scaly appearance, and its long square tail is not apparent when folded. This dainty little dove coos gently and feeds in flocks, sometimes in company with the even smaller ground doves, which are scarcely larger than a sparrow.

White-crowned sparrows are common in the shrubby borders of desert ponds and streams.

Sparrows are numerous and are among the fine singers of the desert. The black-throated or desert sparrow ranges from eastern Oregon, southwest Wyoming, and southern Idaho southward through the desert to Mexico. Almost anywhere in the thorny brush you may expect to hear its sweet song that ends in a trill. In the southern deserts its associates include the verdin, the scaled quail, and the roadrunner. When danger threatens or the desert sparrows are excited, they call continuously or even sing while they fly excitedly from one bush to another.

The white-crowned sparrows are the aristocrats of the family. The Gambel white-crowned sparrow is distinguished from the other races of this species by the white stripe which extends forward to the bill. Many of these birds appear from their Alaskan and Canadian breeding grounds in October and November to spend the winter in the desert. The sage sparrow associates with the white-crowned sparrow and winters in the desert. It breeds over a large territory from Washington, Wyoming, and Nevada to Arizona and Baja California. Other species that breed in the desert are the savannah sparrow, vesper sparrow, lark sparrow, chipping sparrow, fox sparrow, and song sparrow.

A bird you are sure to see in the Sonoran Desert is the cactus wren, which has several notable attributes. First, it is the largest of the wrens, being almost the size of a robin. Second, although its brownish body with black-spotted breast is anything but aristocratic, and its voice is a clatter of monotonous *chug chug chug* notes, and its movements are slow and deliberate in contrast with the saucy, pert scolding of the house wrens, it has achieved the distinction of being the state bird of Arizona. And it has conquered the villainous cholla cactus.

The female builds a flask-shaped nest in the needlelike thicket of cholla spines, starting with a landing platform on the outside and ending with a chamber lined with grass, feathers, and silky soft plant materials. There she and her eggs and babies are safe from coyotes, rats, and hawks, but not from some of the most inquisitive and persistent snakes. The male builds platform nests on the tops of cacti and in thorny bushes.

Another nearly impregnable nest is built by the verdin. This yellow-headed gray bird, smaller than a finch, weaves a grapefruit-sized ball of spiny twigs, plant stems, and grass leaves in mesquite, cat's-claw, and other thorny bushes. The entrance hole is on the side. The interior is lined with down and feathers.

*This cactus wren has just emerged from her nest in the spiny
protection of a cholla cactus.*

Close by, the male builds a less elaborate nest, in which he
roosts during the cold desert nights.

One could go on endlessly with the cast of bird characters in
the desert. The black phoebe likes the vicinity of water, where
mud may be obtained for mixing with grass to construct adobe
nests on cliffs and under bridges. Two orioles are handsome birds
to look for: the Scott oriole resides in the Joshua tree forests, and
the Arizona hooded oriole hangs its basket nest from the limbs
of desert trees. In spring and autumn you may see several species
of migrating hummingbirds, including the black-chinned, the
ruby-throated, the rufous, and Costa's hummingbird. These
winter mostly in Mexico.

The openness of the desert and the visibility of many of its
creatures could lead one to wonder how prey species—including

insects, reptiles, rodents, and small birds—escape decimation by the predator birds. Among the winged predators, the hawks, eagles, owls, shrikes, and roadrunners are models of evolutionary efficiency. And yet, an equilibrium between predator and prey exists. The obvious explanation is that prey species have evolved to minimize the success of their predators. Hence, when we study predator birds, it is instructive to consider the adaptations and life habits by which their prey maintain viable populations.

Quail, for example, are subject to predation by hawks, but they avoid excess mortality of the species by producing large clutches of eggs and young. Also, they are adept at hiding among shrubs when danger threatens. And their habit of banding together in coveys is confusing to enemies. I once saw a bobcat charge from his hiding place into a flock of quail that scattered in all directions into the sagebrush. The bobcat's "flock shooting" resulted in failure, as it does for many human bird hunters. If he had chosen one bird as his target he might have succeeded.

The predators themselves adapt to the seasonality of food resources. In good times they concentrate on animals that are abundant. The California gulls, for example, are notable for their efficiency in control of locust swarms and outbreaks of field mice. In bad times predators such as the eagles shift their attention to carrion or to sick, crippled, and infected animals ranging in size from rabbits to young antelope and deer. This removal of the unhealthy is not an undesirable pressure on prey; it reduces competition for forage among herbivores.

Eagles are the most majestic birds in the desert sky. The American or bald eagle, symbolized by its white head in adulthood, now is rare. The golden eagle, which originally ranged over most of the continent, also is disappearing from the landscape. Apparently DDT is reducing the eggshell thickness and lessening the productivity of these magnificent birds. Thallium sulfate in bait for coyote control also is killing eagles that eat the meat distributed by predator-control operators. Ranchers and hunters kill eagles illegally. On slim circumstantial evidence they sometimes blame eagles for the death of calves and lambs when actually the livestock have died because of disease, accident, mammal predators, or even rattlesnake poisoning. Thus the eagle pays the penalty for being one of nature's scavengers.

The greatest scavenger birds of the desert, of course, are the vultures. These birds, incorrectly called "buzzards," are dark, eagle-like creatures with small naked heads that are black in youth and red at maturity. The turkey vulture is widely distributed from Canada to Mexico; the black vulture is more common in the eastern United States, although it is a resident bird from Texas to southern Arizona.

Vultures have been the subject of much speculation and legend because of their repugnant habit of eating the reeking carcasses of the dead. Their very appearance, while sitting with opened wings and drooping heads, marks them as the undertakers of the animal world. At rest they are ugly and monstrous; at work on a carcass they are ravenous in their gorging of malodorous flesh. Sometimes they eat until they can scarcely fly. If molested by enemies, they regurgitate upon them a horrible stinking mess. Yet in flight they are without peer in the bird world.

It is by magnificent soaring that the vultures locate their food. In early autumn I have counted as many as thirty turkey vultures sitting in a dead cottonwood tree near the town of Silver Lake, Oregon. After an hour of basking in the morning sun they begin their leisurely spiral into the sky as the air currents begin to rise. They follow one another in slow circles until some are mere dots; then, one by one, individuals glide away over the desert.

Once, in this eastern Oregon land of sagebrush, I watched a turkey vulture drop from a great height to an antelope carcass east of the Hart Mountain Wildlife Refuge. Soon another vulture dropped to the feast, and then another and another, over a period of half an hour, until eleven of the great birds had landed. Thus they cooperated by covering an enormous territory and then sharing food when it was found by their marvelous eyesight.

The distance at which a bird can see from different heights was computed a number of years ago by Colonel Richard Meinertzhagen, a British army colonel. At only 500 feet the distance to the visible horizon is 27 miles; at 2,000 feet, the distance is 55 miles. By simple calculation it is easy to demonstrate that a few dozen vultures soaring in endless circles can survey hundreds, if not thousands, of square miles each day. Thus these birds, who seldom kill, perform valuable service in desert sanitation.

The hawks, falcons, and owls also are efficient predators. None are more capable than the prairie falcons. From their nests and perching places on pinnacles and rocky buttes the prairie falcons fly in wide circles or climb to great heights, from which they plunge with dazzling speed to harry hawks, ravens, and even eagles. Once, during the hunting season, a fast-flying mallard at which I was taking aim suddenly exploded in a burst of feathers and plummeted to the ground. It had been struck dead by a peregrine falcon. The usual prey of the falcons, however, are ground squirrels and rabbits, and many small birds including quails, meadow larks, sparrows, and doves. The victims have little chance against the swooping swallow-like flight of the falcons.

Hawks are accepted by people who live in the desert because of their services in balancing the snake and rodent population. The Swainson hawk, a handsome creature with a reddish-brown band on its white chest, pays its debt to the saguaro cactus which supports its bulky nest by controlling the rabbits, ground squirrels, mice, and grasshoppers that eat the saguaro seedlings. Also, it is not uncommon to see this hawk flying to its nest with a live snake dangling from its talons.

The red-tailed hawk also is widely distributed in desert country. It is a graceful, slow flier, but swoops upon its prey with unerring accuracy. Snakes, rodents, lizards, birds, grasshoppers, and even skunks, are acceptable provender. Smaller fare, especially grasshoppers, is the specialty of the little sparrow hawk.

At night the hooting of the great horned owl gives evidence that this marauder is abroad, searching for rabbits, rodents, and skunks. The tiny elf owl, no larger than a house sparrow, comes out of its hole in a tree or saguaro to forage for moths and other insects of the night. The ludicrous burrowing owls stand on abandoned prairie-dog mounds by day and stare at people who stare back at their long legs and short tails. Their nests are built below ground in rodent burrows. When the young are partly grown, they emerge and stand with their parents in amusing family groups of five to seven or more owls of different sizes.

Probably the most intriguing bird of the desert is the roadrunner. Everyone seems to know something about it, and, in addition to its amazing habits and accomplishments, it has acquired various names: "Clown of the Desert," "Chaparral cock," "Ground cuckoo," and *paisano,* or "fellow countryman," in Mexico. In New Mexico the roadrunner is the state bird.

One of the roadrunner's extraordinary features is its appearance. Two of the four toes on each foot point forward, and two point backward. The X-like footprints leave you guessing as to which way the bird went. The shaggy crest on its head and the long loose-jointed tail, which serves as a brake and a rudder, set the roadrunner apart from all other birds. Its running ability is legendary; there are stories of how roadrunners used to race stagecoaches and keep up with them at fifteen miles per hour.

The roadrunner's diet is varied. It specializes in lizards and small snakes. If the lizard is too long to go down, the bird swallows what it can and then goes about its business with the tail of the lizard hanging out of its mouth until the front end is digested. Lizards are hunted especially in midmorning, when they are most active. Large insects, eggs, and young birds also are acceptable items on the roadrunner's menu.

Although the roadrunner is a ground cuckoo, it does not lay eggs in the nests of other birds, as some of its relatives do. Its nest is a saucer-shaped affair, built of twigs in a cholla or thorny shrub or tree. The three to six eggs are incubated for eighteen days. Then the young are fed with a seemingly endless supply of small lizards, crickets, and other soft-bodied insects.

Since the roadrunner lives the year round among its favorite chollas, smoke trees, pinyon and juniper trees, and mesquite bushes, there comes a season when food is scarce, the temperature drops, and the bird needs to conserve its energy. For this it has some remarkable behavioral traits and physical attributes. In the dark it may undergo hypothermia, or lowering of body temperature. By sunning, which is a common practice summer and winter, internal temperature can be returned to normal with minimum metabolism. A recent study has shown that by drooping its wings and holding its plumage erect to expose the patches of black skin on its back, the roadrunner saves energy at the average rate of 551 calories per hour.

Roadrunners have a low level of activity in early morning, which correlates with their sunbathing time. A peak of activity occurs before sunset, possibly in relation to heavy predation on insects. Roadrunners are strictly diurnal and are stimulated to activity by bright light. In darkness they are totally inactive. This explains why roadrunners, which occasionally are admitted to houses as pets, sometimes roost beside striking clocks and amid household activities without being disturbed by noise.

Roadrunners exhibit other interesting behavior. They put on the crippled-bird act in the presence of a presumed enemy. They become tame and frequent gardens or backyards in small towns.

And they are punctual almost to the minute in their daily rounds, either around people's homes or in the desert. The one thing the roadrunner lacks is a decent voice; its principal sound is a clatter made by clicking its mandibles, or a series of unmusical *coo*'s heard most frequently during the nesting season.

Of all the resident birds of the sagebrush deserts the sage grouse are best adapted for life in the heat of summer, the capricious weather of spring and fall, and the cold of winter. For a time they seemed to be vanishing Americans. In the early days of settlement they inhabited the land in countless thousands. In the Gunnison River country in western Colorado hunters used to kill enough to fill a wagon in half a day. In 1886 Dr. George Bird Grinnell saw sage grouse so numerous in Bates Hole, Wyoming, that he likened their flights to those of passenger pigeons. When flying from a high bluff, the front rank of birds had to leave before succeeding tiers could launch themselves into the air.

When I camped in this same area sixty years later, I saw not one sage grouse in a whole day of tramping through the desert. The place had been overgrazed by livestock, the eagles and hawks had been shot, the grasshoppers had been baited with poisoned bran, and the prairie dogs had been exterminated. In that same period I traveled over much of the Great Basin Desert and found that the birds were almost unknown by hunters, and, to a considerable extent, by scientists. Biologists then were assigned to study their food habits, life histories, and population trends. Hunting seasons were abolished and habitat improvements were initiated in at least seven western states. Finally the almost-mythical birds staged a comeback, and much was learned about their fantastic nuptial rituals.

These birds are the largest of the American grouse. The hens weigh about three pounds, and a mature cock may weigh as much as six pounds. In the sagebrush they are silent drab birds, almost indistinguishable from their surroundings. In the hand they are beautiful creatures with mottled backs and olive-green neck patches which show as white pouches when inflated during the courting season. The spiked tail feathers spread into a speckled fan when the cock is on display. The toothed comb scales on the feet, the feathered legs that resemble pants, and the loose fluffy plumage enable the birds to walk in snow and brave the howling blizzards that blow across the northern deserts. Food in winter is no problem, since sagebrush leaves provide all the necessary dietary requirements.

The bizarre courtship of the sage grouse is one of the strangest sights in nature. The cocks appear on the strutting grounds in February and continue their early-morning performances until April. Some of these ancestral booming grounds are possibly hundreds of years old. The grouse are reluctant to abandon them, even when roads are built through them or they are plowed. The booming sounds made by the males and the social organization within the assemblage of variously aged cocks and numerous hens are almost impossible to comprehend at first.

In the wilderness of the desert 300 birds with snow-white breasts, fanned-out tails, and plumed necks strut and parade, each in an individual circle, while inflating and deflating their bare bulbs of yellowish breast skin. Accompanying this strutting are burbling, plopping, pumping sounds that thump against the silence of the dawn. The big adult "master cocks," which may constitute only 5 percent of the total male population, are center stage, while the "sub-cocks" remain less demonstrative or perform at the periphery of the booming ground. The master cocks perform three-fourths of the matings, and the sub-cocks do the rest. Young immature cocks must wait for another season before entering into the polygamous society in which the females accept mating without being pursued and at a time of their own choosing.

If you get up early and arrive at the booming grounds before daylight, there are many localities in which you may see some of this strangest action in the bird world, since the grouse are found from British Columbia to Saskatchewan and in Idaho, Oregon, Utah, Nevada, and New Mexico. Their breeding ceremony may be seen each morning for a period of two months or more. Each session lasts from one to three hours, if the birds are not molested by predators or people. The grouse are not greatly disturbed by a parked automobile, and from that vantage point you may see the aggressiveness of the master cocks. If snow is on the ground and the moon is bright, the performance sometimes starts in early evening and lasts for an hour or two.

Sometimes the cocks come together with slapping wings which may even produce broken bones. You may hear the grunting sounds as the breast pouch fills with air, is tossed up and down—

accompanied by inflation of the yellowish bare spots on the pouch—and then deflated with a *ker-pop.* Then you may see bevies of a dozen females posturing within a circle of males.

The somber-colored females make their nests beneath sagebrush plants sometimes far removed from the booming grounds. The eight to one-dozen greenish-buff eggs, flecked with brown, blend with the background. The downy young follow the hens to grassy areas where they thrive on new vegetable growth and supplement their diet with insects.

A roll call of the birds that find congenial habitats around desert waters produces an astounding number of species. A list of birds found in the Malheur National Wildlife Refuge in eastern Oregon contains 228 species found on the refuge since it was established in 1908. The Bear River Migratory Bird Refuge, on the delta of Bear River where it empties into Great Salt Lake in Utah, is host to a million ducks during the fall migration. Gadwalls and redheads nest here in the marshes, and other dabblers and divers include mallards, pintails, teals, canvasbacks, goldeneyes, and buffleheads. Geese are common, and shorebirds include the distinctive stilts and avocets. California gulls are especially abundant in this region, and along with white pelicans, double-crested cormorants, and Treganza great blue herons they nest in huge colonies on the islands in Great Salt Lake.

Other desert lakes that support fabulous numbers of birds include Harney Lake in Harney County and the lakes east of the Warner Mountains in Oregon. Summer Lake, which lies under the Winter Rim bordering the western edge of the Oregon desert, is a rewarding place for the study of American avocets, redwing blackbirds, coots, cinnamon teals, grebes, Canada geese, mallards, marsh hawks, and gulls. Pyramid Lake, Nevada, also hosts the California gulls and a fabulous colony of white pelicans on Anaho Island. The Salton Sea in California is a haven for thousand of gulls, terns, widgeons, and other waterfowl.

The rivers, streams, lakes, and marshes of the desert provide a multitude of habitats for summer-resident birds. The edge effect between water and desert supplies water, shelter, and food for birds that eat insects, crustaceans, worms, frogs, rodents, snakes, and fish. The list of birds using these habitats includes waterfowl, shorebirds, owls, golden eagles, hawks, and a multitude of songbirds.

Along the fluctuating shorelines of desert lakes, especially those with interspersed open water and emergent vegetation, you may expect to see the killdeer, American avocet, common snipe, spotted sandpiper, Wilson's phalarope, mourning dove, belted kingfisher, violet-green swallow, and long-billed marsh wren. Among the cottonwoods and the riverbank trees and shrubs you may find hairy and downy woodpeckers, Say's phoebe, tree swallows, black-capped chickadees, common bushtits, sage thrashers, numerous warblers, and a host of sparrows. Among those that nest in the vicinity of water and in the surrounding sagebrush, greasewood, and rabbitbrush desert are the American goldfinch, Savannah sparrow, sage sparrow, chipping sparrow, white-crowned sparrow, and song sparrow.

Those of us who were born and raised in the East or on the

California gulls nest on large desert islands in the lakes of Utah, Oregon, and Nevada. On these islands they have few enemies except hawks and snakes, which occasionally prey on the eggs and chicks. (Photo courtesy of Nevada State Fish and Game Commission)

*White pelicans at the mouth of the Truckee River where it flows
into Pyramid Lake, Nevada. These birds nest by the thousands on the
ground on Anaho Island in the lake.*

midwestern prairies associate geese with spring and autumn,
when the great migrations take place between the wintering
grounds in the south and the prairie nesting places in Canada.
Since the Ice Age geese also have been coming and going from
the Arctic to the lakes in Oregon, the Sacramento Valley of
California, and the west coast of Mexico. Both ducks and geese
move across Idaho to the Columbia River and then south through
Oregon and Utah to California. Many Canada geese, however,
nest and remain as residents in eastern Washington, eastern
Oregon, and the Bear River refuge in Utah. Their nests are made
on the saltgrass flats, among weeds, and on muskrat houses,
where the surrounding water protects the eggs from foxes, coyotes, skunks, and other animals.

Even more numerous than the geese are the gulls that nest
in great colonies on islands in the desert lakes and travel as
far as seventy-five miles for food. Ring-billed gulls commonly

nest in the marshy lands around lakes in the northern sagebrush deserts, and Franklin's gulls occasionally nest in the Harney Basin in eastern Oregon. But the most numerous are the California gulls, made famous in history because of their destruction of Mormon crickets attacking the crops of the pioneers in Great Salt Lake Valley in 1848. Later the report of Captain Howard Stansbury recorded the first evidence that gulls, cormorants, and herons nested in great colonies on Antelope Island, Gunnison Island, and Egg Island.

With regard to Gunnison Island, Stansbury wrote on May 8, 1850: "The whole neck and shores on both the little bays were occupied by immense flocks of pelicans and gulls. . . . They literally darkened the air as they rose upon the wing, and, hovering over our heads, caused the surrounding rocks to re-echo with their discordant screams. The ground was thickly strewn with their nests, of which there must have been some thousands."

The white pelicans and California gulls still nest in colonies in Utah and Nevada. When the cui-ui were spawning in Pyramid Lake northeast of Reno, I used to buy a license at the Indian agency and cast a treble hook into the water-boils in the lake near the mouth of the Truckee River until I had hooked the legal three fish. When I, and other fishermen, cleaned our catch the gulls came in great numbers to scavenge the remains of the fish. Offshore the pelicans cruised in white flotillas, apparently curious about our activities. At other times they stood on the sandbars for hours on end, in solid acres of white, apparently doing nothing. Occasionally a pair or a dozen would volplane for a landing, during which they resembled army bombers flying in formation. At other times they circled high in the heavens, the huge flocks becoming momentarily invisible as they turned in unison and then appearing as scintillating flecks of white against the blue sky. No birds of the desert are more picturesque than the pelicans.

When pursued the chuckwallas inflate and wedge themselves in rock crevices so tightly no amount of pulling can dislodge them.

CHAPTER 10

Reptiles and Amphibians of the Desert

Lizards are not only the most abundant vertebrates in the deserts of the world, but important links in the food chain. Many species are insectivorous; some eat almost any kind of insect; others specialize on ants or termites; a few are cannibalistic and feed on other lizards; some eat bird and reptile eggs; and others subsist primarily on plants. Lizards in turn are eaten by snakes, coyotes, skunks, roadrunners, and hawks.

Almost every desert habitat has its typical lizard species. Some kinds associate with rocky areas, some prefer sandy soil, others live principally in creosote shrublands, and a few live near water. In Australia the species *Amphibolurus maculosus* lives on barren salt flats of dry lake beds. Our little desert night lizard lives under the debris and fallen trunks of Joshua trees. It is essentially nocturnal, but becomes active in daytime in winter under favorable temperature conditions. Different species of lizards also occur together in many localities, but their habitat preferences and behavioral characteristics differ so that they do not compete with one another.

Unlike birds and mammals, lizards are ectothermic animals: they acquire most of their body heat from outside sources, including radiation from the sun, conduction from the substrate and surrounding objects, and convection from the air. Some lizards use panting for evaporative cooling. Many species periodically dash into burrows for release of body heat. Some are adept at clinging to the shady sides of stems and at aligning their bodies in the most advantageous positions to avoid excessive heating by the sun, or, conversely, to take advantage of its warmth.

191

Lizard behavior has endless variety. Most species have definite home territories which they defend by aggressive displays, including head bobbing, erection of spines, and actual fighting. Many lizards dig burrows and occupy them at night and in time of danger. Others use holes dug by other animals. Some bury themselves in sand, where they remain overnight. The "sand swimmers," when pursued by enemies, virtually swim into the sand and seem to disappear instantaneously. The zebra-tailed lizard (*Callisaurus draconoides*) prefers open flats and relatively level areas where it can use its great speed to escape. It has been clocked at eighteen miles per hour. At high speed it runs on its hind legs and, owing to the black and white "zebra" stripes on the underside of its tail, presents a flash of color which disappears when it stops abruptly.

You will not be long in the desert without seeing lizards, especially during the spring and summer months. If you are patient, you will see them hunting by sight and catching their prey by running, or you may even see them jumping at flying insects. Some are capable of such speed that they appear as a blur when crossing the sand or jumping from rocks to hide beneath bushes. It is easy to understand why some of their enemies, such as the hawks, roadrunners, and coachwhip snakes, are successful predators: they, also, are fast-moving animals.

One of the fastest of all the desert lizards is the collared lizard (*Crotaphytus collaris*), which moves on two feet like a Lilliputian dinosaur running at top speed. It is found from Idaho to Baja California and eastward to Missouri and Texas. The two black collar markings, which do not extend over the back of the neck, are distinctive. Its relative, the reticulate collared lizard (*C. reticulatus*), is characterized by a dorsal network of light markings and a series of large black spots on the back. It ranges from southern Texas into Mexico. Collared lizards inhabit rocky places in sagebrush, creosote-bush stands, and cactus communities, where they prey on grasshoppers, moths, spiders, and other lizards.

In contrast with the speed of the collared lizard, the slowest of the tribe are the horned lizards, sometimes called "horned toads." These are large-bodied, flat, short-tailed lizards that move so slowly any child can catch them. The Texas horned lizard (*Phrynosoma cornutum*) is well supplied with spines on its head and two rows of abdominal fringe scales. It digs holes in sand to hibernate and emerges in April or May. The eggs are laid in

Yuccas, including the Joshua tree, retain a thatch of leaves on
their stems which provide shelter for lizards and many insects.

The Gila monsters are sluggish lizards, but they can bite if handled. Their bite is poisonous if they are allowed to chew on a person. They are protected by Arizona law.

late spring and summer in burrows, where they are arranged in layers sandwiched between coverings of soil.

Several species of horned lizards inhabit the western deserts. The desert horned lizard (*Phrynosoma platyrhinos*) prefers sandy areas but also inhabits rock outcrops among creosote bushes, cacti, and ocotillo plants. The row of fringe scales on each side of the body is not as pronounced as it is on *P. cornutum*. In the Great Basin the short-horned lizard (*P. douglassi*), a species with very short head spines, occurs on the sagebrush plains. It is also found in the open lava-dust areas and in loose soil habitats in eastern Oregon. The short-horned lizard gives birth to living young. Like their parents the little youngsters blend into their background, and, when they are not scurrying around for food, are almost invisible.

Ants are the favorite food of horned lizards, although they

also eat other insects and spiders. Sometimes they remain beside an anthill for an hour, snapping up the insects as they emerge. I am always reminded, when I see one of these animals, that it does a great deal of tedious work in catching its food and then in turn is eaten in one gulp by hawks, roadrunners, snakes, other lizards, foxes, or coyotes. It does, however, have a form of defense that some mammals apparently find offensive: it can eject blood from its eye membrane to a distance of several feet.

In the warm southwestern deserts two species of large sluggish lizards are found: the Gila monsters *Heloderma suspectum* and *H. horridum*, which average eighteen inches in length, although exceptional specimens may be as long as two feet. These lizards, characterized by orange or yellow spots or bands on their thick bodies, are poisonous to humans who are foolish enough to allow them to bite while being handled. In the same regions the salamander-like banded gecko (*Coleonyx variegatus*), only four or five inches long, hides beneath rocks or fallen tree branches

The fringe-toed lizard is one of the most handsome of the desert saurians. Fringes of scales on the hind feet aid the animal in running over sand, in which it can bury itself almost instantly.

by day and emerges at night to feed on insects, which it stalks and then catches with a quick jump. Unlike other lizards, which hiss when annoyed, the gecko utters a soft squeaking note. The desert night lizard (*Xantusia vigilis*) also forages at night, and it hides by day beneath yucca debris and in the dried leaves on the yucca plants themselves.

One of the commonest of the small lizards is the side-blotched lizard (*Uta stansburiana*). A black spot behind the forelimb is a distinguishing mark of the animal, which is only one and three-quarters to about two inches in snout-vent length. The male in a torpid state is drab and virtually without markings but develops blue flecks and becomes spotted when it warms up. The fringe-toed lizard (*U. notata*) has an edging of scales on the hind feet to aid it in running over the sand.

In the Colorado and Mohave deserts you may see the long-tailed brush lizard (*Urosaurus graciosus*), which spends much of its time in shrubs and trees. Its tail is twice as long as its body. The desert spiny lizard (*Sceloporus magister*) prefers to dwell in the vicinity of water, but also lives in extremely dry deserts from Nevada and Utah to Baja California and Sonora. Its pointed, keeled scales give it an extremely rough appearance.

A sand dweller that appeals to me as one of the most beautiful of lizards is the Mohave fringe-toed lizard (*Uma scoparia*). It is a smooth-bodied animal marked with a fine dark reticulum of white circles with black centers. The belly is white or pale greenish yellow. This lizard can bury itself in the sand in a blur when escape seems to be necessary.

The giant among lizards of the Southwest is the rock-dwelling chuckwalla (*Sauromalus obesus*), which grows to a length of eighteen inches and is stouter than the Gilas. The body is broad and somewhat flattened, with folds of skin hanging down from the neck and sides. The blunt tail is covered with small, closely spaced scales. If you chase one of these lizards, you will learn why it lives in rocky areas. When it reaches a crevice, it inflates itself and wedges its body firmly into the opening so that it cannot be removed by hawks, coyotes, or other animal enemies. The Indians who catch chuckwallas for food deflate them by puncturing them with a sharp-pointed stick or tool.

The chuckwalla is a sunbather and a vegetarian. Because of its large size more time is required to heat its body in the rays of the morning sun. One of its favorite foods is the flowers of the incense bush (*Encelia farinosa*), which it obtains by climbing into the shrub. Leaves of other plants, including desert mallow, creosote bush, and various annuals, are also eaten. If not disturbed after eating time, the chuckwalla may take still another nap on its favorite rock pile. If alarmed, it may jump from rock to rock in a mad dash to safety. If caught, it can do a good job of biting, since it has heavy jaws adapted for chewing off pieces of vegetation.

Snakes are widespread and numerous in the desert. Some are strictly desert dwellers, especially those that live in sandy habi-

The coachwhip snake is common in the Mohave Desert. It is a daytime traveler and frequently is seen climbing in bushes in search of eggs and young birds in the nest.

tats. Others merely endure the desert, or have evolved special features for specific environmental conditions. In spite of their abundance, snakes are not commonly seen by daytime visitors. Many desert snakes only come out of the earth when rains and floods force them to the surface. Other kinds dig burrows but spend part of the time aboveground, or they live in animal dens and rock crevices and appear in the open infrequently. In addition, the great majority of desert snakes are nocturnal, being unable to tolerate brilliant sunlight and high temperatures.

Among the daytime or diurnal snakes are the coachwhip (*Masticophis flagellum*) and the western patch-nosed snake (*Salvadora hexalepis*). The gopher snake (*Pituophis melanoleucus*) is occasionally seen in daytime, but the common kingsnake (*Lampropeltis getulus*) tends to appear only at dusk and during the night. This time of appearance is probably related to the habits of nocturnal snakes which the kingsnake eats.

The various kinds of desert rattlesnakes are generally nocturnal. An exposure of seven to ten minutes in the desert sun will kill the sidewinder (*Crotalus cerastes*) and the western diamondback rattlesnake (*C. atrox*). The prairie or western rattlesnake (*C. viridis*) appears to be less susceptible to heat prostration, at least on the shortgrass prairie where I have encountered most individuals of this species. G. E. Klipple and I once prevented a prairie rattlesnake from leaving a bare hot gravel road near Nunn, Colorado, for forty-six minutes. The thermometer at a nearby government research station registered 97° F., and the road was much hotter than that. The only reaction we could observe was that the snake grew more vicious by the minute. It rattled furiously and struck repeatedly at the long-handled shovel with which we herded it to prevent its escape. It did not die of the heat.

Most people want to know about their chances of being bitten by rattlesnakes in the desert. Actually, the likelihood of being bitten is slight if you are observant, keep away from bushes while walking, and wear shoes or boots that protect your legs below the knees. You should avoid walking close to rocky ledges, placing your hands in holes where you cannot see, sitting down without looking, or placing sleeping bags near rock piles or caves which rattlesnakes may use as dens. In snake-infested country you should avoid walking around at night; or at least, wear boots and carry a flashlight, since most rattlesnakes are nocturnal and are most active at moderate temperatures.

A rattlesnake bite is serious, especially if the person bitten is a child or is in poor physical condition. Medical attention should be sought; if it is not immediately available, a snakebite kit should be used and the directions followed carefully. But there should be no panic such as might be inspired by ridiculous tall tales concerning the virulence of snake poison. These fabulous tales are legion. One that comes to mind is the story of how a cowboy allowed a rattlesnake to bite his lariat. The rope swelled to a diameter of six inches and became completely rigid. Later it was sawed into six-foot lengths and used for fence posts.

Although snakebites are by no means rare, especially in the southern and western states, venomous snakes cause fewer than fifty deaths annually in the United States. Most victims of rattlesnake bite recover when proper first aid is given, followed by subsequent medical care. But the bite of any rattlesnake is a medical emergency and requires the earliest possible treatment.

The bite of most rattlesnakes causes immediate pain, which is followed by swelling about the injured area within ten minutes.

The Mohave rattlesnake ranges widely from Texas to the Mohave Desert. It is also common far southward in Mexico. It feeds on rodents and lizards. The venom of this snake is more toxic than that of any other North American rattlesnake.

Without treatment, swelling may involve an entire leg or arm within one hour and may continue for more than twenty-four hours. Weakness, sweating, faintness, and nausea are commonly experienced. Lymph nodes may become enlarged and painful. Vesicles may form on the skin within three hours, and bleeding may occur from gastrointestinal, urinary, or respiratory tracts.

Bites by the Mohave rattlesnake are extremely serious, since it has the most toxic venom of all North American rattlers— approximately ten times as lethal as the venom from the western diamondback. Bites by the Mohave rattlesnake oftentimes show little local reaction or pain, but are followed later by severe difficulty in breathing. The bad-tempered diamondback, however, because of its size (a maximum of seven feet compared to an average of three feet for the Mohave rattler), carries a larger amount of venom and its bite is also very serious.

Since the venoms of the various rattlesnakes are different, it is important to identify, if possible, the species of snake that does the biting. The markings of the western diamondback are less conspicuous in the desert, where it matches its background to an uncanny degree. The diamonds often have a dusty appearance with indistinct light edges. Two light diagonal stripes appear on the sides of the head; the tail has distinct black and white rings;

The sidewinder is noted for its peculiar form of locomotion, which leaves J-shaped marks on the sand. This rattlesnake has horns above its eyes.

and the belly is cream to pinkish buff, or sometimes gray. The general coloration is gray, buff, or light brown. The diamondback inhabits terrain that varies from rocky hills to flat desert and coastal sands.

The sidewinder is most common in sandy flats and dunes and lies buried during the day, usually in the partial shade of a bush, with only its head exposed. The tracks of this snake, unmistakable when seen in the sand or in road dust, can often lead one to its resting place. Sidewinding, a form of locomotion that reduces slippage on sand or other loose material, leaves a series of J-shaped marks.

The Mohave rattlesnake (*Crotalus scutulatus*) is greenish or yellowish with distinct diamond-shaped markings resembling those of the diamondback and prairie rattlesnakes. It is distributed from West Texas to the Mohave Desert of California and southeastward into Mexico.

About twenty-five species of rattlesnakes are recognized. Most of these are in the southwestern United States and northern Mexico. One species ranges into southern South America, and two are found east of the Mississippi River. One species, on an island in the Gulf of California, does not develop a rattle. All are important in the desert food chain, since they eat kangaroo rats, gophers, rabbits, ground squirrels, mice, birds, lizards, and frogs. Their life histories, adaptations, and the vivid folklore surrounding them are fascinating. Most of this is told in Laurence Klauber's *Rattlesnakes: Their Habits, Life Histories, and Influence on Mankind*, which has been called the greatest snake book of the century.

Most desert snakes, however, are harmless and equally interesting. The desert worm snake, or blind snake (*Leptotyphlops humulis*), is an intriguing creature because of small size—adults measure nine to twelve inches in length—and its vestigial eyes, which are merely black dots beneath ocular scales. The body diameter is the same for the entire length of the snake, and the tail is rounded so the rear and front ends of the animal are alike. It prefers sandy or loose soil in moist situations, and generally eats ants and termites.

One of the gentlest snakes of the desert is the rosy boa (*Lichanura trivirgata*). The glossy scales are so small that it feels smooth or almost silky when handled. It also feels heavy for its size. Adults reach two to three feet in length. The rosy boa's basic color is purplish-gray, but its name is derived from the three reddish stripes that extend its full length. For defense it rolls itself into a rubberlike ball with its head inside.

A daytime wanderer, because of its choice of lizards as food, is the western patch-nosed snake (*Salvadora hexalepis*), which ranges from northwestern Nevada to Baja California and Sonora. This slim brown snake seldom exceeds three feet in length. An enlarged scale on its snout is believed to be of aid in digging the eggs of lizards and other snakes. One of its probable enemies is the larger and faster snake-eating coachwhip, but apparently the fact that the patch-nosed snake is active early in the morning, when temperatures are too low for coachwhips, enables them to coexist.

Two desert snakes other than the rattlers are poisonous but are not dangerous to humans. The California lyre snake (*Trimorphodon vandenburghi*) has fangs in the back of its mouth, but it would have to chew on a finger or toe to inject its venom, which is used in nature to subdue lizards and small mammals. Living in rocky crevices, it also occasionally catches bats.

The other venomous but rarely dangerous serpent in the desert is the Arizona coral snake (*Micruroides euryxanthus*), conspicuous because of the elongate body with yellow- or white-bordered red rings. Its black snout distinguishes this species from the similarly colored nonpoisonous sand snakes and shovel-nosed snakes. Few bites have been reported, but all coral snakes, of which some forty American species have been recognized, should be treated with care.

The movements and home ranges of snakes are difficult to study because of the snakes' secretiveness, their protective coloration, and their nocturnal habits. But a revealing research project led by Harold F. Hirth has shown that some desert snakes travel widely during the summer months and return to their dens by some unknown directional sense in early autumn. The research workers tagged a total of 196 snakes with radioactive tantalum as they emerged from hibernation in a den in the Great Basin west of Grantville, Utah. Then, as the snakes moved away from the den during the summer, they were detected with scintillometers that could locate them at a maximum distance of nine meters on the ground surface and three meters when they were thirty centimeters below the surface. Thus snakes that crawled into rodents' burrows could be found and their locations mapped.

The study showed that Mormon racers (*Coluber constrictor mormon*) remained closer to the den than rattlesnakes and whipsnakes. More than half of the racers recaptured in July and August were 250 meters or more away from the den and were found underground as often as on the surface. When found on the ground, they most commonly were in grass or under sagebrush or rabbitbrush. A few were located basking in these shrubs from 0.3 to 1.0 meters above the ground.

Ten of the sixteen Great Basin rattlesnakes (*Crotalus viridis lutosus*) retaken in this study in the summer were between 900 and 1,200 meters from the den. Most were found, night or day, under or near a sagebrush or rabbitbrush; a few were found coiled in downy chess (*Bromus tectorum*). The greatest travelers were striped whipsnakes (*Masticophis taeniatus taeniatus*); recaptures of these fast-moving snakes were made at distances of 1.5, 3.2, and 3.6 kilometers from the den. As many whipsnakes were recaptured in shrubs as on the ground.

The den where these three species of snakes hibernated also

The rosy boa is seldom seen. It is a gentle snake and can be handled easily. In defending itself it may roll into a ball with its head inside.

was used for overwintering by night snakes, gopher snakes, ringneck snakes, and long-nosed snakes. The summer dispersal of these species was not studied, but the idea was expressed that spatial separation and migration of snakes reduces competition for food as well as predation by hawks, and possibly badgers, which were seen near the entrance to the den.

Snakes in the desert, of course, have many enemies. Coyotes, foxes, eagles, hawks, and owls prey on them, especially the young ones. Roadrunners are adept at killing snakes. And larger mammals, including deer and peccaries, occasionally destroy them. On the other hand, snakes depend upon a multitude of creatures for their own food, including ants, rodents, eggs, birds, frogs, toads, rabbits, and other snakes.

Most of us are inclined to think of frogs, salamanders, and, to some extent, toads as animals of ponds, streams, and moist places. But surprisingly, they are successful in dry places, including the desert. And thereby hangs a tale of interesting adaptations to temperature, evaporation, and unpredictable rainfall. In the desert the number of frogs and toads emerging after rain is almost beyond comprehension. In western Australia frogs have emerged in such multitudes as to impede the passage of trains when the rails became slippery with crushed bodies. In our southwestern deserts the night sometimes becomes raucous with the loud penetrating cries of hundreds of male spadefoot toads, audible for a distance of one or two miles. Yet for months, or even years on end—during prolonged rainless periods—not an amphibian may be seen. All this time they remain in hibernation, each in its earthen cell, waiting until the rain softens the soil.

The Anura (frogs and toads) have the widest distribution of all the Amphibia, extending from arctic regions to the deserts of Africa, Australia, and America. With such a range of environments they necessarily possess many physical and metabolic attributes that enable them to persist in a variety of habitats. One anomalous feature is that their skins are permeable to water and hence they cannot resist evaporation. They seldom or never drink, but, on the other hand, they can absorb water through their skins, even if it is available only from damp soil or dew on desert vegetation. They even outdo the camel in their ability to withstand desiccation—of as much as 50 percent of their body weight. Couch's spadefoot toad (*Scaphiopus couchii*) of our southwestern deserts can lose up to 48 percent before it dies.

As the Amphibia lose water their body fluids become more concentrated. The kidneys of toads cease to form urine when dehydration takes place, and the concentration of body fluids increases without adversely affecting contraction of muscular tissue or locomotion. Urea apparently is stored in a relatively nontoxic form which can be excreted when more favorable moisture conditions return to the desert. The bladders of frogs and toads also can store water which can be recycled in the animal's body. In addition, a portion of the pituitary gland produces hormones which affect water metabolism by increasing retention of the water and the rate of fluid intake through the skin. When moisture is available, the animals can restore as much as 45 percent of their weight in a short time.

Desert frogs and toads escape the daytime heat by hiding in cracks in the soil or rocks, by burrowing in sand, by seeking refuge in holes made by other animals, and by subterranean estivation during long periods between rains. The spadefoot toads dig their own burrows, from which they emerge at night during periods of favorable weather. Rain in quantity brings them forth for breeding, and when ponds and pools are filled with water the desert resounds with their voices.

The male desert toad (*Bufo punctatus*) sings with a birdlike trill as he sits in shallow water. In the beam of a flashlight the vocal sacs of these toads appear as shining white bubbles. Eggs are deposited in shallow water by the females in short strings or singly. The tadpoles metamorphose quickly into tiny toads which hop about on the hot soil, sometimes in such numbers that they resemble an invasion of tiny grasshoppers.

In season, you may hear the voice of the Woodhouse toad (*Bufo woodhousii*) in the sagebrush desert of Utah, the mesquite flats of New Mexico, the freshwater pools of Arizona canyons, and the irrigation ditches from Oregon to California. The sound is a trill or sometimes a prolonged *w-a-a-a-h*. After rains in Texas and south into Mexico you may hear the louder trill of the Sonoran toad (*Bufo compactilis*), which is a burrowing toad that often associates with Couch's spadefoot.

Numerous other toads and frogs live in arid lands. The Pacific tree toad (*Hyla regilla*) ranges from British Columbia to Idaho and Nevada and southward to Baja California. It finds shelter among rocks, in rodent burrows, under bark, and in moist places near ponds and streams. It is so adaptable that it has been found in Death Valley and at elevations exceeding 11,000 feet. The California tree frog (*Hyla californiae*) occurs from southern California to near Rosario, Baja California. It is found in niches in rocks and spends little time in water except when breeding. The voice of these frogs has been described as a quacking note. They breed in freshwater pools and streams.

The giant among toads is the Colorado River toad (*Bufo alvarius*), which reaches a length of seven inches. It has been the subject of exaggeration concerning both its size and the volume of its voice. Cowboys have reported seeing specimens as big as a hat, and their cries have been described as a deafening roar. It is probable that the listeners heard a congress of spadefoot toads, which call in a chorus of loud *Wah*'s from desert pools at breeding time. The Colorado River toads live near the water's edge, especially in the valleys of the Gila and Colorado rivers. Since their large bodies expose considerable surface area to drying, they are among the most aquatic of the toads.

The eggs of the Colorado River toad are laid in ropelike strings more than thirty feet long, each containing several thousand eggs. The eggs hatch rapidly, and the tadpoles metamorphose into young toads in not much more than a month. The young eat small insects, but large adults consume a great variety of large insects, including grasshoppers, beetles, and moths. They also eat centipedes and small lizards. The skin secretions of these toads are toxic to small animals. Dogs that bite or mouth them become sick or paralyzed and sometimes die.

Among the secretive amphibians of the desert are the salamanders, which are unfamiliar creatures to most people. The nuptial dances of salamanders and their double lives as larvae and adults have fascinated biologists for years. They are primitive animals with a geological history that goes back to Tertiary times. Those of us who have lived east of the Missouri-Mississippi river drainage know such salamanders as the mudpuppies of lakes, ponds, and streams and the two-foot (or longer) hellbender. The widely distributed tiger salamander (*Ambystoma tigrinum*), common in the prairie region, also occurs in the desert. The races *mavortium* and *californiense* live in prairie-dog tunnels and in ground-squirrel burrows. They also live beneath water tanks for stock, where overflow from windmill pumps keeps the soil moist. In the rainy season they travel to ponds where breeding occurs.

A new species, the desert slender salamander (*Batrachoseps aridus*), recently has been described by Arden H. Brame, Jr. It occurs in a small canyon on the lower desert slopes of the Santa Rosa Mountains, where it lives beneath limestone layers in the presence of perennial water seepage. Brame speculates that four species of slender salamanders in this genus, distributed from Oregon to California, may represent fragmentations of a species which was widespread in geologic times.

Aeons ago frogs, toads, and salamanders climbed out of their watery environment and adapted to dual habitats of land and water. They still divide their lives between land and water, and the result is a two-way transfer of energy from ponds and streams to the land and back again. As links in the food chain, they prey upon many animals, including earthworms, mollusks, insects, fish, small snakes, and one another. In turn they are eaten by snakes, birds, fish, and mammals. The burrowing species also perform the service of cultivating and aerating the soil and making channels that allow water to penetrate and plants to grow.

One of the durable, interesting, and seemingly lackadaisical

The desert tortoise is an inoffensive creature. Its den provides shelter for uninvited guests including rabbits, rodents, snakes, insects, and lizards. It is a vegetarian.

creatures of southwestern arid lands is the desert tortoise (*Gopherus agassizi*). When mature its high arched shell is twelve inches or more in length. The elephantoid hind legs, with their flat feet, are among its distinctive features. The tail is short. The gular horn, which is a forward projection of the underpart of the shell, is elongated in the males and serves as a weapon to overturn other males at breeding time. The brown domed carapace, with its scutes with growth rings, has a sculptured appearance.

The desert tortoise, one of the few land turtles, is the one seen by travelers in southwestern Nevada, southwestern Utah, southern California, and southward to southern Sonora. It is most commonly encountered on highways. In the Mohave Desert I have seen numerous remains of desert tortoises, crushed by drivers who sometimes deliberately kill these increasingly rare animals.

The desert tortoise frequents areas where the soil permits construction of suitable temporary and permanent burrows. Dunes are generally avoided because the sand is unstable, but rocky areas are acceptable if the soil is satisfactory. Winter homes, where the animals hibernate for as long as six months, are dug into banks or beneath bushes to a length of ten to thirty feet. The tunnel entrance and the burrows have flat floors and arched roofs or ceilings. All sorts of uninvited guests use these burrows, including rattlesnakes, burrowing owls, spiders, lizards, mice, pack rats, and numerous kinds of insects—and once I saw a hog-nosed skunk emerge. I assume that the skunk would also not be reluctant to eat tortoise eggs if it could find where the clutch was laid. The tortoise, however, being well armored, probably is not very much bothered by these freeloaders in its den.

The desert tortoise, primarily a vegetarian, forages on succulent forbs, grass leaves, flowers, and wild fruits, including those of some of the cacti. A captive tortoise, kept by U. G. Nichols, ate all the snails in her yard, and it is probable that the tortoise takes some animal food in the desert. Prowling for food usually takes place during the cooler parts of the day. When the heat is great, the tortoise takes shelter beneath bushes or rocks, or in shallow burrows only three or four feet long.

Most of the water needed by desert tortoises is obtained from the vegetation they eat, although they do drink when water is available—and can increase their weight by more than 40 percent with a single long drink. Water economy, however, is not a great problem for the tortoise, since its thick shell prevents excessive evaporation and it burrows in the earth during the heat of the day. In addition, the tortoise's urinary bladder is believed to be a storage organ in which semisolid urates are stored for long periods of time; thus, voiding of metabolic waste is unnecessary when moisture from food or rain is scarce. When captured, the reptile has a disconcerting habit of emptying its bladder of a surprising amount of liquid.

Tortoises grow slowly and live for many years. When the eggs hatch, the young are miniature copies of the adults, only about one and a half inches long. Although it is known that the adults eat vegetation, I have found no information on the diet of young tortoises. If they follow the habits of their distant relatives, the ornate box turtles, they eat insects, especially those that come to droppings of large desert mammals. The young tortoises themselves are subject to predation by foxes, coyotes, snakes, hawks, and roadrunners, since their shells remain soft for five or six years. They do not become sexually mature until they attain the age of twelve to twenty years.

Courting by the males includes much head bobbing and bumping of the female by the male's gular horn. One observer reports that the male also bites the female's legs and places his front feet on top of her carapace before copulation. The clutch of approximately five eggs is deposited in a hole dug in the soil by the hind legs to a depth of three or four inches. Hatching occurs in about three months, although it has been found to vary from 80 to 118 days.

When you see one of these inoffensive creatures basking by its den, traveling across the desert, or eating flowers, leave it to its own devices. It is protected by law in some localities, and as a pet it will ultimately die or escape to be killed on city streets or the highways. Remember that as a group the turtle tribe has been around for nearly 200 million years, but man's stupidity can cause it to vanish from the earth. If we decimate the turtles, and a multitude of other creatures, one by one, the desert will no longer be the desert and we will have lost another great natural heritage.

Prehistoric Indian drawings show man in the desert and the animals he hunted. Many of these drawings are found in the vicinity of game trails.

CHAPTER 11

Man and the North American Deserts: History and Future

The prehistory of man in the Americas is largely shrouded in mystery. At some unknown time in the past the ancestors of the Indians came to the New World, probably by way of the great featureless plain between Siberia and Alaska, when the sea was low. This drift of humans, begun some 25,000 years ago, or even earlier, possibly followed the Rockies southward until it reached into South America. The time of eastward and westward migration to the Atlantic coast, the Great Basin, and the Pacific coast remains in obscurity.

The first human inhabitants of the area we now know as desert apparently came when the climate was more humid and lakes, rivers, plants, and animals offered many advantages for existence. Fragments of tools and weapons, animal remains, and even human skeletons preserved in caves give evidence that early man lived by the shores of lakes and near streams, where water, wood, and animal life were abundant. These ancient hunters must have lived contemporaneously with the late Pleistocene mammals. Artifacts such as spear points and tools have been discovered together with bones of mammoths, camels, extinct horses, and bison, and even the skins of ancient prairie dogs.

With the passing of the Ice Age prehistoric man was forced to adapt to increasingly arid conditions. The desert cultures advanced by stages from the use of chipped stone artifacts to migratory hunting and gathering and, finally, to an essentially agricultural village life which also involved pottery making, weaving, stone carving, and religious and social ceremonies. Over thousands of years the early inhabitants of the desert region increased in numbers, separated into family groups, bands, and tribes, and established a variety of cultures suitable to their different localities. Many of these cultures were destroyed by natural or man-made disasters, including droughts, floods, volcanic eruptions, and invasions by hostile tribes (themselves perhaps fleeing from other hostile groups in the surrounding fertile lands). Much of the history of these peoples is lost to us forever, but some of it can be at least partially reconstructed thanks to the efforts of geologists, anthropologists, and other interested scholars.

Scientists can, for example, determine the diet of prehistoric groups through the analysis of human coprolites—fecal material preserved in an organic state. Thus, we know that in the eighth century the inhabitants of Lovelock Cave, Nevada, ate an amazing variety of foods, including plant matter, mollusks, insects, fish, birds, and mammals. The vegetable part of their diet alone included cattail pollen, seeds, and fiber; grass seeds of wild rye, scratchgrass, witchgrass, and saltgrass; and nuts, seeds, achenes

Indian artifacts made of obsidian are exposed when lake beds in southeastern Oregon become dry and the fine soil particles are blown away by the wind.

and tubers of pines, sedges, reeds, shrubs, and desert forbs. Fish, presumed to have been caught in Humboldt Lake, included the tui chub, Tahoe sucker, and Lahontan speckled dace. Fragments of bird skins give evidence of meals of coots, ducks, and other waterfowl. The coprolites also contain hairs of bears, squirrels, mice, rabbits, antelope, and deer.

This was a hunting and food-gathering economy that wrought few changes on the environment. These people were a part of nature and adapted themselves to whatever resources could be harvested, whether they were plants, fish, or mammals. They traveled according to the seasons and the supplies of food in the desert, in the lakes, or on the valley slopes. At best, their existence was precarious, and their culture was not advanced. Permanent villages, if they existed, probably were occupied only in the river valleys and on the margins of large freshwater lakes.

The Mohave Indians, on the other hand, were farmers, raising beans, squash, maize, sunflowers, tobacco, gourds, and grasses. Scientists have located their irrigation systems by means of aerial photography. Aerial infrared scanner images combined with soil and pollen analysis have been used to find their agricultural plots.

About the time of Christ the inhabitants of Mesa Verde and the San Juan River Valley in the Four Corners country, where Colorado, Utah, New Mexico, and Arizona come together, became weavers of baskets and sandals. The Basketmakers persisted for some 750 years, gradually developing different ways of life and new skills in weaving, tool making, and the fabrication of jewelery and other ornaments. By A.D. 700 they were building pit houses with adobe-plastered walls.

Near the end of the Basketmaker period a new type of house construction, marking the beginning of the Pueblo period, began in the San Juan area. Subterranean structures gave way to single-room structures in groups that formed small villages. The round *kiva*'s, which visitors now see at Mesa Verde and other sites in the Southwest, were used for ceremonial occasions, the *sipapu*—hole in the floor—leading to the underground spirit world.

As the Pueblo period reached its height, elaborate multistoried houses were built, irrigation was practiced, and there was notable specialization in the arts of weaving and pottery making. And then suddenly abandonment of the pueblos began, with periods of reoccupation until great drought, and possibly other disasters, brought about almost complete depopulation of the Four Corners country by the end of the thirteenth century. Where the people went is somewhat of a mystery. Probably they became the *Anasazi* (Ancient Ones) who regrouped in Arizona and New Mexico, built cliff dwellings on the sides of canyons, and farmed in the desert. Their towns were the pueblos discovered by the early Spanish explorers.

The Indians never conquered the desert, nor did they consider nature their enemy. Instead they used the resources around them —the desert plants and animals—and, in some instances, they also used available water for crop irrigation. The products of the environment furnished food, drink, clothing, medicine, ornaments, and shelter. The native plants provided seeds, nuts, fruits, fresh vegetables, tonics, fibers, and building materials.

Numerous medicinal plants were utilized, and their uses varied from cures for social diseases, sterility, digestive disturbances, and infections to narcotic treatments derived from the juices of mescal beans, milkweeds, and Jimson weeds. Dyes came from mountain mahogany roots, tree bark, and nuts. And shelters, tools, and weapons were made from willows, mesquite trees, cottonwoods, saguaro ribs, and ocotillo.

These uses of natural products left much of the desert unaltered before the advent of the explorers. The Indians, however, did set fires, especially in the forested mountains and in the desert grasslands when they hunted game animals. But these probably were no more frequent than fires set by lightning. And the Indians did practice extensive irrigation in the Salt River Valley in Arizona. But nowhere did they stop the flow of rivers with mighty dams and silt-catching reservoirs.

The early white explorers recorded little of the true nature of the desert. They were not greatly interested in the beauty of the landscape, its plants, mammals, birds, and reptiles. Instead they sought gold and dominion over the land. One of the first white men to explore the desert was Álvar Núñez Cabeza de Vaca. In 1528, on his journey from the Gulf of Mexico into the Sonoran Desert, he heard rumors of Quivira, a fabulous kingdom to the north where there existed the legendary Seven Cities of Cibola full of gold, silver, and jewels. In an attempt to substantiate these rumors Marcos de Niza, a Franciscan friar, and Esteven, a

The influence of the missions and of Spanish architecture still remains in the deserts of the Southwest.

Negro (who had earlier traveled with Captain Pánfilo de Narváez from the Gulf of Mexico to the west coast) made an expedition to the vicinity of the Zuñi pueblos in New Mexico without finding golden cities. But the quest for gold was not ended.

In 1539 Francisco Vásquez de Coronado rode along the coast of Mexico with some 5,000 sheep and 150 cattle. The difficulty of travel resulted in abandonment of many of these animals and probably contributed to the beginning of the desert cattle industry. Coronado's famous journey continued in 1540–1542 from Mexico through what is now southeastern Arizona, across New Mexico, southwestern Texas, and Oklahoma to the present site of Dodge City, Kansas.

One of the last of the great Spanish explorers, Juan de Oñate, crossed the Rio Grande at El Paso and took formal possession of

New Mexico in 1598. His journey continued across New Mexico and Arizona to the Gulf of California. With him went 7,000 cattle in addition to horses, sheep, and goats. When Indians slew some of Oñate's men, the Spanish took revenge at Acoma, where they killed 3,000 to 6,000 Indians.

After this, the desert remained essentially unexplored for another century. Ultimately the missions, presidios, and pueblos established by the Franciscans, Dominicans, and Jesuits became the centers from which modern cities developed. But in the long transition period between the development of missions and permanent settlement, only local disturbances in the landscape were made by gold miners, graziers, and local Indian cultures. Not until the 1800's did men such as Jim Bridger, Jedidiah Smith, Peter Skene Ogden, and other fur trappers give accounts of the Indians and of beaver, deer, antelope, raccoons, and trout.

A few decades later, better-equipped expeditions began to explore the desert. Captain Benjamin Bonneville crossed the Bear Lake country in Utah in 1836 and mentioned the swamps, although his botany and zoology were unscientific. John C. Frémont, who explored Utah three times, was one of the first to give detailed accounts of what he saw in the desert. Then, in the year 1847, Brigham Young led his little band of Mormon pioneers

On December 16, 1843, the Frémont Expedition struggled from the snowy heights of "Winter Ridge" to the grass-lined shores of "Summer Lake" at the edge of the desert in south-central Oregon. The reports of this expedition gave impetus to settlement in the Northwest and in the Oregon desert.

down into the land of Zion in the valley of Great Salt Lake, where they were to fulfill the promise from the Old Testament, "And the desert shall blossom as the rose."

These people came to escape persecution, to live in peace, and to be self-sustaining. They succeeded well, and they conquered that part of the desert with farms and towns and monuments to their religion. Their occupation was not a wanton destruction of the face of the earth for greed or profit, but the establishment of a new pattern of life. The real pressure on the arid lands of the West came later, from the rim of the desert and from hundreds and even thousands of miles away.

The first great pressure came from the treasure seekers in pursuit of dreams of gold and silver. As one discovery after another was made in the mountains and deserts, these reckless adventurers made history and left their mark on the land. They built boom towns that later became ghost towns. The roads, railroads, and settlers remaining after the miners had clawed the earth left their impact around the gold camps, in state politics, and in the financial markets. When James Marshall found gold in California in 1848, the rush for riches by sea and land brought men, women, and whiskey from all corners of the earth. The discovery of gold in the Sierra Nevada foothills produced a steady stream of Sonorans from Mexico. These Mexicans were experienced miners; their crude equipment and techniques dominated the California Gold Rush until steam-powered machinery and company mines replaced them at a later date. Chihuahuans and other Mexicans also flooded into California by land and sea, with consequent changes in mining, commerce, and language. California became a bilingual state by law, and it remained as such until 1878. Thus people who had roots in the desert soil of Mexico dominated the Southwest for many years.

Gold and silver discoveries throughout the West, and as far north as Alaska, continued to draw men to pass through the desert or to stay in it. In 1861 a gold rush came to the John Day and Powder rivers in Oregon. In 1868 silver was found in Utah. In 1859 the Big Bonanza on the Comstock Lode was uncovered. In 1900 new finds resulted in the creation of the town of Tonopah, Nevada. And even as late as 1933 there was a rush to the Mohave Desert, but the dream of vast riches faded once more.

The desert, however, had other minerals of value. By 1900 the value of copper mined in the Sonoran Desert exceeded the value of gold and silver by 300 percent. Later Arizona became the leading copper producer of the nation. Now, in New Mexico, you can stand at the edge of one of the largest copper mines in the world, the Santa Rita open pit copper mine. The pit is over a mile across and one-fifth of a mile deep. Other huge copper deposits are worked at Bingham, Utah; Ely, Nevada; Ajo, Bagdad, Ray, and Superior, Arizona.

There are numerous other mineral resources in the desert, and their development invariably leaves marks on the landscape. Silver now is obtained primarily in connection with copper mining. Mercury, berylium, iron, magnesium, manganese, lead, zinc, boron, and antimony are mined at one place or another in Utah, Nevada, Arizona, and New Mexico. Even borax, which formerly was hauled from Death Valley behind twenty-mule teams, is still being removed from deposits in the Mohave Desert. Borates are obtained from lake brines, such as those at Searles Lake, or from underground and pit mines, especially the latter at Boron, California.

Saline minerals result from high evaporation in the desert. From the concentrated brines come bromine, iodine, calcium chloride, potassium salts, sodium chloride, sodium carbonate, and sodium sulfate. In addition, the California Desert at Mountain Pass in San Bernardino County yields rare-earth minerals which are used in the manufacture of stainless steel, glass, and color television tubes, and in oil refining.

At Mountain Pass there is the rare-earth mineral bastnasite, a fluorocarbonate containing cerium, lanthanum, neodymium, praeseodymium, samarium, gadolinium, and Europium. With the electronic tools now available to the geologist, there is little doubt that the desert in future years will be forced to yield increasing amounts of minerals as explorers probe more deeply into its ancient metamorphic and plutonic rocks.

The most widespread and cataclysmic change in the desert in modern time has resulted from unrestricted grazing. Excessive use by sheep and cattle for more than one hundred years has denuded the grass cover over thousands of square miles, and has resulted in disastrous floods, channelization of streams and dry washes, invasion of noxious trees, shrubs, and annual plants,

Overgrazing by sheep and cattle have reduced the productivity of the desert over hundreds of millions of acres. Excessive numbers of animals have depleted grasses and forbs and allowed the less palatable shrubs to remain.

and modification of desert fauna. Allegedly to protect livestock, predatory animals have been poisoned, with consequent increases in rodents. Through mismanagement, monopoly by stockmen, and political influence, the desert in many places is only one-tenth as productive for livestock as it was when white men first came on the scene.

The livestock invasion of the desert came from several directions. Cattle arrived on the East Coast with the English settlers and gradually moved westward. The Hudson's Bay Company introduced livestock into Oregon and Idaho, and some of these, through several generations, spread southward into the Great Basin, where the Mormons encountered them in 1847. The Mormon settlers themselves introduced cattle and sheep into Utah, some of which were brought overland from California. The Spanish, even before Coronado's journey, brought cattle, sheep, horses, and swine to Mexico. From all these sources the explorers, missionaries, and colonizers introduced the livestock industry into New Mexico, Arizona, Texas, and California.

Tumbledown buildings and abandoned wells are evidence that homesteaders on the desert were unable to support themselves on the 160 acres allowed by the Homestead Act of 1862.

It was inevitable that sheep would occupy the desert because of their mobility in herds and their preference for shrubs and forbs as browse plants. The desert was an ideal place for winter grazing where snow was shallow but sufficiently abundant to furnish needed drinking water. As spring advanced, the herds could be moved to higher altitudes, following the appearance of fresh forage. With the greening of meadows and shrublands in the high mountains, the bands of sheep summered in lush forage until the snows and cold of autumn drove them back to winter-feed on the desert. A map of the sheep trails in the Intermountain West shows lines radiating like spiderwebs from the numerous mountain ranges into the surrounding desert.

Cattle in the desert increased greatly after barbed wire was invented by Joseph Glidden. This Illinois farmer apparently was the first man to put barbs on smooth wire. His product, called

"The Winner," was patented in 1874. Infringements on his patent resulted in lawsuits that lasted for nearly twenty years. In the meantime a host of other inventors developed and patented many types of barbed wire, of which more than 700 are now known.

It has been said that barbed wire, instead of the six-gun, really tamed the West. Fencing with barbed wire in the 1880's led to control of cattle and water holes and to use of the open range, which previously had been dominated by the stockman who arrived first or was fastest on the draw. Range wars between cattlemen and sheepmen followed the fencing, but ultimately the bloody battles ceased and the industry settled down to specific ownership of the more desirable lands, obtained by purchase from the railroads, which had been granted large acreages of government land, or by homesteading. The Homestead Act of 1862 allowed one to obtain 160 acres of government land by paying a registration fee, living on the land for five years, and beginning cultivation. Fences on homesteaded land then offered the means for controlling movements of livestock, seasons of grazing use, and segregation of bulls, cows, and young animals. But even with fencing, overuse of the native forage continued, especially on the public domain.

Unrestricted grazing took its toll in many ways. In one generation the desert in the public domain in Utah was depleted. Throughout the Great Basin the ability of desirable forage plants to reproduce and compete with noxious species was impaired by heavy grazing. Inferior plants, not palatable to livestock, crowded out the native perennials. Halogeton (a poisonous forb), Russian thistle, and downy chess, also known as "cheatgrass," became the principal cover on hundreds of thousands of square miles.

Downy chess, a winter annual grass, germinates in the fall, winters in the seedling stage, and then flowers, fruits, and dries in late April or May. Then it becomes a critical fire hazard. But burning does not destroy its seeds, which drop to the ground as the plant matures. Native shrubs, however, are killed by fire and may not reoccupy the land for a human generation or more.

By overgrazing, man has extended the arid environment—denuding the grass cover and thereby providing opportunity for the invasion of velvet mesquite, junipers, creosote bush, and plants that are poisonous to livestock. This upset in the balance of plant life in the desert will require generations for repair. Even under the best of management, palatable desert shrubs require from twenty-five to forty years to return to good condition. Improvement in protecting both the desert and the needs of ranchers is possible. It must be effected if either are to survive.

Man's recent impact on the desert is many-faceted. Having recently completed a 4,000-mile journey through the American desert, I find it difficult to comprehend all the changes that have occurred since I first saw it more than forty years ago. True, there are still many beautiful landscapes, but many others have been marred by noisy, ultra-busy, smoke-covered cities. The pressure of agriculture, made possible by irrigation, is uprooting the "wasteland" that once made a variegated pattern of fascinating desert life. They call it "reclamation," but a better term would be "claiming," since that is what dams, irrigation reservoirs, cities, military maneuvers, pollution, and vandalism are doing to the desert.

At present much desert land still remains to be "claimed," if water can be made available by such grandiose schemes as bringing Columbia River water south across the desert. One proposal for water transfer is a pact between California and Nevada to boost water supplies in the Lake Tahoe, Truckee River, Carson River, and Walker River basins by diverting additional water away from Pyramid Lake. Another proposal is to develop methods of desalting seawater. Ultimately, the predicament of too little water for American industry will have to be met by reusing the water—recycling it and discharging it unpolluted.

The survival of the desert is further threatened by the appeal it seems to have for the military. One of the most destructive military exercises in America was the "Desert Strike" during World War II, in which maneuvers occurred over some 14 million acres at a cost of $54 million. The tracks left by George S. Patton's tank exercises are still visible. Some of the shrubs, however, are now being replaced by seedlings, and desert animals are reoccupying some of the disturbed areas.

The effects of many other military practices in the desert have never been publicly evaluated. Millions of acres are held in reserve as Ordnance Test Stations, Military Reservations, Missile Ranges, and Proving Grounds, to which the public is denied access for hunting, camping, photography, wildlife study, or other forms of recreation. Occasionally the lid of secrecy regarding activities in these desert reserves is lifted by a scientist or a concerned congressman.

Considerable controversy, for example, followed the killing of more than 6,000 sheep in Skull Valley, Utah, allegedly by deadly VX nerve gas scattered accidentally by an Army test plane. Fred Anshutz, who sustained the greatest loss of sheep, filed a claim against the Army, and it was approved for $376,685. The public media also have reported that the Army contaminated a remote area of the Dugway Proving Grounds with deadly anthrax germs, "to determine how long it might present a hazard." Tests by Britain during World War II had already indicated that contamination by anthrax bacteria can make an area uninhabitable for more than 100 years.

Recently George B. Hartzog, Jr., director of the National Park Service, reported that sonic booms made by supersonic military aircraft are destroying prehistoric ruins in the southwestern United States. In testimony before the House subcommittee on national parks and recreation, Hartzog said that pilots fly above the desert floor in Death Valley National Monument to earn membership in the "I Flew Below Sea Level Club." In this regard, on my last visit to Death Valley, my wife and I were listening to a lecture by the park ranger. Just as he reached a climax of description of the solitude and silence of the desert, a sonic boom shook the building to its foundation. No one laughed.

The desert also is being shaken by nuclear blasts termed "very important" to national defense. The Atomic Energy Commission usually reports no leakage of radiation from these detonations at the Nevada Test Site, but the earth bulges, cracks appear momentarily, and shock waves are felt in Las Vegas and Beatty, Nevada, and in Salt Lake City 350 miles distant. Seismographs register the shocks at a Richter magnitude of 6 to 6.5; a major earthquake rates at 7 or more. Larger shocks are planned for the future.

The cities in the desert are far apart but they influence the desert in many ways. They are, unfortunately, associated with pollution, waste, and vandalism. Desert cities and their people are no worse than cities and people in other parts of the nation, but their effects are felt on a hinterland that until recently was a wilderness of natural beauty.

The large cities are not greatly different from those we know in other parts of the nation. Most have tall buildings, modern banks, giant supermarkets, traffic problems, airports, and atmospheric pollution. Eyesore housing developments, used-car lots, trailer courts, and industrial plants around the urban peripheries exemplify the phenomenon of growth that is characteristic of America.

Salt Lake City, on the edge of the Utah desert, is one of the best-planned cities in the West. The financial and distribution center for much of the Great Basin area, it is notable for its beautiful Temple Square and for being the center of the Mormon religion. Santa Fe, New Mexico, is notable for its Indian culture and Spanish architecture. In contrast, Albuquerque is a commercial city, modern like most eastern cities. Tucson and Phoenix, Arizona, oases for the health seekers, are devoted to tourism, and derive income from electrical industries, copper mining, and crops in the irrigated valleys.

In Nevada, Reno and Las Vegas are noted for their gambling and motel operations and tourism. Boise, the capital of Idaho, at the northern edge of the great sagebrush desert, a military post in 1864, now is a quiet city in the midst of grazing, dairying, fruit-growing, and lumbering communities. Most of the smaller cities and the multitude of towns and villages in the desert have interesting histories. And most now are respectably dull places where people live in peace with one another, away from the turbulent problems and activities of the megalopolis.

The cities, of course, occupy relatively small portions of the desert. But they are bringing a great invasion—people. The agricultural centers are shrinking the desert landscape. As the human dispersion continues, it is creating problems of waste disposal, resource development, highways, power lines, pipelines, and smog. And beyond the western mountains—poised like some gigantic tidal wave—the California coastal metropolitan complex, from Santa Barbara through Los Angeles to San Diego, is bursting through the passes to escape the social tensions and pollution of the urban maelstrom. But with what effect on the desert?

Smog now blows through the pass between San Gorgonio and the San Jacinto Mountains, covering the California Desert with a dirty haze. Phoenix and Tucson are producing their own smog.

And now a giant power-plant complex in the Four Corners area of New Mexico, Arizona, Colorado, and Utah threatens to pollute the air, water, and landscape, which will be strip-mined for coal, in one of the nation's cleanest and most scenic areas.

Man's conquest of the desert is being pressed on other fronts. Scenic pollution by jet planes is one of them. I have waited for hours in the Utah desert for the contrails of transcontinental planes to disappear from the blue sky so I could photograph a scene in its natural beauty without evidence of man's presence. But the condensation trails widen and do not disappear. And what is more serious, recent studies have shown that, for example, a 500-meter-thick contrail sheet increases the infrared emission from the sheet by 18 percent but decreases the solar power through the sheet by 15 percent. Thus, contrail persistence reduces available thermal power at the earth's surface, and modifies the climate and the life cycles of living creatures.

On another front, man is eyeing the desert as a sink for his garbage, radioactive wastes, and combustion products. Unrestricted burning of fields and forests also is contributing to pollution of the desert air. The Oregon seed growers, for example, fire their cereal-grain fields on days approved by the Department of

Air pollution from industry, mining, urban areas, and jet planes is steadily increasing over the desert.

Environmental Quality. And the "smoke management" plan recently developed by the U.S. Forest Service, forest-protection agencies, the forest industry, and the Oregon Department of Environmental Quality coordinates the burning of slash but imposes few restrictions when wind direction is away from populated areas.

When I first visited the desert, more than forty years ago, I never thought of it as a fragile environment. It stretched as far as the eye could see, and its varied terrain, bordered on every side by gray and purple mountains, seemed to be an ageless part of the world. It was not until later, when I had devoted a large part of my life to the professional study of grazing management, that I realized how cattle and sheep had caused much of the barrenness of the desert. From my own studies, and from the research of other scientists, I learned how easily the desert is scarred and how slowly it heals.

Unlike the prairies and the forests in more humid climates, where vegetation renewal begins quickly on disturbed or cut-over areas, the desert is essentially lacking in plant succession. If a desert plant community is denuded and allowed to remain undisturbed, the plants that ultimately return are the offspring of the original species. There is no discrete series of weed, grass, shrub, or tree stages to succeed one another—preparing or ameliorating the soil, or shading the environment for the next stage to follow. The restored community in the desert is the one that was there in the beginning. Its reappearance may take years, or even centuries. Thus, abandoned roads in the desert are not yet healed over after fifty years or more of nonuse.

Motorcycles, dune buggies, and four-wheel-drive vehicles rip up the soil, promote wind and water erosion, and disturb the wild animals of the desert. Bulldozers, tractors pulling anchor chains or cables, and giant root cutters pull down trees and drag unwanted shrubs from the soil to reduce competition with grass so that more livestock can graze. Sagebrush spraying with 2, 4-D generally improves the area temporarily for grazing, since sage competes with grass for moisture in the soil. But killing of the sagebrush also usually makes the grass more accessible for further overgrazing, and it spells "sundown" for the sage grouse, which have long been considered trophy birds by hunters.

At first glance the desert does seem to be unlimited and incapable of destruction. But a closer look reveals the spreading scars of road construction, utility rights-of-way, ghetto campgrounds, city garbage dumps, aqueducts, pipelines, power plants, strip mines, and irrigation facilities. When water comes to the desert, agriculture follows. Then filling stations, and houses, and little towns appear. These grow into larger towns and finally into cities that sprawl out into the desert. Then the silence and tranquillity disappear. These planless movements of humanity and man's expansion of technology are considered by some people to be progress.

The promoters of progress speak of the desert as a wasteland which must be made to bloom for human need. We already have precedents for what happens when the environment is made to bloom. Consider what has happened in the once beautiful Los Angeles Basin—people now are moving out because it no longer is a place for healthy existence. Consider the consequences of constructing the Aswan High Dam on the Nile River. It irrigated the Egyptian desert but it also killed the sardine fisheries in the eastern Mediterranean Sea and bred snails by the billions in the irrigation canals. From the snails parasitic blood flukes, or schistosomes, spread through the Egyptian population.

Other examples of man's "progress" can be cited: the Dust Bowl of the 1930's; the oil spill in the Santa Barbara Channel; the creation and degradation of the Salton Sea; and now, the coal strip-mining and power plants in the deserts of the Southwest. Is the desert destined to be stripped, despoiled, and ravaged for immediate gain before we plan its use and preservation with consideration of all its aspects: biological, sociological, psychological, and economic?

The majority of people come to the desert as an escape from urbanism. But they bring their urbanism with them. The camping boom brings flotillas of trailers and camper vans, and television sets, and electric guitars, and garbage to the crowded park sites. The affluent stay in air conditioned inns to avoid the heat and tribulations of the blowing sands, the laundry problems, and the necessity of cooking meals. To some of these a swimming pool and a cocktail bar are necessities. To others a guided bus tour, or an opportunity to lie in the sun and acquire a tan, are sufficient pleasures. To the motorcyclist the desert offers hills and thrills—trails to climb on roaring machines. And to the vandals the desert offers freedom for garbage dumping, target shooting, and burning the dried thatch from desert palm trees.

Civilization has filled the material wants of millions of people and has left vacuums of time in which they can fulfill desires for new experiences. Many feel a vague but powerful urge to exist, at least temporarily, in a habitat of natural beauty in association with plants, animals, mountains, and sunshine—a world that exists for many of us only in our inner consciousness. In my interviews and contacts with desert visitors I find innumerable people who are searching for breathing space and communication between themselves and nature. To these true lovers of the desert, life is not a conquest of nature for growth or industrial advancement. To them, a beetle, a bird song, or a cherished landscape is a happy moment of escape from the mania of production which now plagues America.

I think of some of the hobbyists as people who appreciate the tangible and intangible values of the desert. They range from snake collectors to rock hounds who find fascinating materials that give them pleasures and memories even after they return home. The original rock hounds, of course, were the grizzled old hermits and prospectors left over from the Gold Rush days, who plodded about with their burros, spending months alone in the desert. They were looking for gold and silver instead of agates, thunder-eggs, opal, and all the other oddities now sought by gem hunters.

The biological attractions of the desert result in many non-consumptive uses, such as viewing, photography, and wild life study. The dollar value of visits for these purposes has been estimated at between $6 and $17 million for the California Desert alone. No one knows the intrinsic value of these visits, which take many forms. Snake and lizard collectors, for example, are numerous, and their activities indicate the growing interest in herpetology. With modern cameras and lenses, photographers record all aspects of the desert, from scenic views and flowers to the activities of birds, mammals, and insects. Other people take paint and canvas and spend hours and days catching the moods of the cactus, the dunes, and the desert mountains.

There are even specialists who take equipment to capture the auditory thrills of the desert. Recently I met a man in the Arizona desert who was intent on recording the voices of birds, coyotes, and other animals. While other people sat around their campfires, he toted his parabolic reflector and sound-recording equipment to the top of a distant knoll. Then, when the shrill, high-pitched *yap-yap-yap* of the coyotes began in the dusk of evening, he focused on the crescendo of greeting that came from coyotes on other hills.

The push to the desert is bound up with ownership of the land, with human pressure from beyond the desert's rim, and with the obsession of the American public for perpetual growth. Conquest of nature seems to be desirable, and since the desert has not yet been despoiled to the extent of the Pacific beaches, the campgrounds of Yosemite Valley, or the redwood forests, it looms as a last frontier for residential retirement developments, industrial expansion, and the commercial growth that accompanies population movements.

It is inevitable that the desert will grow less livable in the future, just as the cities of America are now less livable than they were ten years ago. The population of the eleven western states is expected to double in the next thirty years. The expansion will occur largely on the 175 million acres owned by the federal government—much of it desert land. Federal land managers estimate that a million acres per year will be needed by local governments and business to meet this expansion. Much of this land will be public domain, which is under the control of the Bureau of Land Management of the Department of the Interior. Plans now are being made to classify some 10 million acres for ultimate disposal and to transfer some 3 million acres to local government and private sources during a period of five years.

The designers of these developments are primarily motivated by materialistic concepts. The land speculators, highway builders, and electric-power interests are urging local leaders to press for growth by exploitation of this new environment. A whole cluster of nuclear reactors, for example, has been proposed for the Boeing test site at Boardman in the east-Oregon desert. According to the promoters, water needed to cool the reactors could be used to irrigate thousands of acres of land. But why put this land into crop production while the Department of Agriculture is subsidizing producers throughout the nation to keep thousands of acres idle in order to control surpluses and prices?

On millions of acres controlled by the Bureau of Land Management, management is practically nonexistent because the grazing monopoly helps keep the appropriations low. Grazing permits are obtainable only through inheritance or purchase of property that already has a history of being involved in grazing on federal lands. The fees charged under these permits are priced at only a fraction of the value of grazing on commercial property. In many instances ranchers post "No Trespassing" signs and deny access to the rightful owners—the public—for fishing, hunting, or recreational purposes.

Land grabs and attempted raids on public lands in the western states have been common for many years. Many approaches are used. An example is the recent attempt to trade 109,000 acres of land in the Elko district of Nevada for less than 600 acres of private land needed for the Point Reyes National Seashore north of San Francisco. For each acre owned within the boundaries of the park tract Nevada would lose 187 acres of open-space land to ranchers, developers, or corporations.

One of the tragedies of the desert, and of our whole environment, has been the public acceptance of environmental deterioration and the belief that progress is synonymous with unrestricted use of natural resources. At meetings of national and international societies plenary sessions are held with emphasis on hydrology, mineral resources, land utilization, irrigation, desalinization, and waste-water management. Relatively little emphasis is placed on natural history, the quality of life, or man's need for an unpolluted, un-urbanized environment.

Traditionally people have gone camping to escape the complexity of urban life, to experience a change of scenery, and to enjoy a period of time in natural surroundings only slightly modified by man and his culture. But recent studies indicate that camping now is becoming a social experience. The majority of campers go to highly developed campgrounds. Some go to these congested places because they are afraid of more primitive experiences. Some go because they are acclimated to visiting patterns at home. And some go because they are unaware of the attractions of the natural flora, fauna, geology, or natural history of the desert.

Still others go to congregated areas because of an undefined urge to display their "play world" to other people. Even the facial expressions of water skiers, who end their runs near shore, differ according to the presence or absence of friends and other observers on the shore. For another example, William R. Burch, Jr., in a sociological study of campers, described fire building as an important form of "symbolic labor in the campground." Apparently the campfire not only influences visiting patterns, even among strangers, but wood collecting provides the recreationist with productive work that "legitimizes" his leisure-time activity.

The increasing number of socially oriented campers may not be as destructive to the desert environment as some recreation managers have visualized. The goal of the manager must be to provide recreation for the people who will come, whether their great numbers are desirable or not. By providing highly developed campgrounds for the multitudes who prefer this kind of experience, the more primitive areas with their isolation and beauty will remain slightly used and will provide the quality of recreation desired by the visitor who seeks natural wonders rather than a social experience.

The future of the desert and the preservation of its multitudinous resources is very much in doubt. Man now is inextricably tied to the desert through urbanization, agriculture, exploitation of mineral deposits, manufacturing, and increasing pressure by recreationists. Constantly changing circumstances are altering its social geography. The influx of people from other states, seeking a warm dry climate and an environment still relatively free of pollution and human congestion, is bringing the city syndrome to the desert.

In some areas of the Southwest the dam builders and the well drillers are nearing the end of their exploitation, since there is little additional water in the Colorado River to be used, and the water table under the wells is dropping beyond profitable reach. Industry, mining, agriculture, and people in the Tucson, Arizona, area now are pumping water out of the ground faster than it is being recharged by underground flow. Agriculture, which employs less than 2 percent of the more than one-quarter of a million people in the area, uses nearly half the entire water supply.

Obviously, agriculture in desert areas such as this one will have to move elsewhere, or more efficient use and recycling of water will have to be achieved. Ultimately, water may come from the sea, or there may be revolutionary developments in hydraulic engineering, or rainfall may be increased by cloud seeding. Or the people may rise up in community action, as in Boulder, Colorado, and demand a population ceiling for the area. Whatever happens, there is going to be change in future use and management of the desert.

Protection of the desert is imperative in view of all the pressures on its lands for use by people with many interests. We are beginning to understand the genesis of some of these pressures. And with understanding may come patterns for the education, management, and control of the activities of individuals, industry, and urbanization.

Many of the problems in managing the desert arise from the attitudes of individuals, the strategy of developers, and "environmental illiteracy." Pollution problems, for example, are proliferating with ever-increasing complexity faster than we are solving them. Environmental degradation occurs before we recognize it. Causal relationships between pollution and environmental damage are hard to demonstrate, and many industries are cynical in their promises not to harm the environment. Always there is the motive of maximum profit. And exploitation is constantly predicated on the need for immediate benefit to the local economy, with no thought that the desert is not a continuously recycling life-support system.

Steps now are being taken to preserve the potential of the desert, but many of the efforts are uncoordinated, and some are directed toward solution of problems arising from uses of minor resources. Even these actions are important, since they represent a beginning in the whole field of desert protection. The state of Nevada, for example, now requires that you pass a cram course in trophy hunting before you can receive a permit to hunt and kill a desert bighorn. A trophy ram must be at least seven years old and meet prescribed measurements accepted by most sportsmen and state game departments.

The indoctrination course for hunters drawing a permit requires demonstration of ability to tell the age of rams, based on such criteria as curl and diameter of the horn, shape of the rump, and presence or absence of a knob on the back of the head. This selectivity of hunters, along with the limitation of numbers of permits sold, ensures that older rams will be taken and the young fertile rams will be spared to propagate the herds, which, in Nevada, include some 2,000 desert bighorns.

A broader approach to ultimate nondestructive use of the

desert is the systems-analysis technique now being instituted by personnel of the International Biological Program. Numerous scientists will study terrestrial ecosystems in the Chihuahuan Desert near Las Cruces, New Mexico; in the Sonoran Desert near Tucson, Arizona; in the Great Basin near Milford, Utah; and in the sagebrush vegetation near Richland, Washington. Detailed studies also will be made of plants, herbivorous mammals, birds, insects, and soil organisms involved in the fixation and cycling of nitrogen.

These scientists within a few years hope to predict for all levels of the desert ecosystem the likely effects of any possible modification of the environment. They will do this with data and equations programmed into computers capable of incorporating innumerable reactions from changes in levels of physical and biological factors in the environment. Thus, the effect of removing badgers, snakes, rodents, sagebrush, cactus, or groundwater, or the impact of grazing, mining, camping, road building, or even air pollution can be translated into judgments on how to use desert lands wisely without destroying their character.

The California State Office of the Bureau of Land Management has taken an important step toward management of the desert. The first phase of its effort, called the California Desert Study, was concerned primarily with recreational use of the desert public-domain lands of California. A report on the second phase of the study, "The California Desert . . . A Critical Environmental Challenge," documents the inescapable fact that all resources and uses must be considered in terms of the total desert environment if sound land-management decisions are to be made. Out of this continuing study a Desert Plan can be evolved which will set a pattern for overall use, development, and preservation of one of the great remaining resources of the nation. We need similar plans for all of our American deserts to insure that we do not waste our heritage, but leave it in condition to be passed on to future generations for their physical and spiritual benefit. In our planning to preserve the desert we will have to go beyond its borders to solve some of its major problems.

One of these problems is that everywhere there is smoke and smog. I know where it comes from and where it goes. I have followed it thousands of miles by automobile and in airplanes from the cities across the open country. No longer can we tell our children the fable that the haze of Indian Summer comes from campfires among the tepees. The deadly air pollution all over this country will never permit the air to be clean and pure again until we realize the ecological and physiological consequences of our technology and take action to restore our environment.

APPENDIX

How to See the Desert

Some people go to the desert just to see what it is like. Others go there to be in communion with the spirit of nature, where all of the human senses may come to life. To do this, you must walk upon the desert's sands, gingerly touch its prickly plants, listen to the songs of its birds, and smell the sweetness of its flowers. You must brace yourself against the wind, sit in the shelter of rocks, explore shady canyons, and endure the midday heat to experience the desert's many moods.

To see the desert best, you must travel leisurely, or better still, tarry a while at points of special interest. One look at the rolling dunes, for example, is not enough. You need to see them around the clock: in the rosy dawn, when the animal tracks of night are still visible on their sands; in midmorning, when you can walk on them and become intimate with their forms and intricate ripple marks; in the wind, when sand grains are showering over their cornices, building the massive drifts forward; and at sunset, when the splendid scenic colors slowly surrender to shadows creeping up from the interdunal swales.

A day in cactus land or in Joshua-tree country is not enough. Even a week is insufficient for intimate exploration of the local hills, valleys, rock outcrops, and desert waters. But a week of leisurely wandering will allow you to become better acquainted with the most abundant plants, birds, and reptiles, and the vistas of broad basins and distant mountains.

To reap the rewards of a wide variety of desert environments in a larger territory, you should spend two weeks, or even a month, in such places as Death Valley, or the Organ-Pipe Cactus

National Monument, or the Malheur National Bird Refuge. Spring or autumn, when the weather is fine and wildlife is most active and abundant, are the most rewarding seasons for the serious, intelligent visitor.

To see the many kinds of living things in the desert, you must be abroad at different times of the day or night. But being abroad does not mean that you should be in constant motion. On moonlit nights, if you sit motionless on a blanket or portable stool, you can watch the activities of kangaroo rats, pocket mice, scorpions, coyotes, rabbits, skunks, pack rats, toads, bats, and moths. A silent watch, day or night, near a water hole can be productive, since many desert animals schedule regular visits there for food and drink. Even in the heat of day a silent vigil in the shade of rocks or trees will reveal the presence of birds, mammals, reptiles, and insects that would remain unnoticed if you were in motion. When you have been looking for an hour, some of these will materialize out of apparent nothingness, and you will realize that they have been there all the time, maybe looking at you.

To find these tranquil places, you must get off the freeway, from which you get only flickering glances at the land. Budget some time to go the long way around. Follow the back roads that wander along the contours of the slopes, spiral up mountainsides, or meander across the flats. Linger a while to watch a rainstorm as the black clouds gather and the raindrops come down in such torrents that the dry washes become turbulent rivers. The fury of the storm is something to be remembered. And so is the fragrance of the clean air when the rain stops and the clouds open to let the sunlight flash down from a glorious blue sky onto green and yellow slopes and vermillion cliffs. Then the red, yellow, and white cactus flowers seem more beautiful than roses.

If you camp in the desert, even in summer, expect some of the nights to be cool. Winter in the southern deserts has many nippy nights, but you sleep well, and wake to the tang of balmy mornings and sunny days. Winter in the northern deserts has many exhilarating days for hiking and observing birds and other wildlife. But camping there is only for the rugged, experienced adventurer, and you should be forewarned that blizzards may howl out of the north, bringing death with freezing winds that sometimes blow unceasingly for several days and nights. Spring is the best time to see the northern deserts, for then the profusion of green growth and wild flowers is at its best.

DESERT SURVIVAL

There are dangers in the desert. There are rattlesnakes, scorpions, stinging insects, floods, treacherous sands, rocks, heat, and dryness. But these cannot compare with the dangers on our highways and in the cities, where the ugliness of mugging, theft, murder, smog, noise, and confusion are always present. Automobiles in the United States kill hundreds of people each week, more than die in many years from all the natural dangers in the desert. Bees kill more people annually than all the snakes in the nation. Still, fatalities do occur in the desert, largely because people do not prepare for a safe and enjoyable experience in this different environment.

If you are going into strange country, the best principle is to avoid danger instead of experiencing the nightmare of extricating yourself from a difficult situation. Your car or other vehicle should receive careful consideration—its wheels are better than your legs for getting out of the desert, especially if you go far into the back country. See that your motor and tires are in excellent condition before you start. And take an extra supply of water for the radiator.

You should never venture into the desert without an axe, a shovel, tow rope, tire pump, water cans, extra oil, and a set of tools and equipment for minor repairs. On many occasions I have used my shovel to dig sand away from my car and to smooth paths over the banks of dry washes to avoid high centering. Once, during the night, a pack rat built a stick nest between the motor and the radiator of my truck. When the motor started, the fan belt broke, and tools were necessary to install the spare fan belt which I always carry in desert country. I also look at the motor before I start it in the morning.

When driving unfamiliar roads, remember that the length and steepness of slopes can be deceiving; if your motor starts to lug, shift to a lower gear. If it heats, stop, turn into the wind, and let it idle while you dash water on the radiator. And do not drive down a slope so steep that you cannot climb out again. If there is vapor lock, place wet rags on the fuel pump. And if you are driving in loose sand, do not reduce the air pressure in tubeless tires to flatten them for better traction. Tubeless tires with low pressure will come off the rims.

Carry a map on trips away from the main highways. Study the terrain, roads, streams, hills, mountains, and distances traveled. Orient yourself with these features and know where you are at all times. Look back frequently so that you will recognize the country on your return trail—this applies especially when you are walking. If your car fails, your map will indicate the direction and shortest distance to travel for help. But do not walk unless you are certain that other travelers or rescuers will not come your way.

Walking in the hot desert, even for pleasure, is more efficient if you follow a few rules for saving energy and avoiding excessive water loss. When air temperature exceeds body temperature, the body tends to keep cool by sweating. If the moisture lost by sweat evaporation exceeds 5 percent of body weight, thirst is followed by nausea, dizziness, difficult breathing, and heart pounding. Dehydration beyond 15 percent may be fatal. In order to avoid dehydration a man may drink as much as two gallons of water per day when the maximum temperature is 120° F.; without water he can expect to live for two days.

On the hot desert walking is best done in the morning and after 6:00 P.M. Even if you are in good physical condition, walk slowly, go around obstructions instead of over them, avoid climbing steep slopes, and rest a few minutes each quarter of an hour. When walking in sand, lean forward, keep your knees slightly bent, place the whole foot on the sand, and clasp your hands behind your back to save the energy that otherwise would be expended in swinging your arms.

Wear loose-fitting clothes in the desert, to hold down sweat evaporation. Rest in the shade, and if you must lie down, do it off the ground by reclining on a bush or pile of shrubbery, if it is available. Temperatures above the ground may be 50° cooler than at the surface. Take salt tablets sparingly, even if water is available, since excessive amounts of salt can reduce sweating and body cooling. Eating while walking in high temperatures also diverts water needed for sweating. Alcohol greatly increases dehydration and should be avoided.

Among the greatly exaggerated dangers of the desert are the poisonous creatures, which have been the subject of superstitions and misunderstanding for many years. There are snakes, scorpions, spiders, Gila monsters, ants, wasps, bees, and bugs in the desert, and the careless person can be injured by some of these. But most of the poisonous creatures, excepting the rattlesnakes and a few species of scorpions, cause only temporary pain and inconvenience. Even the bite of the large desert centipede, although painful, is not cause for intense fright or hysteria. Bathing its bite, and those of some of the insect stings, in ammonia will bring relief, and an antiseptic such as iodine will reduce the likelihood of infection.

Scorpions should be avoided by refraining from picking up rocks or boards with bare hands. Boots should be worn when you are abroad at night, since at that time scorpions are on the surface of the ground searching for prey. Only two scorpions in Arizona are deadly, but there are several in Mexico. The scorpion sting causes restlessness, increased heart rate, and difficult breathing. The recommended treatment includes application of a tourniquet for a few minutes, between the area of the sting and the heart, and cooling of the sting area with ice packs. Scorpion antivenin is available in hospitals, and if the injured person is a child, medical attention should be sought immediately.

The large hairy tarantulas are among the most interesting and least harmful of the desert spiders. Many children keep them as pets, and if they are teased to bite, the principal danger is from bacterial infection. The black widow spider, however, which is widespread throughout the United States, has a painful bite which can cause death. The black widow is glossy black. On the underside of the round abdomen is a bright red spot shaped like an hourglass. This spider and the brown recluse spider, with the violin-shaped spot on the head end, should be avoided by using care in and around outhouses, old buildings, and piles of clothing. In campgrounds the undersides of the seats in pit toilets should be examined, since this is a favorite place for web spinning to catch flies attracted by odors.

I have seen no records of fatalities caused by coral snakes in the desert. This type of snake, although poisonous, is so small that an adult person would have to insert a finger in its mouth in order to be bitten. Rattlesnakes, however, are a danger in many parts of the United States as well as in the western and southwestern states and Mexico. More than fifteen kinds of rattlesnakes live in the desert, and the best procedure is to take reasonable precautions to avoid them and to respect them when you see them.

Protective clothing, especially leather boots, is insurance

against most snakebites on the feet and lower legs. Another precaution is to look before you step and never to climb over rocks or ledges by placing your hands above your head without looking. At night, walk with a flashlight to see if rattlesnakes are lying in your path. And at all times avoid walking near bushes where rattlesnakes may be curled up in sleep. On sandy areas do not place your hands on the ground or sit near bushes without checking for sidewinders, which like to bury themselves during the day.

If you go afield in the desert, carry a suction-type snakebite kit and know how to use it before the necessity arises. This involves use of a tourniquet, making incisions through or near the fang punctures, and applying suction to the cuts. The patient should receive medical help as soon as possible.

Cryotherapy, which involves keeping the bitten hand or other member of the body in ice or iced water, is not recommended by the majority of medical authorities. Keeping the injured part cool (40° to 50° F.) may be of some value in slowing circulation, but should not be prolonged in view of the already oxygen-deficient tissues.

Although some of the snakes and other creatures of the desert are poisonous, most of the animals are harmless and have their place in the delicate adjustment of nature. If you know some of the basic principles of outdoorsmanship, keep your self-reliance, and remain observant, you should have little fear of the desert. If you go prepared, travel there can be an interesting and enjoyable experience.

THINGS AND PLACES TO SEE

The desert is so vast, and people who wish to see it have such varied interests, that only a few items for the inquisitive traveler can be listed here. Almost anywhere along the highways, outstanding vistas and scenic values are present. Even with a short stop you can examine the varied plant life and the beauty of desert flowers, shrubs, and trees. Some of the birds, insects, and common daytime animals are nearly always present. And with the aid of tourist guides and maps, short journeys away from the superhighways will lead you to desert lakes, streams, Indian ruins, unusual geologic formations, ghost towns, and points of historic interest. Of course, if you are environmentally oriented, you will want to extend your visit for days or even weeks to deepen your understanding of the desert, to acquire intimate knowledge of some of its principles, processes, and creatures, and to experience its ever-changing moods.

For these longer visits there are national parks and monuments dedicated exclusively to the desert. Numerous wildlife refuges maintained for wildlife conservation and administered by the Bureau of Sport Fisheries and Wildlife of the Department of the Interior provide exceptional opportunities to see resident and migratory birds, small mammals, and, in some instances, larger mammals such as desert bighorns. Other outstanding areas for observation and study of desert life are maintained as museums, parks, and recreational areas by states, counties, and private organizations. Private clubs, associations, and other groups—for example, rock-hound organizations—maintain lists of tours and localities of interest to their members.

If you intend to explore the appealing land of the desert, you should obtain guidebooks and maps with emphasis on the places and things you want to see and do. These are available in such variety as to satisfy the needs of almost any visitor in the western deserts. For an overall picture of the recreation possibilities in the desert, try to obtain a copy of *Room to Roam—A Recreation Guide to the Public Lands,* published by the U.S. Department of the Interior, Bureau of Land Management, Washington, D.C. This is available from the Superintendent of Documents, U.S. Government Printing Office, Washington, D.C., 20402, for 75¢. This publication contains a long list of places of interest in the West, keyed to regional maps showing main highways, rivers, and larger cities. Another useful reference is *Guides to Outdoor Recreation Areas and Facilities,* published by the Department of the Interior, Bureau of Outdoor Recreation, Washington, D.C., 20240. This is not a guidebook, but a listing of guidebooks and publications for broad regions and for each state. It gives addresses of private, state, and federal organizations, along with prices of guides, if there is a charge.

If you want information about national parks and monuments, write to the Public Inquiry Section, National Park Service, Washington, D.C., 20240. For information about state-owned campgrounds, write to the Tourism Bureau, State Capital, at the capital city. For details about dam and watershed projects and campgrounds, write to the Technical Liaison Officer, Department of the Army, Office of the Chief Engineer, Washington, D.C., 20315. Outdoor guides and campground atlases are available in wide variety at bookstores and magazine stands, and from some of the major oil companies. These tabulations include descriptions of many local historical, biological, and recreational areas.

The desert areas described in the following pages represent only a few of the places where you may go to acquire an initial acquaintance with the desert. If you become a desert lover, you will go on from these to search out new vistas and attractions in the hinterlands far from the noise, tension, and technology of modern civilization.

ARIZONA

Here you will find desert as most Americans visualize it. A good place to start is at the Arizona-Sonora Desert Museum in Tucson Mountain Park, fourteen miles west of Tucson. A day or two spent in examination of the plants and animals native to the Sonoran Desert will give you knowledge of desert wildlife that would require years of searching in the wilderness. In this outdoor museum you can see foxes, coyotes, peccaries, coatimundis, boogum trees, cacti, rodents, and underground exhibits of ants, prairie dogs, and snakes. Many of the desert birds also can be seen close up. For field acquaintance with the desert, visit the Saguaro National Monument and roam among the giant cacti, where woodpeckers, lizards, jackrabbits, and colorful lizards abound. For fantastic scenic displays of Sonoran Desert vegetation and panoramas of mountains and plains, see the Organ-Pipe Cactus National Monument on the border between the United States and Mexico. This is 140 miles south of Phoenix and 142 miles west of Tucson. Here you can see organ-pipe cactus, teddybear cholla, barrel cactus, cat's-claw, mesquite, ironwood, and a multitude of showy forbs in season. The cactus wrens nest in the chollas beside your trailer, and white-winged doves scurry over the ground. If you take the Puerto Blanco Drive you will follow historic trails, see desert springs, and see a great variety of birds at the man-made oasis at Quitobaquito. In this arid region you can sense the variety of the desert and the impact of human use by shopping in Nogales, in Sonora, Mexico, or by visiting the Santa Catalina Mountains, Salt River Valley, Yaqui and Papago villages, San Xavier Mission, the large copper mines, and the

Santa Rita Experimental Range. Prehistoric Indian cliff dwellings are present in Canyon de Chelly National Monument. The Petrified Forest National Monument near Holbrook has large fields of petrified logs in the midst of the Painted Desert, a stark land of colored rocks. Kofa Game Refuge near Yuma supports some 400 bighorns in rugged mountains that rise sharply above the desert.

CALIFORNIA

California has a great variety of desert habitats ranging from the endless miles of creosote bush in the Mohave Desert to the spectacular Joshua trees, to the parched lands below sea level in Death Valley and around the Salton Sea. The Joshua Tree National Monument is habitat for plants and animals of both Great Basin and Sonoran desert affinities. Spectacular wild-flower displays occur on sandy soils in rainy seasons. Mesquite, ocotillo, and California fan palms add variety to the landscape. Rocks of several geological eras are exposed, including Pinto gneiss and gray or pinkish quartz monzonite. Animals range in size from antelope ground squirrels and side-blotched lizards to desert bighorns. Death Valley, lowest point on the continent, and possibly the hottest spot in the world in summer, supports 600 kinds of plants and many animals specialized for life in a harsh environment. Evidences of prehistoric man and of early mining activities, including borax production, are widespread. All of the great divisions of geologic time and most of their subdivisions, along with recent volcanism, are available for study. Pupfish, survivors of fish in prehistoric lakes, swim in Salt Creek. Anza-Borrego Desert State Park includes one of California's last frontiers— weird, colorful, and still primitive. Here are elephant trees, canyons, springs, volcanic hills, pictographs, and wild burros on the borders of Clark Lake. Lesser areas of interest are Salton Sea State Park near Mecca, 200 feet below sea level; Palm Canyon, Palm Springs, and Kelso Sand Dunes on the Mohave Desert. Other dunes occur near El Centro and Yuma, Arizona.

IDAHO

Thousands of square miles are covered with sagebrush on the Snake River Plains in southern Idaho. This is productive grazing country, since many grasses and colorful forbs mingle with the pigmy forests of sage. West of the Teton Range lava outcrops occur in many places. The Craters of the Moon National Monument near Arco is a volcanic area of craters, caves, and lava flows. The Bruneau Sand Dunes, 15 miles south of Mountain Home, also are of interest because they reach a height of 425 feet. In general, the sagebrush lands of Idaho have a more luxuriant vegetation than those of the Great Basin owing to the abundance of bluebunch wheatgrass, Idaho fescue, and western wheatgrass.

NEVADA

This is the land of sagebrush, shadscale, winterfat, and Mormon tea. It is also the land of parallel mountain ranges separated by long slopes extending down from the foothills to ancient lake beds that are miles and miles across. The vistas are magnificent. Wildlife varies from a multitude of birds to pack rats, coyotes, rabbits, pronghorns, and desert bighorns. The waters of the state contain a fascinating variety of fish, including the cui-ui of Pyramid Lake. Anaho Island in this lake is the breeding ground for thousands of white pelicans and multitudes of California gulls. The Desert Game Refuge near Las Vegas supports one of the largest desert bighorn populations in existence. Sheldon National Antelope Refuge in Washoe County has a large pronghorn population. If you drive south toward Beatty, Nevada, on the way to Death Valley, you will see Joshua trees, indicating the gradual transition from the Great Basin Desert vegetation to the Mohave Desert environment. Lake Mead National Recreation Area in Nevada and Arizona has a length of 115 miles at maximum capacity of the reservoir. This lake, and Mohave Lake behind Davis Dam, present attractions for fishermen and water enthusiasts.

NEW MEXICO

There is much of history here, beginning with the legend of the Seven Cities of Cibola, which attracted Spanish explorers. The many mission churches testify to early explorations of the desert. During the seventeenth and eighteenth centuries New Mexico was the heart of the Spanish empire in the Southwest. In the mosaic of scenery you can see the desert grasslands in the eastern part of the state and on the uplands, where grama and other grasses grow in dense stands. Westward, the exotic plants of the desert become numerous. Along U.S. Highway 66 you can see olive-green creosote bushes, mesquite trees, cacti, yuccas, Apache plumes, and century plants. Don't look for saguaro cacti— you'll see them in Arizona. But there are 400 species of birds, including roadrunners and 5 kinds of doves. The White Sands National Monument in Tularosa Basin contains the largest known gypsum desert in the world. Plants are remarkably adapted to life among the wavelike dunes. Fourwing saltbush and iodine bush are common here. Some of the animals are bleached to blend with their gypsum background. In contrast, similar animals in the awesome black wasteland of the Carrizozo malpais have dark pelages for camouflage in the black, rough-surfaced lava. Since bats are well represented in the desert, the place to see them in swarms is the famous Carlsbad Caverns, where some 15 species live. Ancient pueblo ruins may be seen at Gran Quivira, Abo, and Quarai.

OREGON

Much of eastern Oregon is sagebrush country. The dry bed of Alford Lake, east of Steens Mountain, is an extensive alkali flat, mostly devoid of vegetation. Local areas in southeastern Oregon also are dominated by greasewood, with bare ground between the shrubs. Wind and water erosion exposes many Indian arrow points and other artifacts made of obsidian. Pronghorns, jackrabbits, badgers, skunks, and other small mammals live in these desert lands. Mule deer come down from the bordering mountains to spend the winter. Marshlands and small lakes in this section of the desert attract thousands of geese, ducks, and gulls, along with grebes, great blue herons, and yellow-headed blackbirds. Desert plants, mammals, and birds can be seen, especially in the Malheur Wildlife Refuge and in the vicinity of Hart Mountain Wildlife Refuge east of Lakeview, Oregon. The lava fields, volcanic cones, and ice caves south and east of Bend, Oregon, tell the story of recent geological formations. The road between Burns, Oregon, and McDermit, Nevada, offers unexcelled vistas of unbroken sagebrush stands that cover the rolling hills for dozens of miles. Along the road from Bend to Burns you can see classical examples of the transition from juniper forests to sagebrush desert. Bobcats, coyotes, doves, and quail abound in this area.

TEXAS

In most of Texas grassland originally dominated the landscape. Short-grass prairie characterized the Panhandle area, and farther south and east stands of tall-grass prairie alternated with forests in the area known as the Cross Timbers. In western Texas desert grassland characterizes the nonmountainous landscape. The Monahans Sands, near Monahans on U.S. 80 in the western part of the state, are desertlike dunes. The best examples of desert terrain in Texas are found in Big Bend National Park along the sweeping bend of the Rio Grande River between the United States and Mexico. This is one of the wildest unspoiled areas left in the United States. Parts of the area still are virtually unexplored. Large canyons, volcanic rock formations, semiarid plains, arroyos, washes, and mountain belts provide habitats for many life zones, including desert cactus communities. Desert scrub covers large areas but is not monotonous. Desert grassland occurs on the lower slopes of the Chisos Mountains. Chinograss (*Bouteloua breviseta*) and sotol are characteristic. Creosote bush, various yuccas, ocotillo, lechuguilla, and annual flower gardens in the rainy season add to the variety of plants characteristic of the Chihuahuan Desert.

UTAH

Utah has a great variety of desert habitats that vary from the barren lands of the Bonneville Salt Flats west of Salt Lake City to endless miles of Great Basin Desert dominated by big sagebrush. Scattered over the desert province are many spectacular geologic formations. The Arches National Monument, north across the Colorado River from the picturesque old Mormon pioneer town of Moab, has many stone arches, windows, spires, and pinnacles. These weird forms have been carved by running water, wind, rain, frost, and heat. Many kinds of birds, rodents, and small reptiles provide interesting material for nature study. The Canyon Lands National Park and the Indian ruins at Hovenweep National Park provide worthwhile diversions for the desert traveler. And the brooding stone monoliths of Monument Valley in the land of the Navajo Indians produce unforgettable memories of desert scenery. Of course, Great Salt Lake, more than one-quarter pure salt, is the remnant of that gigantic prehistoric Lake Bonneville which once covered most of the Great Basin. Bear River Migratory Bird Refuge, on the delta of Bear River where it empties into Great Salt Lake, reminds us that water still flows into the desert. Visitors at the refuge can drive around the dike roads and see millions of ducks, geese, grebes, and shorebirds in season. Some 20,000 whistling swans may be present in mid-October. Herons, egrets, gulls, muskrats, beavers, jackrabbits, skunks, and badgers also are found here.

WASHINGTON

The northern rim of the desert occurs in eastern Washington, where sagebrush mingles with the grasses of the once magnificent Palouse Prairie. The prairie has been plowed and planted to wheat, but the sagebrush-grass community of the ecotone, or transition zone, between prairie and desert persists as remnants on the stony hills and flats of the scablands, around the dry falls of Grand Coulee, along the steep slopes above the Yakima River, and in the Horse Heaven Hills west of Kennewick and south of Prosser. The Ginkgo Petrified Forest, near Ellensburg, contains the greatest number of petrified species found anywhere and is a reminder that the place has not always been an arid land.

WYOMING

The lower elevations of the Wyoming Basin in the southwest quarter of the state and the Bighorn Basin west of the Bighorn Mountains resemble the Great Basin in their aridity and vegetation. Annual precipitation averages less than ten inches, the soils are alkaline, and the dry depressions support greasewood and other alkali-tolerant shrubs. On the lighter soils enriched with lime or gypsum, which may develop into a caliche hardpan, the vegetation is mostly sagebrush or shadscale. Shale outcrops are common, and where parent material produces sand, dunes develop. A good example is the dune country some thirty-four miles north of Rock Springs. East and west of Wamsutter along U.S. Highway 30 the soils are red and the area is known as the

Red Desert. Many pronghorns can be seen from the road in this part of Wyoming. Sage grouse also are abundant on the brush-covered hills. The Continental Divide crosses this desert, but the topographic relief is so gentle that few people are aware of it unless they see the sign near the highway. The transition from midcontinent prairie to desert also is gradual and extends over a distance of many miles.

MEXICO

Much of Mexico consists of mountains and high plateaus. The northern highlands extend approximately 700 miles south from the borders of Arizona, New Mexico, and western Texas. This is a dry region with mountains and arid plains, which vary from nearly pure sand desert through extensive growths of organ-pipe cactus and saguaros to thorny shrubs and grassy plains with scattered trees. The Baja California region has few good roads, although with proper equipment it is possible to drive from Ensenada to La Paz. The coastal region is extremely arid and is characterized by many kinds of cacti, including the giant cardón, which reaches a height of sixty feet. Regular camping facilities as we know them are absent in the Mexican deserts, and there are risks in traveling in this rugged and unfamiliar region. It is best not to go alone with a single vehicle, and it is essential to carry ample gasoline, water, and food. For fantastic scenery, weird plants, and unusual animals this desert is unexcelled by any other on the North American continent.

BIBLIOGRAPHY

American Ornithologists' Union. *Check-list of North American Birds.* Baltimore: Lord Baltimore Press, Inc., 1957.

Andrewes, Christopher. *The Lives of Wasps and Bees.* New York: American Elsevier Publishing Company, 1969.

Aneshansley, Daniel J., and Eisner, Thomas. "Biochemistry at 100° C.; Explosive Secretory Discharge of Bombardier Beetles (*Brachinus*)." *Science,* 165:61–63, 1969.

Anonymous. *Poisonous Snakes of the World: A Manual for Use by U.S. Amphibious Forces.* Department of the Navy, Bureau of Medicine and Surgery. U.S. Government Printing Office, Washington, D.C.: 1965.

Axelrod, Daniel I. "Climate and Evolution in Western North America during Middle Pliocene Time." *Evolution,* 2:127–144, 1948.

Barbour, Michael G. "Age and Space Distribution of the Desert Shrub *Larrea divaricata.*" *Ecology,* 50:679–685, 1969.

Bartholomew, George A., and Dawson, William R. "Body Temperature and Water Requirements in the Mourning Dove, *Zenaidura macroura marginella.*" *Ecology,* 35:181–187, 1954.

———— "Temperature Regulation in Desert Mammals." In *Desert Biology,* edited by G. W. Brown, Jr., vol. 1, pp. 395–421. New York: Academic Press, 1968.

Beatley, Janice C. "Dependence of Desert Rodents on Winter Annuals and Precipitation." *Ecology,* 50:721–724, 1969.

———— "Survival of Winter Annuals in the Northern Mohave Desert." *Ecology,* 48:745–750, 1967.

Behle, William H. *The Bird Life of Great Salt Lake.* Salt Lake City: University of Utah Press, 1958.

Benson, Lyman. *The Cacti of Arizona.* Illus. by Lucretia Breazeale Hamilton. Tucson: University of Arizona Press, 1969.

———— *The Native Cacti of California.* Stanford: Stanford University Press, 1969.

Benson, Seth B. "Concealing Coloration among Some Desert Rodents of the Southwestern United States." *University of California Publications in Zoology,* 40:1–70, 1933.

Bentley, P. J. "Adaptations of Amphibia to Arid Environments." *Science,* 152:619–623, 1966.

Borror, Donald J., and De Long, Dwight M. *An Introduction to the Study of Insects* (rev. ed.). New York: Holt, Rinehart and Winston, 1964.

249

Brame, Arden H., Jr. "A New Species of *Batrachoseps* (Slender salamander) from the Desert of Southern California." *Contributions in Science*, Los Angeles County Museum of Natural History, no. 200, November 13, 1970.

Brandt, Herbert. *Arizona and Its Bird Life*. Cleveland: The Bird Research Foundation, 1951.

Brogan, Phil F. *East of the Cascades* (3rd ed.). Portland, Oregon: Binfords & Mort, Publishers, 1965.

Brown, G. W., Jr. (ed.). *Desert Biology*, vol. 1. New York: Academic Press, 1968.

Brown, James H., and Bartholomew, George A. "Periodicity and Energetics of Torpor in the Kangaroo Mouse, *Microdipodops pallidus*." *Ecology*, 50:705–709, 1969.

Buechner, H. K. *The Bighorn Sheep in the United States: Its Past, Present and Future*. Wildlife Society Monograph, no. 4, 1960.

Bureau of Land Management. *The California Desert—A Recreation Study of the Desert Public Domain Lands of California*. Prepared by the California State Office of the Bureau of Land Management and the Western Regional Office of the National Park Service, 1968.

Carlisle, D. B. "Triops (Entomostraca) Eggs Killed Only by Boiling." *Science*, 161:279, 1968.

Carpenter, C. C. "Patterns of Social Behavior in the Desert Iguana, *Dipsosaurus dorsalis*." *Copeia*: 396–405, 1961.

Carter, F. "Bird Life at Twentynine Palms." *Condor*, 39:210–219, 1937.

Cloudsley-Thompson, J. L. *Desert Life*. New York: Pergamon Press, 1965.

———— *Spiders, Scorpions, Centipedes, and Mites*. New York: Pergamon Press, 1958.

Cole, Arthur C., Jr. *Pogonomyrmex Harvester Ants—A Study of the Genus in North America*. Knoxville: University of Tennessee Press, 1968.

Costello, David F. *The World of the Ant*. Philadelphia: J. B. Lippincott Company, 1968.

Cowles, Raymond B. "Observations on the Winter Activities of Desert Reptiles." *Ecology*, 22:125–140, 1941.

Darrah, William Culp. *Powell of the Colorado*. Princeton: Princeton University Press, 1969.

Dawson, W. R.; Shoemaker, V. H.; and Licht, P. "Evaporative Water Losses of Some Small Australian Lizards." *Ecology*, 47:589–594, 1966.

Dayton, William. "Important Western Browse Plants." U.S. Department of Agriculture, Miscellaneous Publication, no. 101. Washington, D.C.: 1931.

Dodge, Natt N. *Flowers of the Southwest Deserts*. Globe, Arizona: Southwestern Monuments Association, 1965.

———— *Poisonous Dwellers of the Desert*. Globe, Arizona: Southwestern Monuments Association, 1968.

Dunbier, Roger. *The Sonoran Desert: Its Geography, Economy, and People*. Tucson: University of Arizona Press, 1968.

Emerson, Fred W. "An Ecological Reconnaissance on the White Sands, New Mexico." *Ecology*, 16:226–233, 1935.

Emmel, Thomas C. and John F. "Selection and Host Plant Overlap in Two Desert Papilio Butterflies." *Ecology*, 50:158–159, 1969.

Farb, Peter. *Face of North America: The Natural History of a Continent*. New York: Harper & Row, Publishers, 1963.

Fautin, R. W. "Biotic Communities of the Northern Desert Shrub Biome in Western Utah." *Ecological Monographs*, 16:251–310, 1946.

Fenneman, N. M. *Physiography of the Western United States*. New York: McGraw-Hill Book Company, 1931.

Ferris, Roxana S. *Death Valley Wildflowers*. Death Valley, California: Death Valley Natural History Association, 1962.

Gregor, Howard F. "Push to the Desert." *Science*, 129:1329–1339, 1959.

Hadley, Neil F., and Williams, Stanley C. "Surface Activities of Some North American Scorpions in Relation to Feeding." *Ecology*, 49: 726–734. 1968.

Hall, E. Raymond. *Mammals of Nevada*. Berkeley: University of California Press, 1946.

———— and Kelson, K. R. *The Mammals of North America*, 2 vols. New York: The Ronald Press, 1959.

Heinrich, Bernd. "Thoracic Temperature Stabilization by Blood Circulation in a Free-flying Moth. *Science*, 168:580–582, 1970.

Heizer, Robert F., and Napton, Lewis K. "Biological and Cultural Evidence from Prehistoric Human Coprolites." *Science*, 165:563–568, 1969.

Hirth, Harold F.; Pendleton, Robert C.; King, Arthur C.; and Downard, Thomas R. "Dispersal of Snakes from a Hibernaculum in Northwestern Utah. *Ecology*, 50:332–339, 1969.

Hunt, Charles B. *Physiography of the United States*. San Francisco: W. H. Freeman and Company, 1967.

Jaeger, Edmund C. *The California Deserts* (4th ed.). Stanford: Stanford University Press, 1965.

———— *Desert Wild Flowers*. Stanford: Stanford University Press, 1968.

———— *Desert Wildlife*. Stanford: Stanford University Press, 1961.

———— *The North American Deserts*. Stanford: Stanford University Press, 1957.

Kavanau, J. Lee, and Ramos, J. "Roadrunners: Activity of Captive Individuals." *Science*, 169:780–782, 1970.

Klauber, Laurence M. *Rattlesnakes: Their Habits, Life Histories, and Influence on Mankind*, 2 vols. Berkeley and Los Angeles: University of California Press, 1956.

Krutch, Joseph Wood. *The Desert Year*. New York: William Sloane Associates, 1952.

LaRivers, Ira. *Fishes and Fisheries of Nevada*. Reno: Nevada State

Fish and Game Commission, 1962.

Larson, Peggy. *Deserts of America.* Englewood Cliffs, N.J.: Prentice-Hall, Inc., 1970.

Little, Elbert L., Jr. *Southwestern Trees—A Guide to the Native Species of New Mexico and Arizona.* U.S. Department of Agriculture, Agricultural Handbook no. 9. Washington, D.C.: 1950.

Livingston, B. E., and Shreve, Forrest. *The Distribution of Vegetation in the United States, as Related to Climatic Conditions.* Carnegie Institution of Washington, Publication no. 284. Washington, D.C.: 1921.

Mann, John. "Cactus-Feeding Insects and Mites." Smithsonian Institution, United States National Museum, Bulletin no. 256. Washington, D.C.: 1969.

Meinertzhagen, Richard. "The Speed and Altitude of Bird Flight." *Ibis,* 97:81–117, 1955.

Miller, Alden H., and Stebbins, Robert C. *The Lives of Desert Animals in Joshua Tree National Monument.* Berkeley: University of California Press, 1964.

McDougall, W. B., and Sperry, Omer E. "Plants of Big Bend National Park." National Park Service, U.S. Department of the Interior. Washington, D.C.: 1951.

McGinnies, William G.; Goldman, Bram J.; and Paylore, Patricia (eds.). *Deserts of the World—An Appraisal of Research into Their Physical and Biological Environments.* Tucson: The University of Arizona Press, 1968.

Nichols, U. G. "Habits of the Desert Tortoise, *Gopherus agassizi.*" *Herpetologica,* 9:65–69, 1953.

Norris, K. S. *Lizard Ecology: A Symposium.* Columbia: University of Missouri Press, 1967.

Ohmart, Robert D., and Lasiewski, Robert C. "Roadrunners: Energy Conservation by Hypothermia and Absorption of Sunlight." *Science,* 172:67–69, 1971.

Parker, Horace. *Anza-Borrego Desert Guide Book.* Balboa Island, California: Paisano Press, Inc., 1969.

Pond, Alonzo W. *The Desert World.* New York: Thomas Nelson & Sons, 1962.

Rosenzweig, Michael L., and Winakur, Jerald. "Population Ecology of Desert Rodent Communities: Habitats and Environmental Complexity. *Ecology,* 50:558–572, 1969.

Schmidt-Nielsen, K.; Schmidt-Nielsen, B.; Jarnum, S. A.; and Houpt, T. R. "Body Temperature of the Camel and Its Relation to Water Economy." *American Journal of Physiology,* 188:103–112, 1957.

Shreve, Forrest. *Vegetation of the Sonoran Desert.* Carnegie Institution of Washington, Publication no. 591. Washington, D.C.: 1951.

———— and Livingston, B. E. *See under* Livingston.

————and Wiggins, Ira L. *Vegetation and Flora of the Sonoran Desert.* Stanford: Stanford University Press, 1964.

Sigler, William F., and Miller, Robert Rush. *Fishes of Utah.* Salt Lake City: Utah State Department of Fish and Game, 1963.

Skaife, S. H. *Dwellers in Darkness*. Garden City, N.Y.: Doubleday & Company, Inc., 1961.

Smith, Ronald E. *The Natural History of the Prairie Dog in Kansas*. Topeka, Kansas: Museum of Natural History and State Biological Survey Miscellaneous Publication no. 16, June 1958, and no. 49 (with addenda by Stephen R. Wylie), Sept. 1967.

Stansbury, Howard. *Exploration and Survey of the Valley of the Great Salt Lake of Utah*. Philadelphia: Lippincott, Grambo and Co., 1852.

Steenbergh, Warren F., and Lowe, Charles H. "Critical Factors During the First Years of Life of the Saguaro (*Cereus giganteus*) at Saguaro National Monument, Arizona." *Ecology* 50:825–834, 1969.

Strong, Emory. *Stone Age in the Great Basin*. Portland, Oregon: Binfords & Mort, Publishers, 1969.

Sutton, Ann and Myron. *The Life of the Desert*. New York: McGraw-Hill Book Company, 1966.

Tevis, Lloyd, Jr. "Interrelations between the Harvester Ant *Veromessor pergandei* (Mayr) and Some Desert Ephemerals." *Ecology*, 39:695–704, 1958.

Turner, Raymond M.; Alcorn, Stanley M.; and Olin, George. "Mortality of Transplanted Saguaro Seedlings." *Ecology*, 50:835–844, 1969.

Vorhies, C. T. "Water Requirements of Desert Animals in the Southwest." University of Arizona Technical Bulletin no. 107. Tucson: 1945.

Walker, Boyd W. (ed.). "The Ecology of the Salton Sea, California, in Relation to the Sportfishery." Sacramento: State of California, Department of Fish and Game, Fish Bulletin no. 113. (1961)

Weesner, Frances M. *The Termites of the United States—A Handbook*. Elizabeth, New Jersey: The National Pest Control Association, 1965.

Welles, Ralph E. and Florence B. "The Bighorn of Death Valley." National Park Service, *Fauna of the National Parks of the United States:* Fauna Series no. 6. Washington, D.C.: 1961.

Weniger, Del. *Cacti of the Southwest*. Austin: University of Texas, 1970.

Went, F. W. "Fungi Associated with Stalactite Growth." *Science*, 166:385–386, 1969.

Wheelock, Walt (ed.). *Desert Peaks Guide,* part I. Glendale, California: La Siesta Press, 1964.

Wilson, E. O. "Social Insects." *Science*, 172:406, 1971.

Woodbury, A. M., and Hardy, R. "Studies of the Desert Tortoise, *Gopherus agassizii*." *Ecological Monographs*, 18:145–200, 1948.

Index

Italic page numbers denote illustrations.